Pocket PARIS

TOP SIGHTS • LOCAL LIFE • MADE EASY

Catherine Le Nevez

In This Book

QuickStart Guide

Your keys to understanding the city – we help you decide what to do and how to do it

Need to Know
Tips for a smooth trip

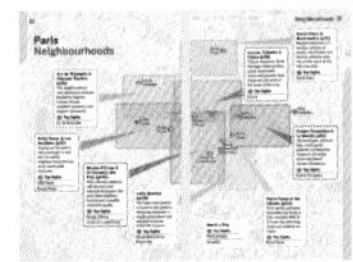

Neighbourhoods
What's where

Explore Paris

The best things to see and do, neighbourhood by neighbourhood

Top Sights
Make the most of your visit

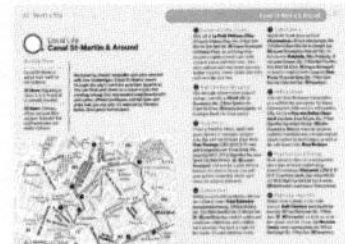

Local Life
The insider's city

The Best of Paris

The city's highlights in handy lists to help you plan

Best Walks
See the city on foot

Paris' Best...
The best experiences

Survival Guide

Tips and tricks for a seamless, hassle-free city experience

Getting Around
Travel like a local

Essential Information
Including where to stay

Our selection of the city's best places to eat, drink and experience:

- Sights
- Eating
- Drinking
- Entertainment
- Shopping

These symbols give you the vital information for each listing:

- Telephone Numbers
- Opening Hours
- Parking
- Nonsmoking
- Internet Access
- Wi-Fi Access
- Vegetarian Selection
- English-Language Menu
- Family-Friendly
- Pet-Friendly
- Bus
- Ferry
- Metro
- Tram
- Train

Find each listing quickly on maps for each neighbourhood:

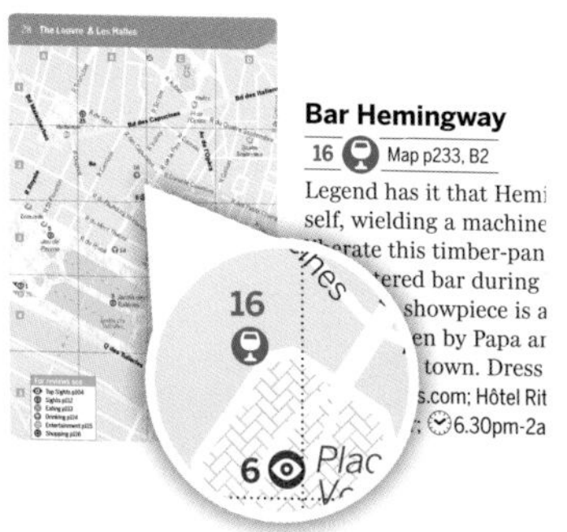
Bar Hemingway
16
Map p233, B2
Legend has it that Hemi
self, wielding a machine
showpiece is a
town. Dress
6.30pm-2a
16
6
Plac

Lonely Planet's Paris

Lonely Planet Pocket Guides are designed to get you straight to the heart of the city.

Inside you'll find all the must-see sights, plus tips to make your visit to each one really memorable. We've split the city into easy-to-navigate neighbourhoods and provided clear maps so you'll find your way around with ease. Our expert authors have searched out the best of the city: walks, food, nightlife and shopping, to name a few. Because you want to explore, our 'Local Life' pages will take you to some of the most exciting areas to experience the real Paris.

And of course you'll find all the practical tips you need for a smooth trip: itineraries for short visits, how to get around, and how much to tip the guy who serves you a drink at the end of a long day's exploration.

It's your guarantee of a really great experience.

Our Promise

You can trust our travel information because Lonely Planet authors visit the places we write about, each and every edition. We never accept freebies for positive coverage, so you can rely on us to tell it like it is.

QuickStart Guide 7

Explore Paris 21

Worth a Trip:

QuickStart Guide

Welcome to Paris

Paris has a timeless familiarity for first-time and frequent visitors, with instantly recognisable architectural icons – the wrought-iron Eiffel Tower, the broad Arc de Triomphe guarding the glamorous Champs-Élysées, the gargoyled Notre Dame cathedral and lamplit bridges spanning the Seine. But against this backdrop, Paris' real magic lies in the unexpected: hidden parks, small museums and tucked-away boutiques, bistros and neighbourhood cafes where you can watch Parisian life unfold.

Eiffel Tower (p24) and Jardins du Trocadéro (p42)
NEALE CLARK / GETTY IMAGES ©

Paris Top Sights

Eiffel Tower (p24)

No other monument is as synonymous with a place as this graceful wrought-iron spire is with Paris. Head to the top for panoramic views over the city, day and night.

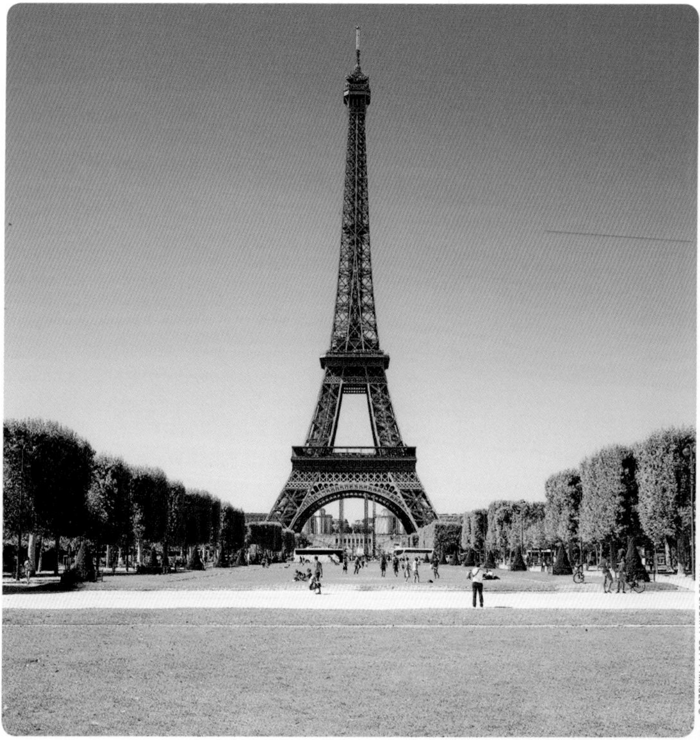

Notre Dame (p114)

A vision of stained-glass rose windows, gothic gargoyles and flying buttresses, Paris' glorious cathedral lies at the heart of the city. Climbing its 400-odd spiralling steps takes you up into its towers.

Louvre (p50)

The *Mona Lisa* and the *Venus de Milo* are just two of the priceless treasures among the 35,000 works of art housed inside this resplendent fortress turned palace turned France's first national museum.

Arc de Triomphe (p38)

Standing sentinel on the Champs-Élysées, this intricately carved triumphal arch epitomises Paris' pomp and ceremony, especially during festivals and celebrations. And yes, you can climb to the top of it too.

Sacré-Cœur (p74)

In the fabled artists' neighbourhood of Montmartre, climb staircased, ivy-clad streets or catch the funicular that glides up to reach the dove-white domes of Paris' crowning basilica.

BRUNO DE HOGUES / GETTY IMAGES ©

Centre Pompidou (p90)

Richard Rogers and Renzo Piano's striking building, with exposed pipes and plumbing, has an exceptional collection of modern, postmodern and contemporary art, topped off by a panorama radiating from the roof.

NEIL FARRIN / GETTY IMAGES ©

JEAN-PIERRE LESCOURRET / GETTY IMAGES ©

Jardin du Luxembourg (p150)

Do as Parisians do: grab a 1923-designed metal chairs and find your own favourite part of the city's loveliest park, filled with chestnut groves, ponds and children's activities.

PAWEL LIBERA / GETTY IMAGES ©

Musée d'Orsay (p148)

Works by some of the most famous artists to have painted in Paris – including Van Gogh, Renoir and Monet – are spectacularly showcased in this turn-of-the-20th-century former railway station.

Musée National du Moyen Âge (p130)

A Roman-era bathhouse (c AD 200) and 15th-century mansion, the Hôtel de Cluny houses France's National Museum of the Middle Ages, famed for its medieval tapestries.

CRAIG PERSHOUSE / GETTY IMAGES ©

BRUNO DE HOGUES / GETTY IMAGES ©

Père Lachaise (p108)

Paris is a collection of villages, and this 44-hectare cemetery of lanes and elaborate tombs qualifies as one in its own right. Famous 'residents' include Oscar Wilde, Jim Morrison and Édith Piaf.

Musée Rodin (p26)

Rodin's seminal sculptures, including *The Thinker,* are placed in the rose gardens, while the 18th-century mansion's interior demonstrates that Rodin's talents encompassed myriad other art forms.

BROOKS KRAFT / CORBIS ©

GRANT FAINT / GETTY IMAGES ©

Versailles (p166)

It's worth venturing outside central Paris to marvel at the extraordinary opulence of this colossal château, which was the seat of the royal court until the start of the French Revolution.

Paris Local Life

Insider tips to help you find the real city

Paris' star attractions certainly justify the hype. But to discover the 'Parisians' Paris', you need to delve into the city's *quartiers*. These quarters are like a patchwork of villages, each with its own evolving character and timeless sense of community.

The Spirit of Les Halles (p56)

- Cookware shops
- Late-night bistros

In the streets where Paris' wholesale markets were located, their spirit lives on, with grocers' stalls, virtually unchanged bakeries, and late-opening and 24-hour bistros, as well as cookware shops where Parisian chefs still buy the tools of their trade.

A Heads-Up on the Haut Marais (p92)

- Emerging designers
- Covered markets

The southern Marais used to attract all the hype, but the *haut* (upper, ie northern) part of Paris' hippest *quartier* continues to explode as an art and fashion hub, with edgy boutiques and galleries popping up amid longstanding neighbourhood haunts enjoying a revival.

Canal St-Martin & Around (p86)

- Offbeat boutiques
- Cool cafes

The banks of this picturesque canal and its surrounds are the epicentre of the city's *bobo* (bourgeois bohemian) culture, where artists, musicians and other creatives catch cutting-edge music and shop at offbeat new and secondhand boutiques.

Art in Montmartre (p76)

- Windmills
- Village squares

Picasso, Renoir and Van Gogh were just some of the seminal artists who once lived and worked in Montmartre, and although this quaint, village-like neighbourhood of higgledy-piggledy streets now teems with visitors, you can find tangible reminders of its artistic legacy that still thrive today.

A Stroll Along Rue Mouffetard (p132)

- Market stalls
- Lively bars

This old Roman road in the Latin Quarter is lined with colourful food-

Canal St-Martin (p86)

market stalls, cheap eateries, quirky shops and student-filled bars. You can easily spend several hours here, but give it a miss on Monday, when the markets are closed.

Southeastern Discovery (p144)

▶ National library
▶ Floating bars

Off the tourist radar, there are lots of reasons to explore this up-and-coming area, including exhibitions at the book-shaped national library, the national cinema institute and the national fashion institute, as well as floating bars or nightclubs and even a floating swimming pool.

St-Germain des Prés' Historic Shops (p152)

▶ Antique dealers
▶ Storied shops

St-Germain des Prés is filled with designer boutiques, but while browsing through them you'll find a trove of history-steeped shops in this soulful Left Bank neighbourhood, as well as the city's first-ever department store and its magnificent food hall, which draws Parisians from across the city.

Other great places to experience the city like a local:

Rue Cler (p34)

Rue des Martyrs (p85)

Marché d'Aligre (p102)

Place de la Madeleine (p70)

'Little Brittany' (p160)

Behind the Butte (p80)

Rue de Lappe (p104)

Pletzl (p99)

Paris Day Planner

Day One

One day in Paris? This itinerary covers the very top sights of the city. Start your visit at the emblematic **Eiffel Tower** (p24) for stupendous views across the city. Back on solid ground, make your way to the **Louvre** (p50), which holds some of the world's greatest art treasures, including the *Mona Lisa* and *Venus de Milo*.

You'll want to spend at least a couple of hours at the Louvre. Once you're finished, head to **Angelina** (p67) for outrageously decadent hot chocolate. Walk it off with a stroll along the Seine, finishing at the Île de la Cité to visit the island's beautiful churches, **Notre Dame** (p114) and **Sainte-Chapelle** (p122). Spend the rest of the afternoon wandering the laneways and poking through the quirky shops of the Île St-Louis, stopping to savour a **Berthillon** (p123) ice cream.

Dine on French classics at **La Tour de Montlhéry – Chez Denise** (p64) or cutting-edge neobistro cuisine at **Frenchie** (p63). After dinner, order the ultimate Bloody Mary at the place it was invented, **Harry's New York Bar** (p67).

Day Two

Start your second day at the **Sacré-Cœur** (p74), taking in vistas from the steps out front and up inside its dome. Spend some time strolling Montmartre's backstreets, checking out bustling **place du Tertre** (p77) and works by the surrealist master at the **Dalí Espace Montmartre** (p79), before lunch at local favourite **Le Miroir** (p85).

After lunch, head to the **Centre Pompidou** (p90) to gaze at its eye-popping exterior and explore its fabulous modern art museum. Spend the rest of the afternoon absorbing the atmosphere of the Marais, checking out the boutiques and galleries in the **haut Marais** (p92) and getting lost in the maze of medieval streets. Learn about Parisian history at the **Musée Carnavalet** (p96) and take a walk along the elevated **Promenade Plantée** (p99).

Le Marais and its eastern neighbour Bastille are the epicentre of Paris' nightlife. Start off with a glass of wine at **Le Baron Rouge** (p102), before moving on to dinner at the beautiful art nouveau **Brasserie Bofinger** (p104). Afterwards, kick off a bar crawl on **rue de Lappe** (p104).

Short on time?
We've arranged Paris' must-sees into these day-by-day itineraries to make sure you see the very best of the city in the time you have available.

Day Three

Spend your third day on Paris' Left Bank. Start at the vast **Les Invalides complex** (p30), incorporating a **military museum** (p30), an exhibition on de Gaulle, and **Napoléon's tomb** (p31). Then visit the **Musée Rodin** (p26), where the artist's sculptures are displayed in a gorgeous mansion and its rose-filled gardens. Continue the artistic theme at the **Musée d'Orsay** (p148), which holds the nation's incredible impressionist and postimpressionist collections.

Wander east through chic St-Germain des Prés, stopping for lunch at **Bouillon Racine** (p159) and checking out the area's **historic shops**. Linger over a coffee at legendary literary hangout **Les Deux Magots** (p172), stroll through the beautiful **Jardin du Luxembourg** (p150). Then mingle with **Sorbonne** (p138) students in the Latin Quarter's **rue Mouffetard** (p132) and visit the **Panthéon** (p136) mausoleum, the resting place for many of France's great thinkers.

After dinner at romantic **Le Coupe-Chou** (p140), head to charming local wine bar **Café de la Nouvelle Mairie** (p141), before catching jazz in the medieval cellars of the **Caveau de la Huchette** (p142).

Day Four

Take in panoramic city views from the top of Paris' iconic **Arc de Triomphe** (p38), then promenade along the grand av des **Champs-Élysées**. Detour for high-end window shopping in the *haute couture* heartland of the Triangle d'Or (**Golden Triangle**; p47), then meander through the World Heritage–listed **Jardin des Tuileries** (p60) to the wonderful **Musée de l'Orangerie** (p60) to view Monet's stunning *Water Lilies*.

Spend the afternoon exploring the buzzing, bohemian **Canal St-Martin** (p86) neighbourhood, starting with lunch on the canalside terrace at **Chez Prune** (p87), before checking out the area's funky boutiques. Then make your way to the world's most visited cemetery, **Père Lachaise** (p109), to visit famous graves including those of Édith Piaf, Oscar Wilde and Jim Morrison.

After dinner at hip bistro **Yard** (p109), or **Chatomat** (p87) in up-and-coming Belleville, check out the area's bars, catch the can-can dancers at the famous **Moulin Rouge** (p85) cabaret or take in a performance at the lavish **Palais Garnier** (p68) opera house.

Need to Know

For more information, see Survival Guide (p204)

Currency
Euro (€)

Language
French

Visas
Generally no restrictions for EU citizens. Usually not required for most other nationalities for stays of up to 90 days.

Money
ATMs widely available. Visa and MasterCard accepted in most hotels, shops and restaurants; fewer establishments accept American Express.

Mobile Phones
Check with your provider before you leave about roaming and French SIM-card options.

Time
Central European Time (GMT/UTC plus one hour)

Plugs & Adaptors
Plugs in France have two round pins. Voltage is 220V AC, 50Hz. Appliances rated US 110V need a transformer to work safely.

Tipping
Already included in prices under French law, though if service is particularly good, you might tip an extra 5% to 10% in restaurants. Round taxi fares up to the nearest euro.

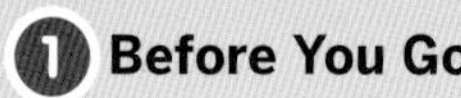

Before You Go

Your Daily Budget

Budget less than €100
- Dorm beds €25–50
- Self-catering supermarkets and markets
- Inexpensive public transport, stand-by theatre tickets

Midrange €100–250
- Double room €130–250
- Two-course meals €20–40
- Affordable museums

Top End over €250
- Historic luxury hotels
- Gastronomic restaurants
- Designer boutiques

Useful Websites

Lonely Planet (www.lonelyplanet.com/paris) Destination information, bookings, traveller forum and more

Paris Info (www.parisinfo.com) Comprehensive tourist-authority website.

Secrets of Paris (www.secretsofparis.com) Loads of resources and reviews.

Paris by Mouth (http://parisbymouth.com) Dining and drinking news and reviews.

Advance Planning

Two months before Organise opera, ballet or cabaret tickets and make reservations for high-end or popular restaurants.

Two weeks before Sign up for a free, local-led tour and start narrowing down your choice of museums.

Two days before Pack your most comfortable shoes – Paris is best explored on foot.

2 Arriving in Paris

Paris' two main airports are its largest, Charles de Gaulle, and the smaller Orly; the quickest and easiest transport options are listed below. Some budget carriers such as Ryanair use Beauvais airport, linked by shuttle bus. Gare du Nord train station is also a major entry point for UK travellers.

From Charles de Gaulle Airport

Destination	Best Transport
Champs-Élysées, Arc de Triomphe	Air France bus 2
St-Germain des Prés (Gare Montparnasse)	Air France bus 4
Bastille (Gare de Lyon)	Air France bus 4
Châtelet–Les Halles, Notre Dame	RER train B
St-Germain des Prés, Latin Quarter (Denfert Rochereau)	RER train B
Opéra	Roissybus

From Orly Airport

Destination	Best Transport
Les Invalides	Air France bus 1
Champs-Élysées, Arc de Triomphe	Air France bus 1
St-Germain des Prés (Gare Montparnasse)	Air France bus 1
St-Germain des Prés, Latin Quarter (Denfert Rochereau)	Orlybus
Châtelet–Les Halles, Notre Dame	Orlyval, then RER train B
Latin Quarter	Orlyval, then RER train B

3 Getting Around

Walking is a pleasure in Paris, but the city also has one of the most efficient and inexpensive public-transport systems in the world, making getting around a breeze.

Metro & RER

Paris' underground network, run by the RATP, consists of two separate but linked systems: the metro and the RER suburban train line. The metro has 14 numbered lines; the RER has five main lines, designated A to E and then numbered, that pass through the city centre and are good for quick cross-city journeys. Each metro line is marked by a number, colour and final destination. You'll save money by purchasing a *carnet* (book) of 10 tickets.

Bus

The extensive bus network is a slower but scenic alternative to the metro, and is easier for those with limited mobility and parents with prams/buggies.

Cycling

The Vélib' pick-up, drop-off bike system has revolutionised travel in Paris, with over 20,000 bikes and 1800 bike stations around 300m apart throughout the city. Subscriptions are super-cheap and the first 30 minutes of use are free.

Boat

The city's most beautiful 'boulevard', the Seine, runs right through the centre of the city. Boat cruises are plentiful; the hop-on, hop-off Batobus has eight stops serving some of Paris' top sights.

Taxi

You'll find ranks around major intersections.

Paris Neighbourhoods

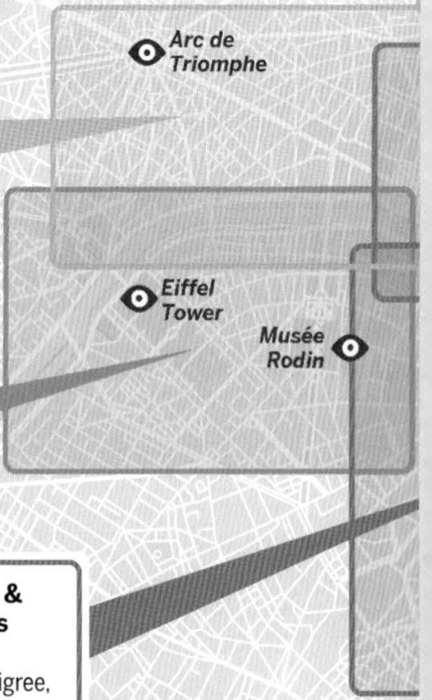

Arc de Triomphe & Champs-Élysées (p36)
This neighbourhood sees glamorous avenues flanked by flagship fashion houses, excellent museums and elegant restaurants.

Top Sights

Arc de Triomphe

Eiffel Tower & Les Invalides (p22)
Zipping up the spire is reason enough to visit, but this stately neighbourhood also has some unmissable museums.

Top Sights

Eiffel Tower

Musée Rodin

Musée d'Orsay & St-Germain des Prés (p146)
With a literary pedigree, cafe terraces and exquisite boutiques, this gentrified neighbourhood retains a soulful, cinematic quality.

Top Sights

Musée d'Orsay

Jardin du Luxembourg

Latin Quarter (p128)
The lively Latin Quarter is home to vast gardens, intriguing museums, a mighty mausoleum and spirited Sorbonne university students.

Top Sights

Musée National du Moyen Âge

Arc de Triomphe

Eiffel Tower

Musée Rodin

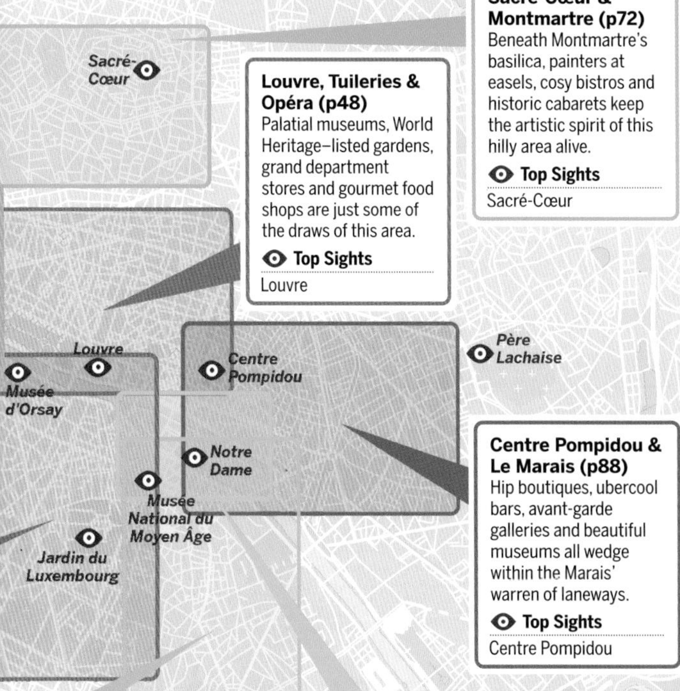

Sacré-Cœur & Montmartre (p72)
Beneath Montmartre's basilica, painters at easels, cosy bistros and historic cabarets keep the artistic spirit of this hilly area alive.

Top Sights

Sacré-Cœur

Louvre, Tuileries & Opéra (p48)
Palatial museums, World Heritage–listed gardens, grand department stores and gourmet food shops are just some of the draws of this area.

Top Sights

Louvre

Centre Pompidou & Le Marais (p88)
Hip boutiques, ubercool bars, avant-garde galleries and beautiful museums all wedge within the Marais' warren of laneways.

Top Sights

Centre Pompidou

Notre Dame & the Islands (p112)
Paris' gothic cathedral dominates the Île de la Cité; romantic little Île St-Louis has charming shops and sublime ice cream.

Top Sights

Notre Dame

Worth a Trip

Top Sights

Père Lachaise

Versailles

Explore **Paris**

Worth a Trip

Jardin des Tuileries (p60)

Explore

Eiffel Tower & Les Invalides

Stretching west along the Seine's southern bank, the broad boulevards and imposing architecture of the Eiffel Tower and Les Invalides area are Paris at its most bombastic. In this *grande dame* of a neighbourhood you can get up close and personal with the city's symbolic tower and discover its evolving history.

The Sights in a Day

A river cruise is the ideal way to start (and/or end) a day in this iconic area, with several companies stopping near the Eiffel Tower. Spend the morning exploring the **Musée Rodin** (p26), allowing time to soak up the serenity of its sculpture garden, then head to **Les Invalides** (p30) to learn about French military history through the ages and pay homage at Napoléon's tomb.

After lunch at **Le Casse Noix** (p33) or a picnic in the **Parc du Champ de Mars** (p32) beneath the Eiffel Tower, check out the indigenous art and striking architecture of the **Musée du Quai Branly** (p31). If you and your olfactory senses are game, you could take a walk below ground in the Paris sewers at the **Musée des Égouts de Paris** (p32).

Sunset is the best time to ascend the **Eiffel Tower** (p24), to experience both the dizzying views during daylight and then the glittering *ville lumière* (City of Light) by night. For mind-blowing mystery degustation menus, head to **Restaurant David Toutain** (p32).

Top Sights

Eiffel Tower (p24)

Musée Rodin (p26)

Best of Paris

Architecture

Eiffel Tower (p24)

Musée du Quai Branly (p31)

Museums

Musée Rodin (p26)

Eating

Restaurant David Toutain (p32)

Choux d'Enfer (p33)

Drinking

Coutume (p34)

Panoramas

Eiffel Tower (p24)

Île aux Cygnes (p32)

Multicultural Paris

Musée du Quai Branly (p31)

Getting There

M **Metro** Bir Hakeim (line 6) or Champ de Mars–Tour Eiffel (RER C)

M **Metro** From Alma Marceau (line 9), it's an easy stroll over the Pont de l'Alma bridge.

Boat In addition to river cruises, the hop-on hop-off Batobus starts and ends its run at the Eiffel Tower.

Top Sights
Eiffel Tower

No one could imagine Paris today without its signature spire. But Gustave Eiffel constructed this graceful tower – the world's tallest, at 320m, until it was eclipsed by Manhattan's Chrysler Building some four decades later – only as a temporary exhibit for the 1889 Exposition Universelle (World Fair). Luckily, the tower's popularity (and use as a platform for radiotelegraphy antennas) assured its survival beyond the fair and its elegant art nouveau webbed-metal design has become the defining fixture of the city's skyline.

Map p28, C2

www.tour-eiffel.fr

Champ de Mars, 7e

lift to top adult/child €15/10.50, lift to 2nd fl €9/4.50

9am-midnight mid-Jun–Aug, 9.30am-11pm, Sep–mid-Jun

M Bir Hakeim or Champ de Mars–Tour Eiffel

Don't Miss

The Trip Up

Lifts (elevators) yo-yo up and down the north, west and east pillars to the tower's three platforms (57m, 115m and 276m); change lifts on the 2nd level for the final ascent to the top. (There's wheelchair access to the 1st and 2nd floors.) If you're feeling athletic, you can climb about 700 stairs in the south pillar up to the 2nd floor for an up-close view of the ironwork.

The Views

Views from the top extend up to 60km. Visibility is hampered by cloud cover and rain, so try to time your visit for a clear day (access is restricted in severe weather). Telescopes and maps placed around the tower pinpoint locations in Paris and beyond.

The Lighting

Each night, the tower's beacons beam an 80km radius around the city (look up from the top platform to see the 6000-watt lamps). And every hour, for five minutes on the hour, the entire tower sparkles with 20,000 lights. It took 25 mountain climbers five months to install the bulbs.

Gustave Eiffel's Office

Historic exhibits throughout the tower include Gustave Eiffel's restored top-floor office, where wax models of Eiffel and his daughter Claire greet Thomas Edison, who visited the tower in 1889.

Story Windows

The 2nd floor's story windows give a nuts-and-bolts overview of the lifts' mechanics.

Pavilions

On the 1st floor, two new glass pavilions house interactive history exhibits. Outside them, peer down through glass flooring to the ground below.

☑ Top Tips

- Save time by buying lift tickets ahead online (staircase tickets must be bought at the tower). Choose a time slot and preprint tickets or use a smartphone that can be read by the scanner at the entrance.
- The top can be breezy, so bring a jacket.

Take a Break

Dine at the tower's 1st-level brasserie **58 Tour Eiffel** (☎01 45 55 20 04; www.restaurants-toureiffel.com; 1st level; 2-/3-course lunch menus €21/26, dinner menus €66/75; ⏲11.30am-4.30pm & 6.30-11pm) or its Michelin-starred 2nd-level gastronomic restaurant **Le Jules Verne** (☎01 45 55 61 44; www.lejulesverne-paris.com; 2nd fl; lunch menus €98/ dinner menus €185-230; ⏲noon-1.30pm & 7.30-9.30pm), or make a toast at the top-floor champagne bar.

Top Sights
Musée Rodin

Auguste Rodin was more than just a sculptor: he painted, sketched, engraved and collected. And his former workshop and showroom, the beautiful 1730-built Hôtel Biron, is more than just a museum. Rodin donated his entire collection to the French state in 1908 on the proviso they dedicate the Hôtel Biron to displaying his works. They're now installed not only in the mansion itself but also in its rose garden, which is one of the most peaceful places in central Paris.

Map p28, G3

www.musee-rodin.fr

79 rue de Varenne, 7e

adult/child museum incl garden €6/free, garden only €2/free

10am-5.45pm Tue & Thu-Sun, to 8.45pm Wed

M Varenne

The Three Shades from *The Gates of Hell*

Don't Miss

The Thinker

Rodin's famous sculpture *The Thinker* (*Le Penseur*) universally symbolises philosophy. The first large-scale cast, made from bronze and marble and completed in 1902, resides in the museum's garden – the perfect place to contemplate this heroic naked figure that was conceived by Rodin to represent intellect and poetry (it was originally titled *The Poet*).

The Gates of Hell

The Gates of Hell (*La Porte de l'Enfer*) was commissioned as the entrance for a decorative arts museum in 1880. Although the museum was never built, Rodin worked on his sculptural masterpiece until his death in 1917. Standing 6m high by 4m wide, its 180 figures comprise an intricate scene from Dante's *Inferno*.

The Kiss

Originally part of *The Gates of Hell*, marble monument to love *The Kiss* (*Le Baiser*) was first titled *Francesca da Rimini* (after the 13th-century Italian noblewoman in Dante's *Inferno*). The sculpture's entwined lovers caused controversy on the work's completion due to Rodin's then-radical approach of depicting women as equal partners in ardour.

Camille Claudel Sculptures

Rodin's protégé, sculptor Camille Claudel, also famously became his mistress. Both teacher and student had a major influence on each other's creations. The world's largest collection of Claudel's sculptures is displayed in the museum.

Collections

In addition to Rodin's own paintings and sketches, don't miss his prized collection of works by artists including Van Gogh and Renoir.

Top Tips

- Save money by purchasing a combined ticket with the nearby Musée d'Orsay (€15 if you visit both on the same day).
- Admission is free on the first Sunday of the month year round.
- Buy tickets ahead online. Preprint tickets or use a smartphone that can be read by the scanner at the entrance.
- Check out more of Rodin's work in Paris' Jardin des Tuileries.

Take a Break

Award-winning goodies include baguettes made in front of you at *boulangerie* **Besnier** (Map p28, H3; 40 rue de Bourgogne, 7e; 7am-8pm Mon-Fri Sep-Jul; M Varenne).

For feisty flavours from southwestern France, try **Le Square** (Map p28, H2; 01 45 51 09 03; www.restaurant-lesquare.com; 31 rue St-Dominique, 7e; lunch/dinner menus from €19.50/26; kitchen noon-2.30pm & 7-10pm Mon-Sat; ; M Solférino).

For reviews see

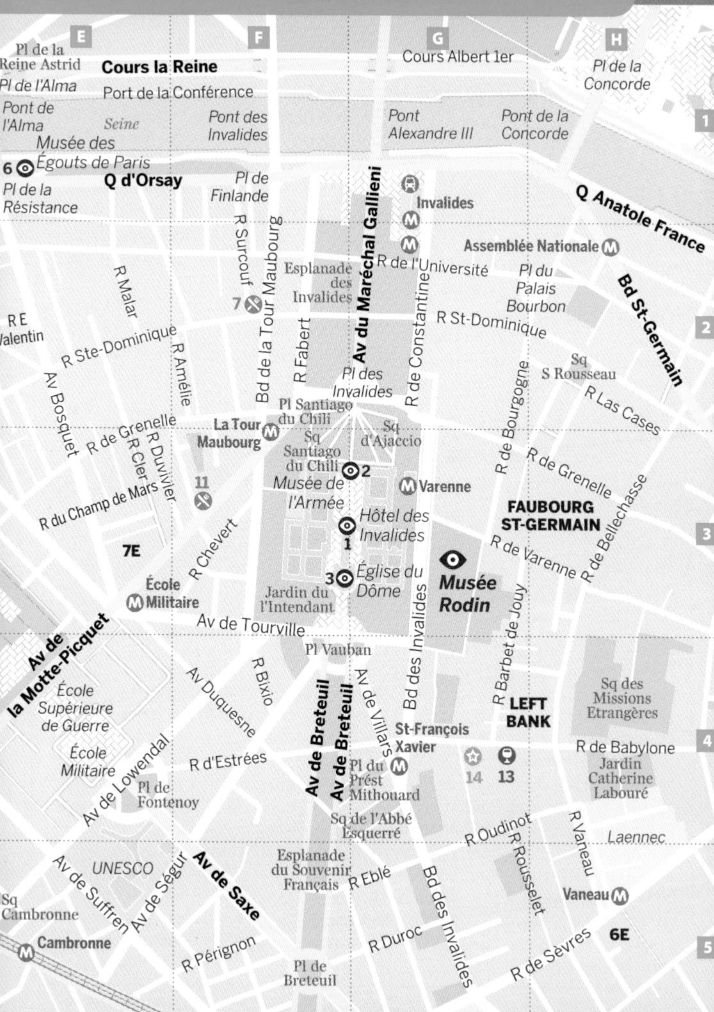

E
F
G
H
1
2
3
4
5
Pl de la Reine Astrid
Cours la Reine
Pl de l'Alma
Port de la Conférence
Pont de l'Alma
Seine
Pont des Invalides
Musée des Égouts de Paris
6
Q d'Orsay
Pl de la Résistance
Pl de Finlande
Cours Albert 1er
Pl de la Concorde
Pont Alexandre III
Pont de la Concorde
Invalides
Q Anatole France
Assemblée Nationale
R Surcouf
Bd de la Tour Maubourg
Av du Maréchal Gallieni
Esplanade des Invalides
R de l'Université
Pl du Palais Bourbon
Bd St-Germain
R Malar
7
R de Constantine
R St-Dominique
R E Valentin
R Ste-Dominique
R Amélie
R Fabert
Pl des Invalides
Sq S Rousseau
R Las Cases
Av Bosquet
Pl Santiago du Chili
R de Bourgogne
R de Grenelle
R Cler
R Duvivier
La Tour Maubourg
Sq Santiago du Chili
Sq d'Ajaccio
R de Grenelle
2
Musée de l'Armée
Varenne
11
R du Champ de Mars
FAUBOURG ST-GERMAIN
Hôtel des Invalides
1
R de Bellechasse
7E
R Chevert
R de Varenne
3
Église du Dôme
Musée Rodin
École Militaire
Jardin du l'Intendant
Bd des Invalides
R Barbet de Jouy
Av de Tourville
Av de la Motte-Picquet
Pl Vauban
R Bixio
Av Duquesne
Av de Breteuil
Av de Villars
Sq des Missions Etrangères
École Supérieure de Guerre
LEFT BANK
St-François Xavier
R de Babylone
École Militaire
Av de Lowendal
R d'Estrées
Pl du Prést Mithouard
14
13
Jardin Catherine Labouré
Pl de Fontenoy
Sq de l'Abbé Esquerré
R Oudinot
R Vaneau
Laennec
R Rousselet
Av de Suffren
UNESCO
Av de Ségur
Av de Saxe
Esplanade du Souvenir Français
R Eblé
Bd des Invalides
Vaneau
Sq Cambronne
6E
Cambronne
R Pérignon
R Duroc
Pl de Breteuil
R de Sèvres

Sights

Hôtel des Invalides
MONUMENT, MUSEUM

1 Map p28, F3

The Hôtel des Invalides was built in the 1670s by Louis XIV to house 4000 *invalides* (disabled war veterans). On 14 July 1789, a mob broke into the building and seized 32,000 rifles before heading on to the prison at Bastille and the start of the French Revolution. Hours for individual sites often vary so check the website for updates.

(www.musee-armee.fr; 129 rue de Grenelle, 7e; adult/child €9.50/free; 7.30am-7pm daily, to 9pm Tue Apr-Sep, hours can vary; M Invalides)

Musée de l'Armée
MUSEUM

2 Map p28, G3

North of Hôtel des Invalides, in the Cour d'Honneur, is the Musée de l'Armée, which holds the nation's largest collection on French military history. Sobering wartime footage screens at this army museum, which also has weaponry, flag and medal displays as well as a multimedia area dedicated to Charles de Gaulle.

(Army Museum; www.musee-armee.fr; 129 rue de Grenelle, 7e; included in Hôtel des Invalides admission; 10am-6pm Apr-Oct, to 5pm Nov-Mar; M Invalides)

Understand

Charles de Gaulle & WWII

The WWII battle for France began in earnest in May 1940 and by 14 June France had capitulated. Paris was occupied, and almost half the population evacuated. General Charles de Gaulle, France's undersecretary of war, fled to London. In a radio broadcast on 18 June 1940, he appealed to French patriots to continue resisting the Germans. He set up a French government-in-exile and established the Forces Françaises Libres (Free French Forces), fighting alongside the Allies. Paris was liberated on 25 August 1944 by an Allied force spearheaded by Free French units.

De Gaulle returned to Paris and set up a provisional government, but in January 1946 he resigned, wrongly believing that the move would provoke a popular outcry for his return. De Gaulle formed his own party (Rassemblement du Peuple Français) and remained in opposition until 1958, when he was brought back to power to prevent a military coup over the uprising in Algeria. He resigned as president in 1969, succeeded by Gaullist Prime Minister Georges Pompidou.

PHILLIPE RUAULT ©

Musée du Quai Branly, architecture by Ateliers Jean Nouvel

Église du Dôme CHURCH

3 Map p28, F3

With its sparkling golden dome (1677–1735), the Hôtel des Invalides' landmark church is one of the finest religious edifices erected under Louis XIV and was the inspiration for the United States Capitol building. It received the remains of Napoléon in 1840; the extravagant **Tombeau de Napoléon 1er** comprises six coffins fitting into one another like a Russian doll.

(www.musee-armee.fr; 129 rue de Grenelle, 7e; included in Hôtel des Invalides admission; 7.30 am-7pm daily, to 9pm Tue Apr-Sep; M Invalides)

Musée du Quai Branly MUSEUM

4 Map p28, D2

No other museum in Paris so inspires travellers, armchair anthropologists and those who appreciate the beauty of traditional craftsmanship. A tribute to the diversity of human culture, Musée du Quai Branly presents an overview of indigenous and folk art. Its four main sections focus on Oceania, Asia, Africa and the Americas. An impressive array of masks, carvings, jewellery and more make up the body of the collection, displayed in a unique interior without rooms or high walls.

(www.quaibranly.fr; 37 quai Branly, 7e; adult/child €8.50/free; 11am-7pm Tue, Wed & Sun, to 9pm Thu-Sat; M Alma Marceau or Pont de l'Alma)

Parc du Champ de Mars

PARK

5 Map p28, D3

Running southeast from the Eiffel Tower, the grassy Champ de Mars – an ideal summer picnic spot – was originally used as a parade ground for the cadets of the 18th-century **École Militaire**, the vast French-classical building at the southeastern end of the park, which counts Napoléon Bonaparte among its graduates. The steel-and-etched glass **Wall for Peace memorial** (2000) was created by Clara Halter.
(Champ de Mars, 7e; M Champ de Mars–Tour Eiffel or École Militaire)

Musée des Égouts de Paris

MUSEUM

6 Map p28, E1

Raw sewage flows beneath your feet as you walk through 480m of odoriferous tunnels in this working sewer museum. Exhibitions cover the development of Paris' waste-water-disposal system, including its resident rats (there's an estimated one sewer rat for every Parisian above ground). Enter via a rectangular maintenance hole topped with a kiosk across the street from 93 quai d'Orsay, 7e.

The sewers keep regular hours except when rain floods the tunnels. Toy rats are sold at its gift shop.
(place de la Résistance, 7e; adult/child €4.40/3.60; 11am-5pm Sat-Wed May-Sep, 11am-4pm Sat-Wed Oct-Dec & Feb-Apr; M Alma Marceau or RER Pont de l'Alma)

Local Life

Île aux Cygnes

Paris' little-known third island, the artificially created Île aux Cygnes (Isle of Swans; Map p28, A4), was formed in 1827 to protect the river port and measures just 850m by 11m. On the western side of the Pont de Grenelle is a soaring one-quarter-scale **Statue of Liberty replica**, inaugurated in 1889. Walk east along the Allée des Cygnes – the tree-lined walkway that runs the length of the island – for knock-out Eiffel Tower views.

Eating

Restaurant David Toutain

GASTRONOMIC €€€

7 Map p28, F2

Prepare to be wowed: David Toutain pushes the envelope at his eponymous new restaurant with some of the most creative high-end cooking in Paris today. Mystery degustation courses include unlikely combinations such as smoked eel served in green-apple and black-sesame mousse, or candied celery and truffled rice pudding with artichoke praline (there are stunning wine pairings available).
(01 45 51 11 10; http://davidtoutain.com; 29 rue Surcouf, 7e; lunch menus €42, lunch & dinner menus €68-98; noon-2.30pm & 8-10pm Mon-Fri; M Invalides)

Understand

Paris Today

While the elegance and spirit of the Paris of Haussmann, Hugo and Toulouse-Lautrec will never disappear, the city is constantly reinventing itself. And Parisians are in the mood for change: the 2014 municipal elections ushered in the city's first-ever female mayor, socialist Anne Hidalgo.

Before taking the top job, Hidalgo was the First Deputy Mayor of Paris under Bertrand Delanoë, who pioneered innovative initiatives including the Vélib' bike-share scheme, Autolib' car-share scheme, Paris Plages 'beaches', and permanent pedestrianisation of the former riverside expressway (now comprising Les Berges de Seine) and the once traffic-choked place de la République (newly transformed into a fountain-filled square).

One of Hidalgo's first high-profile acts as mayor was to take action on the 'love locks' (padlocks attached by couples who throw the key into the Seine as a symbol of eternal love) that decorate (or desecrate) the city's bridges, causing structural damage and collapse. Among Hidalgo's goals are turning unused office space into 60,000 new homes within six years, creating pedestrianised 'eco-districts' in each *arrondissement* (city disctrict) and planting 20,000 trees.

Le Casse Noix — MODERN FRENCH **€€**

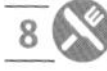

8 Map p28, C4

Proving that a location footsteps from the Eiffel Tower doesn't mean compromising on quality, quantity or authenticity, 'the nutcracker' is a neighbourhood gem with a cosy retro interior, affordable prices and exceptional cuisine that changes by season and by the inspiration of owner-chef Pierre Olivier Lenormand, who has honed his skills in some of Paris' most feted kitchens. Book ahead.

(01 45 66 09 01; www.le-cassenoix.fr; 56 rue de la Fédération, 15e; 2-/3-course lunch menus €21/26, 3-course dinner menus €33; noon-2.30pm & 7-10.30pm Mon-Fri; M Bir Hakeim)

Choux d'Enfer — PATISSERIE **€**

9 Map p28, B3

This kiosk gives street food a whole new spin. The creation of top French chefs Alain Ducasse and Christophe Michalak, it cooks up *choux* (pastry puffs). Grab a brown paper bag of nine *choux salées* (savoury cheese puffs) spiced with pepper, curry or cumin; or go sweet with almond, cocoa, coffee, lemon and vanilla *chouquettes,* with or without cream filling.

(01 47 83 26 67; cnr rue Jean Rey & quai Branly, 15e; sweet/savoury choux bags €5/7, with cream filling €6-17; 10am-8pm; M Bir-Hakeim or RER Champ de Mars–Tour Eiffel)

La Véraison MODERN FRENCH €€

10 Map p28, D5

The elegant simplicity of owner-chef Ulla Bosse's welcoming neighbourhood bistro (bare boards, timber tables, pistachio-coloured walls) belies the outstanding cuisine she creates in her open kitchen. The starters alone – truffled chestnut velouté, foie gras ravioli in cognac sauce, burrata cheese with orange, crispy 'Peking duck' morsels, Thai crab cakes with mango dip – are reason enough to return.

(☎01 45 32 39 39; www.laveraison.com; 64 rue de la Croix Nivert, 15e; 2-/3-course lunch menus €15/18, mains €19-24; ⏲12.30-2pm & 8-10pm Tue-Fri, 7.30-10pm Sat; M Commerce)

Pain & Chocolat CAFE €

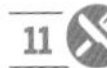

11 Map p28, F3

You'll be glad you forewent that overpriced, underdelivering hotel breakfast when you start the day in proper Parisian style at this delightfully retro cafe. Everything is made on the premises, salads, tartines, egg dishes and cakes, pastries and quiches included. Don't miss the hot chocolate, made from an old family recipe.

(16 av de la Motte-Picquet, 7e; mains €10-22, brunch menus €7-22; ⏲9am-7pm Tue-Fri, 10am-7pm Sat & Sun; M La Tour Maubourg)

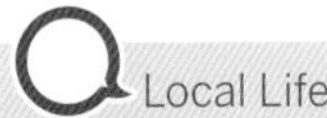

Local Life

Rue Cler

Pick up fresh bread, sandwich fillings, pastries and wine for a picnic along the typically Parisian market street **rue Cler** (Map p28, E3; 7e; ⏲most shops 8am-7pm Tue-Sat, to noon Sun; M École Militaire), which buzzes with local shoppers, especially on weekends.

La Gauloise TRADITIONAL FRENCH €€

12 Map p28, D4

With a name like La Gauloise, you wouldn't expect this venerable, terrace-fronted restaurant to serve anything other than traditional fare, which it does, very well. From the onion soup to the braised stuffed cabbage and duckling served with old-fashioned mashed potato, *îles flottantes* (floating islands) for dessert, and Madeleine cakes with coffee, it refines but doesn't reinvent the classics that make French cuisine iconic.

(☎01 47 34 11 64; 59 av de la Motte-Picquet, 15e; 2-/3-course lunch menus €24.50/29.50, mains €25-36; ⏲noon-2.30pm & 7-11pm; M La Motte Picquet Grenelle)

Drinking

Coutume CAFE

13 Map p28, G4

If you've noticed that the coffee in Paris is getting better lately, it is thanks in no small part to Coutume,

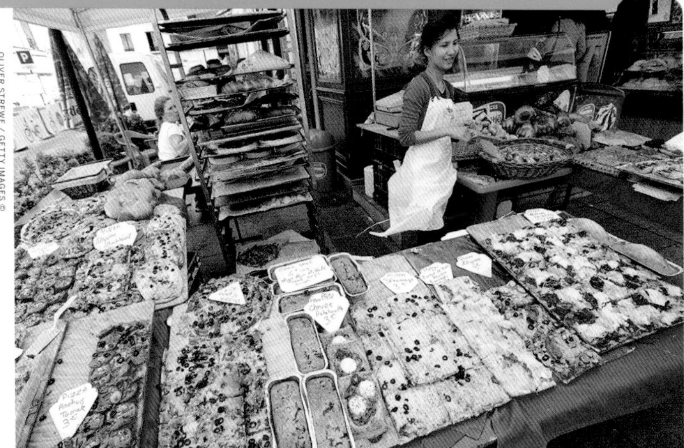

Pastry shop, rue Cler

an artisan roaster of premium beans for scores of establishments around town. Its flagship cafe – a bright, light-filled, post-industrial space – is ground zero for innovative preparation methods including cold extraction and siphon brews. It serves fabulous organic fare and pastries too.
(http://coutumecafe.com; 47 rue Babylone, 7e; ⌚8am-7pm Mon-Fri, from 10am Sat & Sun; Wi-Fi; M St-François Xavier or Vaneau)

Entertainment

Cinéma La Pagode — CINEMA

14 ☆ Map p28, G4

This 19th-century Japanese pagoda was converted into a cinema in the 1930s and remains the most atmospheric spot in Paris to catch arthouse and classic films. Don't miss a moment or two in its bamboo-enshrined garden.
(☎01 45 55 48 48; www.etoile-cinemas.com; 57bis rue de Babylone, 7e; M St-François Xavier)

Explore

Arc de Triomphe & Champs-Élysées

Pomp and grandeur reign: Baron Haussmann famously reshaped the Parisian cityscape around the Arc de Triomphe, from which a dozen avenues radiate like the spokes of a wheel. The most celebrated (and the scene of major celebrations) is the luxury-shop-lined av des Champs-Élysées. The neighbourhood's splendour extends to its *haute cuisine* restaurants and *haute couture* fashion houses.

The Sights in a Day

Climb above the **Champs-Élysées** to the top of the **Arc de Triomphe** (p38), then stroll – and shop – along this famous avenue named for the Elysian Fields ('heaven' in Greek mythology).

After lunch in the beautiful tearoom of the **Musée Jacquemart-André** (p42), wander among the flagship fashion houses of the **Triangle d'Or** (p47) and admire the ornate Asian artefacts at the **Musée Guimet des Arts Asiatiques** (p42) or catch blockbuster exhibitions at the **Grand Palais** (p42). Visit the resident fish at the **Cinéaqua** (p44) aquarium, snap a postcard-perfect photo of the Eiffel Tower from the terrace of the **Palais de Chaillot** (p42) and another from inside its exceptional architectural museum, the **Cité de l'Architecture et du Patrimoine** (p42).

Options for dinner in the area extend from intimate neighbourhood bistros such as **Le Hide** (p46) to gastronomic heavyweights such as **Lasserre** (p45). Later, hit pumping nightclubs such as **ShowCase** (p46).

Top Sights

Arc de Triomphe (p38)

Best of Paris

Architecture

Musée Maxim's (p44)

Cité de l'Architecture et du Patrimoine (p42)

Museums

Musée d'Art Moderne de la Ville de Paris (p44)

For Kids

Aquarium de Paris Cinéaqua (p44)

Multicultural Paris

Musée Guimet des Arts Asiatiques (p42)

Gourmet Shops

Ladurée (p45)

Panoramas

Arc de Triomphe (p38)

Getting There

Ⓜ **Metro** Charles de Gaulle–Étoile (lines 1, 2, 6 and RER A) is adjacent to the Arc de Triomphe.

Ⓜ **Metro** The Champs-Élysées' other stops are George V (line 1), Franklin D Roosevelt (lines 1 and 9) and Champs-Élysées–Clemenceau (1 and 13).

Boat The hop-on, hop-off Batobus stops near the Champs-Élysées by Pont Alexandre III.

Top Sights
Arc de Triomphe

If anything rivals the Eiffel Tower as the symbol of Paris, it's this magnificent 1836-built monument to Napoléon's 1805 victory at Austerlitz, which he commissioned the following year. The intricately sculpted triumphal arch stands sentinel in the centre of the enormous Étoile ('star') roundabout. At the top, some of the best views of Paris stretch east along the *axe historique* to the Louvre's glass pyramid, and west to the modern Grande Arche in high-rise La Défense.

Map p40, B2

www.monuments-nationaux.fr

place Charles de Gaulle, 8e

adult/child €9.50/free

10am-11pm Apr-Sep, to 10.30pm Oct-Mar

M Charles de Gaulle–Étoile

Don't Miss

The Architecture

Inspired by the Roman Arch of Titus, architect Jean-François Chalgrin gave the Arc de Triomphe its imposing stature through its outsized dimensions: a proud 50m high, 45m long and 22m wide.

The Sculptures

The most famous of the four high-relief panels at the base is to the right when you're facing the arch from the av des Champs-Élysées side. It's entitled Départ des Volontaires de 1792 (also known as La Marseillaise). Higher up, a frieze running around the whole monument depicts hundreds of figures.

The Climb to the Top

Scaling 284 steps brings you to the panoramic terrace at the top of the arch. Tickets are sold in the underground passage that surfaces on the northeastern side of the Champs-Élysées.

The Axe Historique

The Arc de Triomphe is the highest point of Paris' line of monuments known as the *axe historique* (historic axis; also called the grand axis). Views swoop east down the Champs-Élysées to the Louvre's glass pyramid, and west along the *axe historique* to the modern, box-like Grande Arche in the high-rise business district of La Défense.

The Tomb of the Unknown Soldier

Honouring the 1.3 million French soldiers who lost their lives in WWI, the Unknown Soldier was laid to rest under the arch in 1921, beneath an eternal flame (rekindled daily at 6.30pm).

Bastille Day Celebrations

The military parade commemorating France's national Bastille Day (14 July) kicks off from the arch (adorned by a billowing tricolour for the occasion).

Top Tips

- Don't try to cross the traffic-choked roundabout above ground! Stairs on the Champs-Élysées' northeastern side lead beneath the Étoile to pedestrian tunnels that bring you out safely beneath the arch.
- Admission to the terrace at the top is free on the first Sunday of the month from November to March.
- Don't risk getting skittled by traffic by taking photos while crossing the Champs-Elysées.
- There *is* a lift (elevator) at the arch, but it's only for visitors with limited mobility or those travelling with young children, and there are still some unavoidable steps.

Take a Break

Right near the arch, **Publicis Drugstore** (Map p40, C2; www.publicisdrugstore.com; 133 av des Champs-Élysées, 8e; 8am-2am Mon-Fri, 10am-2am Sat & Sun; M Charles de Gaulle–Étoile) is great for a meal, drink or snack.

A
B
C
D
1
2
3
4
5
Pl du Gal Patton
R des Acacias
17e
Av Carnot
R du Général Lanrezac
15
R Troyon
20
R du Faubourg St-Honoré
Argentine
Av de la Grande Armée
R Duret
Charles de Gaulle-Étoile
R de Tilsitt
Av Hoche
R Beaujon
Pl G Guillaumin
Av de Friedland
Arc de Triomphe
Charles de Gaulle-Étoile
Av Foch
Pl Charles de Gaulle
Av des Champs-Élysées
R Lord Byron
R Washington
R de Presbourg
Kléber
George V
19
R Vernet
R Paul Valéry
Av d'Iéna
11
Av Victor Hugo
TRIANGLE D'OR
R Galilée
R de Bassano
Av Kléber
R La Pérouse
R Jean Giraudoux
R Quentin Bauchart
R Copernic
Av Marceau
R Pierre Charron
R Lauriston
R de Belloy
Pl des États-Unis
R Marbeuf
R C Marot
Pl Amiral de Grasse
R de Chaillot
Av Pierre 1er de Serbie
R Galilée
R de la Trémoille
Boissière
16e
Lycée Assomption
Av George V
R du Boccador
Av Raymond Poincaré
R Boissière
Musée Guimet des Arts Asiatiques
Musée de la Mode de la Ville de Paris
12
8
3
Sq Brignole Galliéra
R de Longchamp
R de Lübeck
Iéna
Alma Marceau
Pl de la Reine Astrid
Pl d'Iéna
6
Palais de Tokyo
10
Musée d'Art Moderne de la Ville de Paris
Pl de l'Alma
Pl du Trocadéro et du 11 Novembre
Av du Président Wilson
Trocadéro
Av Albert de Mun
Av d'Iéna
Pont de l'Alma
Aquarium de Paris Cinéaqua
R Fresnel
Av de New York
Cimetière de Passy
1
Palais de Chaillot
Pont de l'Alma
Pl de la Résistance
Passerelle Debilly
7
Av des Nations Unies
Q Branly
Pl de Varsovie
Port de la Bourdonnais
Av Rapp
Av Bosquet

For reviews see

Top Sights	p38
Sights	p42
Eating	p45
Drinking	p46
Entertainment	p47
Shopping	p47

Sights

Palais de Chaillot

PALACE

1 Map p40, A5

The two curved, colonnaded wings of this palace and the terrace in between them afford an exceptional panorama of the **Jardins du Trocadéro**, the Seine and the Eiffel Tower. The palace's eastern wing houses the standout **Cité de l'Architecture et du Patrimoine** (www.citechaillot.fr; 1 place du Trocadéro et du 11 Novembre, 16e; adult/child €8/free; 11am-7pm Wed & Fri-Mon, to 9pm Thu; M Trocadéro), devoted to French architecture and heritage. The western wing houses the Musée de la Marine. Also located in this wing is Musée de l'Homme, which is closed for renovations until 2015.

(17 place du Trocadéro et du 11 Novembre, 16e; M Trocadéro)

Musée Jacquemart-André

ART MUSEUM

2 Map p40, F1

If you belonged to the cream of Parisian society in the late 19th century, chances are you would have been invited to one of the dazzling soirées held at this mansion. The home of art collectors Nélie Jacquemart and Édouard André, this opulent residence was designed in the then-fashionable eclectic style, which combined elements from different eras – seen here in the presence of Greek and Roman antiquities, Egyptian artefacts, period furnishings and portraits by Dutch masters.

(www.musee-jacquemart-andre.com; 158 bd Haussmann, 8e; adult/child €11/9.50; 10am-6pm, to 9.30pm Mon & Sat during temporary exhibits; M Miromesnil)

Musée Guimet des Arts Asiatiques

ART MUSEUM

3 Map p40, B4

France's foremost Asian art museum has a superb collection. Observe the gradual transmission of both Buddhism and artistic styles along the Silk Road in pieces ranging from 1st-century Gandhara Buddhas from Afghanistan and Pakistan, to later Central Asian, Chinese and Japanese Buddhist sculptures and art. Part of the collection is housed in the nearby **Panthéon Bouddhique** (19 av d'Iéna, 16e; admission free; 10am-5.45pm Wed-Mon, garden to 5pm) with a **Japanese garden**.

(www.museeguimet.fr; 6 place d'Iéna, 16e; adult/child €7.50/free; 10am-6pm Wed-Mon; M Iéna)

Grand Palais

ART MUSEUM

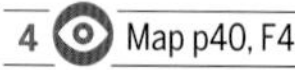

4 Map p40, F4

Erected for the 1900 Exposition Universelle (World's Fair), the Grand Palais today houses several exhibition spaces beneath its huge 8.5-ton art nouveau glass roof. Some of Paris' biggest shows (Renoir, Chagall, Turner) are held in the Galeries Nationales, lasting three to four months. Hours, prices and exhibition dates vary significantly for all galleries. Those listed here generally apply

Palais de Chaillot

to the Galeries Nationales, but always check the website for exact details. Reserving a ticket online for any show is strongly advised.
(www.grandpalais.fr; 3 av du Général Eisenhower, 8e; adult/child €13/9; 10am-10pm Tue-Sat, to 8pm Sun & Mon; M Champs-Élysées–Clemenceau)

Petit Palais

ART MUSEUM

5 Map p40, G4

Like the Grand Palais opposite, this architectural stunner was also built for the 1900 Exposition Universelle, and is home to the Paris municipality's Museum of Fine Arts, the Musée des Beaux-Arts de la Ville de Paris. It specialises in medieval and Renaissance objets d'art, such as porcelain and clocks, tapestries, drawings and 19th-century French painting and sculpture, and also has paintings by such artists as Rembrandt, Colbert, Cézanne, Monet, Gaugin and Delacroix.
(www.petitpalais.paris.fr; av Winston Churchill, 8e; permanent collections free; 10am-6pm Tue-Sun; M Champs-Élysées–Clemenceau)

Palais de Tokyo

ART MUSEUM

6 Map p40, C4

The Tokyo Palace, created for the 1937 Exposition Universelle, has no permanent collection. Rather its shell-like interior of concrete and steel is a stark backdrop to interactive contemporary art exhibitions and installations.

Its bookshop is fabulous for art and design magazines, and its eating and drinking options are magic.
(www.palaisdetokyo.com; 13 av du Président Wilson, 16e; adult/child €10/free; noon-midnight Wed-Mon; M Iéna)

Aquarium de Paris Cinéaqua AQUARIUM

7  Map p40, B5

Paris' aquarium, on the eastern side of the Jardins du Trocadéro, has a shark tank and 500-odd fish species to entertain families on rainy days. Three cinemas screen ocean-related and other films (dubbed in French, with subtitles). Show your ticket from the nearby Musée de la Marine to get reduced aquarium admission (adult/child €16.40/10.40).
(www.cineaqua.com; av des Nations Unies, 16e; adult/child €20.50/16; 10am-7pm; M Trocadéro)

Musée de la Mode de la Ville de Paris MUSEUM

8  Map p40, C4

Paris' Fashion Museum, housed in 19th-century Palais Galliera, warehouses some 100,000 outfits and accessories – from canes and umbrellas to fans and gloves – from the 18th century to the present day. The sumptuous Italianate palace and gardens dating from the mid-19th century are worth a visit in themselves, as are the excellent temporary exhibitions.
(www.palaisgalliera.paris.fr; 10 av Pierre 1er de Serbie, 16e; adult/child €8/free; 10am-6pm Tue, Wed, Fri-Sun, 10am-9pm Thu; M Iéna)

Musée Maxim's MUSEUM

9  Map p40, H4

During *la belle époque,* Maxim's bistro was the most glamorous place to be in the capital. The restaurant has lost much of its cachet (though the food is actually excellent), but for art nouveau buffs, the real treasure is the upstairs museum. Opened by Maxim's owner, fashion designer Pierre Cardin, it's filled with some 550 pieces of art nouveau artworks, *objets d'art* and furniture detailed during 40-minute guided tours (available in English).
(01 42 65 30 47; www.maxims-musee-artnouveau.com; 3 rue Royale, 8e; admission €15; tours 2pm, 3.15pm & 4pm Wed-Sun; M Concorde)

Musée d'Art Moderne de la Ville de Paris ART MUSEUM

10  Map p40, C4

The permanent collection at Paris' modern-art museum displays works representative of just about every major artistic movement of the 20th and (nascent) 21st centuries, with works by Modigliani, Matisse, Braque and Soutine. The real jewel though is the room hung with canvases by Dufy and Bonnard. Look out for cutting-edge temporary exhibitions (not free).
(www.mam.paris.fr; 11 av du Président Wilson, 16e; admission free; 10am-6pm Tue, Wed, Fri-Sun, 10am-10pm Thu; M Iéna)

Eating

Ladurée

PATISSERIE €

11 Map p40, D2

One of the oldest patisseries in Paris, Ladurée has been around since 1862 and was the original creator of the lighter-than-air *macaron*. Its tearoom is the classiest spot to indulge on the Champs. Alternatively, pick up some pastries to go – from croissants to its trademark *macarons,* it's all quite heavenly.

(www.laduree.com; 75 av des Champs-Élysées, 8e; pastries from €1.50; 7.30am-11.30pm Mon-Fri, 8.30am-12.30am Sat, 8.30am-11.30pm Sun; M George V)

Philippe & Jean-Pierre

TRADITIONAL FRENCH €€

12 Map p40, D4

Philippe graciously oversees the elegant, parquet-floored, white tableclothed dining room, while co-owner Jean-Pierre helms the kitchen. Seasonal menus incorporate dishes such as cauliflower cream soup with mushrooms and truffles, sautéed scallops with leek and Granny Smith sauce and melt-in-the-middle *moelleux au chocolat* cake. Given the service, quality and gilt-edged Triangle d'Or location, prices are a veritable bargain.

(01 47 23 57 80; www.philippeetjeanpierre.fr; 7 rue de Boccador, 8e; 4-/5-course menus €40/50, mains €24-26; noon-2.15pm & 7.15-10.45pm Mon-Sat; M Alma Marceau)

Lasserre

GASTRONOMIC €€€

13 Map p40, F4

Since 1942, this exceedingly elegant restaurant in the Triangle d'Or has hosted style icons such as Audrey Hepburn and is still a superlative choice for a twin-Michelin-starred meal to remember. A bellhop-attended lift, white-and-gold chandeliered decor, extraordinary retractable roof and flawless service set the stage for head chef Christophe Moret's and pastry chef Claire Heitzer's inspired creations. Dress code required.

(01 43 59 02 13; www.restaurant-lasserre.com; 17 av Franklin Roosevelt, 8e; lunch menus €90-120, degustation menu €220, mains €82-125; noon-2pm Thu-Fri, 7-10pm Tue-Sat; M Franklin D Roosevelt)

Local Life

Hidden Oasis

Descending rustic, uneven staircases (by the white-marble Alfred de Musset sculpture on av Franklin D Roosevelt, or the upper garden off Cours la Reine) brings you to the tiny, 0.7-hectare **Jardin de la Nouvelle France** (Map p40, F4), an unexpected wonderland of lilacs, lemon, orange, maple and weeping beech trees, with a wildlife-filled pond, waterfall, wooden footbridge and benches to soak up the serenity.

Mini Palais
MODERN FRENCH €€

14 Map p40, F4

Set inside the Grand Palais, the Mini Palais resembles an artist's studio on a colossal scale, with unvarnished hardwood floors, industrial lights suspended from ceiling beams and plaster casts on display. Its sizzling success means that the crowd is anything but bohemian; dress to impress for a taste of the lauded modern cuisine.

(☎01 42 56 42 42; www.minipalais.com; av Winston Churchill, 8e; lunch menus €28, mains €22-45; ⏲10am-2am, kitchen to midnight; Ⓜ Champs-Élysées–Clemenceau or Invalides)

Le Hide
FRENCH €€

15 Map p40, B1

A perpetual favourite, Le Hide is a tiny neighbourhood bistro serving scrumptious traditional French fare: snails, baked shoulder of lamb with pumpkin purée or monkfish in lemon butter. Unsurprisingly, this place fills up faster than you can scamper down the steps of the nearby Arc de Triomphe. Reserve well in advance.

(☎01 45 74 15 81; www.lehide.fr; 10 rue du Général Lanrezac, 17e; 2-/3-course menus €25/34; ⏲noon-2pm Mon-Fri & 7-10pm Mon-Sat; Ⓜ Charles de Gaulle–Étoile)

Bistrot du Sommelier
BISTRO €€€

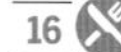

16 Map p40, G1

If you like *haute cuisine* with your wine (rather than the other way around), this refurbished brainchild of star sommelier Philippe Faure-Brac offers superb degustation menus with pre-paired wines. Fridays are an institution, offering a three-course tasting lunch with wine for €55 and five-course dinner with wine for €75 (reservations essential).

(☎01 42 65 24 85; www.bistrotdusommelier.com; 97 bd Haussmann; lunch menus €34-55, dinner menus €70-118; ⏲noon-2.30pm & 7-10.30pm Mon-Fri; Ⓜ St-Augustin)

Drinking

Charlie Birdy
PUB

17 Map p40, E2

This laid-back place situated off the Champs-Élysées is the most inviting pub in the neighbourhood. The usual array of bar food (burgers, hot dogs) is available; DJs hit the decks on weekends.

(www.charliebirdy.com; 124 rue de la Boétie, 8e; ⏲noon-5am; 📶; Ⓜ Franklin D Roosevelt)

ShowCase
CLUB

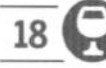

18 Map p40, F5

This huge electro club has solved the neighbour-versus-noise problem that haunts so many Parisian nightlife spots: it's secreted beneath the Pont Alexandre III bridge alongside the Seine. Unlike other exclusive Champs backstreet clubs, the Showcase can pack 'em in (up to 1500 clubbers) and is less stringent

about its door policy, though you'll still want to dress like a star.
(www.showcase.fr; Port des Champs-Élysées, 8e; ⏱11.30pm-6am Thu-Sat; MInvalides or Champs-Élysées–Clemenceau)

Queen CLUB

19  Map p40, D2

These days this doyen of a club is as popular with a straight crowd as it is with its namesake clientele, but Monday's disco nights are still prime dancing queen territory. Although right on the Champs-Élysées, it's not nearly as inaccessible as the other nearby clubs.
(☎01 53 89 08 90; www.queen.fr; 102 av des Champs-Élysées, 8e; ⏱11.30pm-6.30am; MGeorge V)

Entertainment

Salle Pleyel CLASSICAL

20 Map p40, D1

Dating from the 1920s, this highly regarded hall hosts many of Paris' finest classical-music recitals and concerts.
(☎01 42 56 13 13; www.sallepleyel.fr; 252 rue du Faubourg St-Honoré, 8e; ⏱box office noon-7pm Mon-Sat, to 8pm on day of performance, 11am to 2 hours prior to performance Sun; MTernes)

Local Life

Golden Triangle

The designer-heeled **Triangle d'Or** (Golden Triangle; Map p40, D2) harbours historic *haute couture* flagships including Chanel, Christian Dior, Christian Lacroix, Commes des Garçons, Givenchy, Hermès, Jean-Paul Gaultier, Lanvin, Louis Vuitton and Yves Saint Laurent.

Shopping

Guerlain PERFUME

21  Map p40, E3

Guerlain is Paris' most famous parfumerie, and its shop (dating from 1912) is one of the most beautiful in the city. With its shimmering mirror and marble art-deco interior, it's a reminder of the former glory of the Champs-Élysées. For total indulgence, make an appointment at its decadent spa.
(☎spa 01 45 62 11 21; www.guerlain.com; 68 av des Champs-Élysées, 8e; ⏱10.30am-8pm Mon-Sat, noon-7pm Sun; MFranklin D Roosevelt)

Explore

Louvre, Tuileries & Opéra

Carving its way through the city, Paris' *axe historique* passes through the Tuileries gardens before reaching IM Pei's glass pyramid at the entrance to Paris' mightiest museum, the Louvre. Gourmet shops garland the Église de la Madeleine, while further north are the splendid Palais Garnier opera house and art nouveau department stores of the Grands Boulevards.

The Sights in a Day

Navigating the labyrinthine **Louvre** (p50) takes a while, so it's an ideal place to start your day. Other museums well worth a visit include the **Musée de l'Orangerie** (p60), showcasing Monet's enormous *Water Lilies*, and photography at the **Jeu de Paume** (p60), both enveloped by the elegant lawns, fountains and ponds of the **Jardin des Tuileries** (p60).

After visiting the **Église de la Madeleine** (p60), deliberate over the eateries around **place de la Madeleine** (p70). Go behind the scenes of the opulent **Palais Garnier** (p68) opera house. Then shop at the beautiful **Galeries Lafayette** (p70) and **Le Printemps** (p70) department stores and take in the free panoramas from their rooftops.

Two of the hottest restaurants in this 'hood, **Frenchie** (p63) and **Verjus** (p64), offer walk-in wine-bar dining. Afterwards, hit the dance floor of legendary house and techno venue **Le Rex Club** (p68) or catch a jazz session on **rue des Lombards**.

For a local's day in Les Halles, see p56.

Top Sights

Louvre (p50)

Local Life

The Spirit of Les Halles (p56)

Best of Paris

Architecture

Galeries Lafayette (p70)

Louvre glass pyramid (p50)

Forum des Halles (p71)

Museums

Musée de l'Orangerie (p60)

Jeu de Paume (p60)

Eating

Frenchie (p63)

Yam'Tcha (p65)

Getting There

Ⓜ **Metro** The Louvre has two metro stations: Palais Royal–Musée du Louvre (lines 1 and 7), and Louvre–Rivoli (line 1).

Ⓜ **Metro** Châtelet–Les Halles is Paris' main hub, with many metro and RER lines converging here.

Boat The hop-on, hop-off Batobus stops outside the Louvre.

Top Sights
Louvre

It's estimated it would take nine months just to glance at every artwork in Paris' pièce de résistance, one of the world's largest and most diverse museums, stretching along the Seine. Constructed as a fortress by Philippe-Auguste in the early 13th century, the Palais du Louvre was rebuilt in the mid-16th century as a royal residence; and in 1793 the Revolutionary Convention turned it into France's first national museum. Today, it's the resplendent showcase of some 35,000 works.

Map p58, E5

www.louvre.fr

rue de Rivoli & quai des Tuileries, 1er

adult/child €12/free

9am-6pm Mon, Thu, Sat & Sun, to 9.45pm Wed & Fri

M Palais Royal–Musée du Louvre

Don't Miss

Collections

This rambling palace houses priceless treasures from antiquity to the 19th century, within eight curatorial departments: Near Eastern Antiquities, Egyptian Antiquities, Greek, Etruscan and Roman Antiquities, Islamic Art, Sculptures, Decorative Arts, Paintings (split into three main categories: the French school, the Italian and Spanish schools, and the Northern European schools – German, Flemish and Dutch), and Prints and Drawings.

Louvre Pyramid

A new entrance was necessary to accommodate the crowds, but when it was unveiled in 1989, few people thought IM Pei's 21m-high futuristic glass pyramid was in keeping with the centuries-old palace. But the bold juxtaposition works and today no one could imagine the Louvre without it.

Hall Napoléon

The split-level public area under the glass pyramid is known as the Hall Napoléon. In addition to a helpful information booth, there's a temporary exhibition hall, a bookshop, a souvenir store, a cafe and auditoriums.

Mona Lisa

Room 6, 1st floor, Denon Wing

The Louvre's star attraction, Leonardo Da Vinci's early 16th-century painting *La Joconde (Mona Lisa)*, resides in a climate-controlled enclosure that is situated behind a wooden railing and bulletproof glass in the glass-roofed Salle des Etats.

☑ Top Tips

- You need to queue twice to get in: once for security and then again to buy tickets.
- The longest queues are outside the Grande Pyramide; use the Carrousel du Louvre entrance (99 rue de Rivoli or direct from the metro) or the Porte de Lions entrance (closed Wednesday and Friday).
- A Paris Museum Pass or Paris City Passport gives you priority; buying tickets in advance will also help expedite the process.
- Advance tickets are available from Fnac; a new online ticketing system is being implemented.
- Multimedia guides (€5/3) help you get the most out of your visit.

Take a Break

Tickets are valid all day, so you can nip out any time. If the weather's amenable, picnic like a royal in the Jardin des Tuileries (p60).

LOUVRE

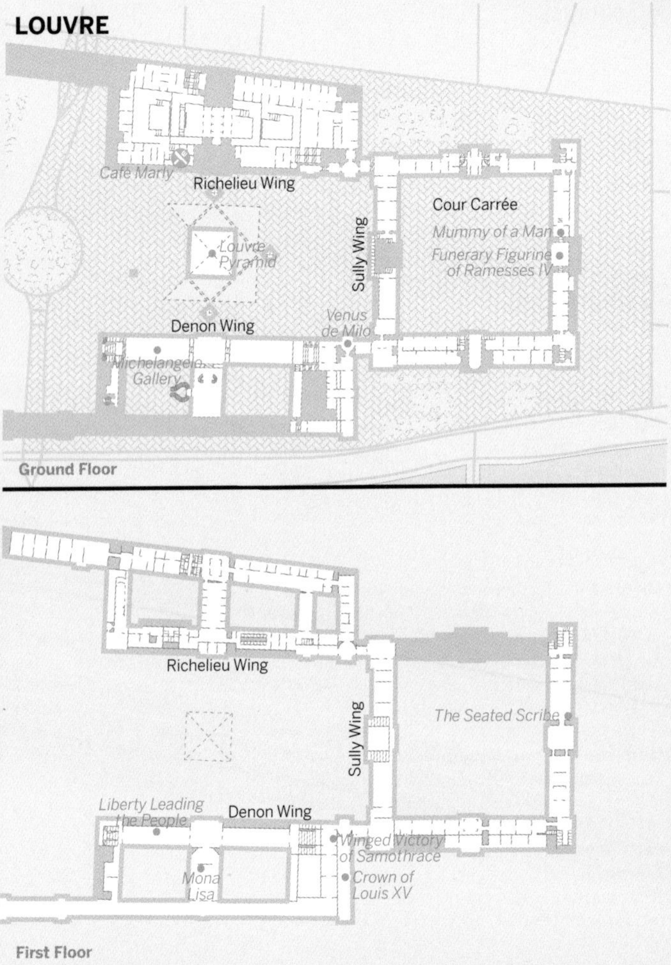

Café Marly
Richelieu Wing
Louvre Pyramid
Sully Wing
Cour Carrée
Mummy of a Man
Funerary Figurine of Ramesses IV
Denon Wing
Venus de Milo
Michelangelo Gallery

Ground Floor

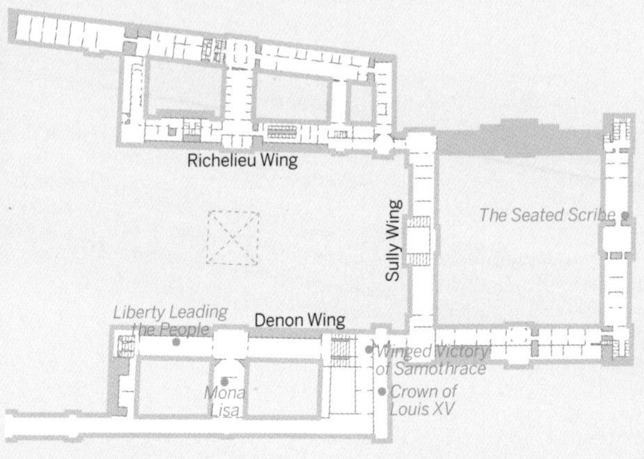

First Floor

Venus de Milo

Room 16, ground floor, Sully Wing

Standing 203cm high, the c 100–130 BC Greek marble sculpture *Aphrodite of Milos*, better known as the *Venus de Milo*, is slightly larger than life size. The graceful statue (discovered in 1820 without its arms) depicts Aphrodite, the Greek goddess of beauty and love.

Winged Victory of Samothrace

Top of Daru staircase, 1st floor, Denon Wing

This c 190 BC marble sculpture of the Greek goddess Nike (Victory), the *Winged Victory of Samothrace* (also known as the *Nike of Samothrace*), was discovered in 1863 (minus her head and arms) and has been displayed at the Louvre since 1884. It's under renovation throughout 2015.

The Raft of the Medusa

Room 77, 1st floor, Denon Wing

Théodore Géricault's large-scale *The Raft of the Medusa* was inspired by the French Royal Navy frigate, the *Medusa,* shipwrecked in 1816 en route to colonise Senegal. The shortage of lifeboats meant a raft had to be built for 150 people, which drifted for 13 days and ultimately saved only 10 lives.

19th-Century French Works

2nd floor, Sully Wing

Works by artists such as Corot and Fragonard are housed on the 2nd floor of the Sully Wing. Look out for Ingres' *Turkish Bath* (Room 60, 2nd Floor, Sully Wing).

Pharaonic Egypt Collections

Sully Wing

The eastern side of the Sully Wing's ground and 1st floors houses the Louvre's astonishing cache of Pharaonic Egyptian art, artefacts and funerary art.

The Seated Scribe

Room 22, 1st floor, Sully Wing

Sitting cross-legged, *The Seated Scribe,* the painted limestone statue with rock-crystal inlaid eyes, dates way back to c 2620–2500 BC. Measuring 53.7cm high by 44cm wide, the unknown figure is depicted holding a papyrus scroll in his left hand; he's thought to have been holding a brush in his right hand that has since disappeared.

Michelangelo Gallery

Room 4, ground floor, Denon Wing

Michelangelo's marble masterpiece *The Dying Slave* is one of many magnificent 16th- to 19th-century Italian sculptures here, along with Canova's *Psyche and Cupid.*

Italian Paintings

1st floor, Denon Wing

Renaissance works by Raphael, Botticelli and Titian are among the Louvre's collection of Italian paintings on the Denon Wing's 1st floor.

Detail of Richelieu Wing

Islamic Galleries

Lower ground floor, Denon Wing

The state-of-the-art Islamic art galleries are housed in the stunningly restored Cour Visconti, topped by a 'flying carpet' roof, and present an overview of artistic creation from the 7th century to the early 19th century.

Northern European Paintings

2nd floor, Richelieu Wing

Directly above the gilt and crystal of the Napoléon III Apartments (1st floor), the Richelieu Wing's 2nd floor allows for a quieter meander through an inspirational collection of Flemish and Dutch paintings spearheaded by works by Peter Paul Rubens and Pieter Bruegel the Elder. Vermeer's *The Lacemaker* can be found in Room 38, while Room 31 is devoted chiefly to works by Rembrandt.

Crown of Louis XV

Room 66, 1st floor, Denon Wing

French kings traditionally had crowns made solely for their coronations, which was the only time Louis XV wore this embroidered satin cap in 1722. Topped by openwork arches and a fleur-de-lis, the crown was originally adorned with pearls, sapphires, rubies, topazes, emeralds and diamonds; in 1729 the stones were replaced with the paste imitations you see today.

Temporary Exhibitions

The Hall Napoléon mounts excellent temporary exhibitions (€13). Note that free admission to the Louvre on the first Sunday of the month from October to March doesn't include temporary exhibitions.

Thematic Trails

The Louvre has an array of innovative, entertaining self-guided thematic trails, from 'Masterpieces of the Louvre' to 'The Art of Eating', as well as the 'Da Vinci Code' tour and many trails that kids will enjoy such as 'A Lion Hunt' (lion sculptures). Trails can be downloaded from the website.

Guided Tours

If you'd like expert guidance, various English-language tours depart from the Hall Napoléon. Reserve a spot up to 14 days in advance where possible, or sign up on arrival at the museum.

Other Palais du Louvre Museums

Rohan Wing

The Louvre shelters three **additional museums** (www.lesartsdecoratifs.fr; 107 rue de Rivoli, 1er; aduld/child €11/free; ⌚11am-6pm Tue-Sun, to 9pm Thu; MPalais Royal–Musée du Louvre): the **Musée des Arts Décoratifs**, featuring furniture, ceramics and glassware; the **Musée de la Publicité**, displaying advertising, including posters dating from the 13th century; and the **Musée de la Mode et du Textile**, showcasing couture and fabrics.

Local Life
The Spirit of Les Halles

In 1137 Louis VI created *halles* (markets) for merchants who converged on the city centre to sell their wares, and for over 800 years they were, in the words of Émile Zola, the 'belly of Paris'. Although the wholesalers moved out to the suburb of Rungis in 1971, the markets' spirit lives on in legacies and local treasures here.

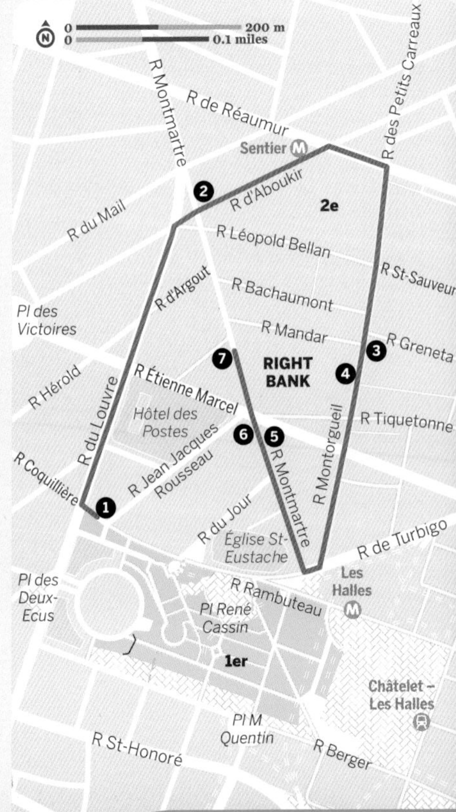

1 Cookware Shopping

Paris' professional chefs still come to this neighbourhood to stock up on knives, whisks, sieves, slicers, ladles, grinders, pastry moulds, pots, pans, chopping blocks, champagne buckets, duck presses and more at venerable cookware shops, including the 1820-established **E Dehillerin** (www.dehillerin.com; 18-20 rue Coquillière, 1er; 9am-12.30pm & 2-6pm Mon, 9am-6pm Tue-Sat; M Les Halles).

❷ Cookbook Shopping

There are more esteemed cookware shops on rue Montmartre, as well as Paris' leading food bookshop **Librairie Gourmande** (www.librairie-gourmande.fr; 92 rue Montmartre, 1er; ⏲11am-7pm Mon-Sat; Ⓜ Sentier) – a perfect place to pick up inspiration. All the classic texts are here, along with cutting-edge collections and cocktail recipe books.

❸ Oyster Market Legacy

A splinter of the historic *halles*, pedestrianised rue Montorgueil was its oyster market. The remaining legacy of its original incarnation is the 19th-century timber-lined restaurant **Au Rocher de Cancale** (☎01 42 33 50 29; www.aurocherdecancale.fr; 78 rue Montorgueil, 2e; mains €10.50-22; ⏲8am-2am daily; Ⓜ Sentier or Les Halles). At this memorable restaurant, virtually unchanged, you can feast on oysters and seafood from Cancale (Brittany).

❹ Picturesque Patisserie

Opened in 1730 the beautiful pastel murals at **Stohrer** (www.stohrer.fr; 51 rue Montorgueil, 2e; ⏲7.30am-8.30pm daily; Ⓜ Les Halles) were added in 1864 by Paul Baudry, who also decorated the Garnier Opèra's Grand Foyer. Specialities invented here include *baba rhum* (rum-drenched brioche) and *puit d'amour* (cream-filled, caramel-topped puff pastry).

❺ Gourmet Goods Shopping

If the foie gras, truffles, caviar and other delicacies at the 1894 *épicerie* (specialist grocer) **Comptoir de la Gastronomie** (www.comptoirdelagastronomie.com; 34 rue Montmartre, 1er; ⏲6am-8pm Tue-Sat, 9am-8pm Mon; Ⓜ Les Halles) tantalise, you can enjoy them at its adjacent restaurant.

❻ Apéro at Le Conchon à l'Oreille

A Parisian jewel, the heritage-listed hole-in-the-wall **Le Conchon à l'Oreille** (☎01 42 36 07 56; 15 rue Montmartre, 1er; ⏲10am-2am Tue-Sat; Ⓜ Les Halles) retains laid tiles from the 1890s, depicting vibrant market scenes of the old *halles*. Hours can vary.

❼ Late-Night Dinner at Le Tambour

Salvaged street furniture and old metro maps make the good-natured bistro and bar **Le Tambour** (☎01 42 33 06 90; 41 rue Montmartre, 2e; ⏲8am-6am; Ⓜ Étienne Marcel or Sentier) a shrine to the soul of Paris and a mecca for Parisian night owls, with food served until 3.30am or 4am.

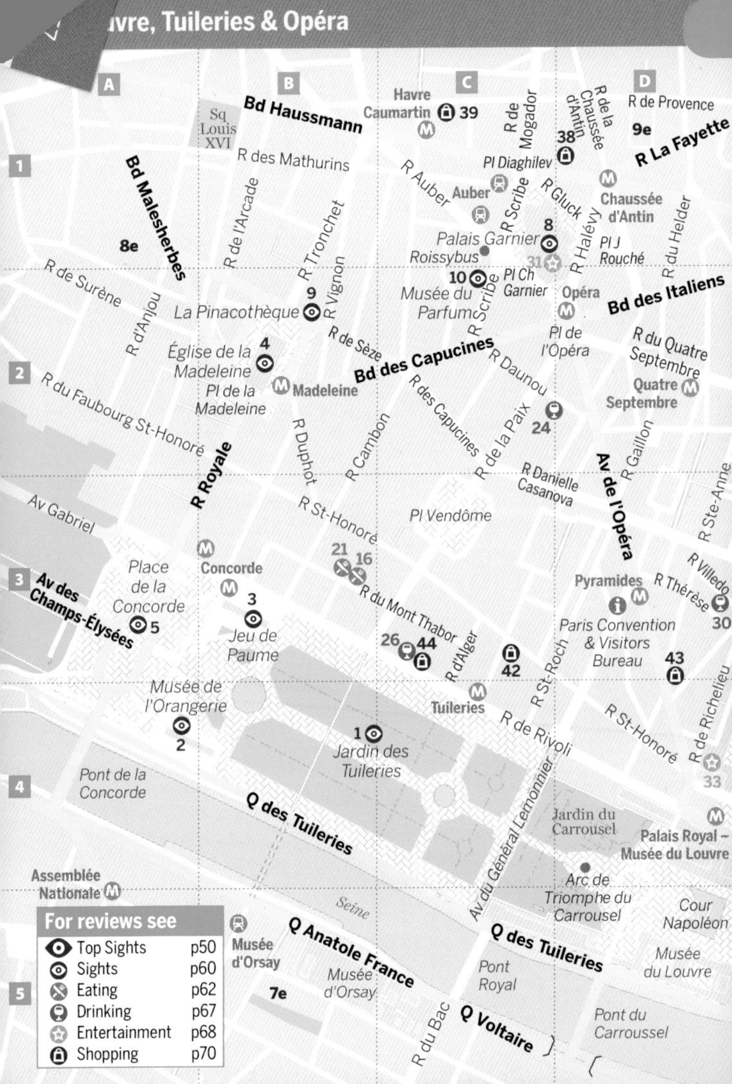
A
B
C
D
1
2
3
4
5
Sq Louis XVI
Bd Haussmann
Havre Caumartin
39
R de Mogador
R de la Chaussée d'Antin
R de Provence
9e
R La Fayette
38
Pl Diaghilev
R des Mathurins
Bd Malesherbes
R de l'Arcade
R Tronchet
R Auber
Auber
R Scribe
R Gluck
R Halévy
Chaussée d'Antin
R du Helder
8e
8
Palais Garnier
Roissybus
31
Pl J Rouché
R de Surène
10
Musée du Parfum
Pl Ch Garnier
Opéra
Bd des Italiens
9
La Pinacothèque
R Vignon
R d'Anjou
4
Église de la Madeleine
R de Sèze
Bd des Capucines
R Daunou
Pl de l'Opéra
R du Quatre Septembre
Quatre Septembre
Pl de la Madeleine
Madeleine
R du Faubourg St-Honoré
R Duphot
R Cambon
R des Capucines
R de la Paix
24
R Gaillon
Av de l'Opéra
R Danielle Casanova
R Ste-Anne
R Royale
Av Gabriel
R St-Honoré
Pl Vendôme
Concorde
Place de la Concorde
21
16
R du Mont Thabor
Pyramides
R Thérèse
R Villedo
30
Av des Champs-Élysées
5
3
Jeu de Paume
26
44
R d'Alger
42
R St-Roch
Paris Convention & Visitors Bureau
43
Musée de l'Orangerie
Tuileries
R de Rivoli
R St-Honoré
R de Richelieu
2
1
Jardin des Tuileries
33
Pont de la Concorde
Q des Tuileries
Av du Général Lemonnier
Jardin du Carrousel
Palais Royal – Musée du Louvre
Assemblée Nationale
Arc de Triomphe du Carrousel
Seine
Cour Napoléon
For reviews see
Top Sights p50
Sights p60
Eating p62
Drinking p67
Entertainment p68
Shopping p70
Musée d'Orsay
Q Anatole France
Q des Tuileries
Musée du Louvre
Pont Royal
7e
Musée d'Orsay
R du Bac
Q Voltaire
Pont du Carroussel

E
F
G
H
1
2
3
4
5
R Laffitte
R le Peletier
R Rossini
R Drouot
R du Faubourg Montmartre
36
R Richer
12
R de Montyon
15
R Trévise
R du Faubourg Poissonnière
R d'Hauteville
10e
R du Faubourg St-Denis
Bd Haussmann
Passage des Panoramas
R Bergère
32
Cité Bergère
Richelieu Drouot
Grands Boulevards
Bd Poissonnière
R de l'Échiquier
19
Bonne Nouvelle
R Favart
R de Richelieu
R St-Marc
R Montmartre
R du Sentier
35
Bd de Bonne Nouvelle
Strasbourg St-Denis
R Feydeau
R de la Lune
R des Jeûneurs
R Poissonnière
La Bourse
Bourse
2e
25
R St-Augustin
R de Cléry
R d'Aboukir
R de Réaumur
R Vivienne
R de la Banque
28
R du Nil
R du Caire
Sentier
22
13
R du Mail
R des Petits Champs
41
Pl des Petits Pères
R d'Aboukir
R Léopold Bellan
Réaumur Sébastopol
14
R de Beaujolais
23
R d'Argout
R Montmartre
R Montorgueil
29
R St-Sauveur
R de Montpensier
Pyramides
Pl des Victoires
20
R Mandar
R Greneta
R St-Denis
Bd de Sébastopol
37
Jardin du Palais Royal
6
RIGHT BANK
R du Louvre
40
R Étienne Marcel
R Tiquetonne
R de Turbigo
R de Valois
Banque de France
Hôtel des Postes
Étienne Marcel
Palais Royal
R Coquillière
R du Jour
Église St-Eustache
3e
Pl Colette
R Croix des Petits Champs
R du Colonel Driant
7
R Mondétour
1er
Pl des Deux-Ecus
Pl René Cassin
34
Les Halles
11
Pl du Palais Royal
R Rambuteau
R St-Martin
R Beaubourg
R Sauval
Châtelet – Les Halles
R St-Honoré
18
17
Jardin de l'Oratoire
Pl M Quentin
R Berger
R Pierre Lescot
Pl Georges Pompidou
Rambuteau
Musée du Louvre
27
R des Prauvaires
R des Halles
Pl M de Navarre
Louvre – Rivoli
Centre Pompidou
Cour Carrée
Pl du Louvre
R de l'Arbre Sec
R du Pont Neuf
Châtelet
Pl E Michelet
R des Lombards
Jardin de l'Infante
R de Rivoli
Châtelet
4e
R du Renard
R du Temple
Q du Louvre
Pont Neuf
Pont des Arts

Sights

Jardin des Tuileries
GARDENS

1 Map p58, B4

Filled with fountains, ponds and sculptures, the formal, 28-hectare Tuileries Garden, which begins just west of the Jardin du Carrousel, was laid out in its present form more or less in 1664 by André Le Nôtre, who also created the gardens at Vaux-le-Vicomte and Versailles. The Tuileries soon became the most fashionable spot in Paris for parading about in one's finery. It now forms part of the Banks of the Seine World Heritage Site listed by Unesco in 1991.

(7am-11pm Jun-Aug, shorter hours rest of year; ; M Tuileries or Concorde)

Musée de l'Orangerie
MUSEUM

2 Map p58, A4

Located in the southwestern corner of the Jardin des Tuileries, this museum, along with the Jeu de Paume, is all that remains of the former Palais des Tuileries, which was razed during the Paris Commune in 1871. It exhibits important Impressionist works, including a series of Monet's *Decorations des Nymphéas* (Water Lilies) in two huge oval rooms purpose-built in 1927 on the artist's instructions, as well as works by Cézanne, Matisse, Picasso, Renoir, Sisley, Soutine and Utrillo. An audioguide costs €5.

(www.musee-orangerie.fr; Jardin des Tuileries, 1e; adult/child €9/6.50; 9am-6pm Wed-Mon; M Concorde)

Jeu de Paume
GALLERY

3 Map p58, B3

The Galerie du Jeu de Paume, which stages innovative photography exhibitions, is housed in an erstwhile *jeu de paume* (royal tennis court) in the northwestern corner of the Jardin des Tuileries and is all that remains of the Palais des Tuileries.

(01 47 03 12 50; www.jeudepaume.org; 1 place de la Concorde, 8e; adult/child €8.50/free; 11am-9pm Tue, to 7pm Wed-Sun; M Concorde)

Église de la Madeleine
CHURCH

4 Map p58, B2

Place de la Madeleine (p70) is named after the 19th-century neoclassical church at its centre, the Église de la Madeleine. Constructed in the style of a massive Greek temple, 'La Madeleine' was consecrated in 1842 after almost a century of design changes and construction delays.

The church is a popular venue for classical-music concerts (some free); check the posters outside or the website for dates.

(Church of St Mary Magdalene; www.eglise-lamadeleine.com; place de la Madeleine, 8e; 9.30am-7pm; M Madeleine)

Place de la Concorde
SQUARE

5 Map p58, A3

Paris spreads around you, with views of the Eiffel Tower, the Seine and along the Champs-Élysées, when you stand in the city's largest square. Its

Place de la Concorde

3300-year-old pink granite obelisk was a gift from Egypt in 1831. The square was first laid out in 1755 and originally named after King Louis XV, but its royal associations meant that it took centre stage during the Revolution – Louis XVI was the first to be guillotined here in 1793.
(8e; M Concorde)

Jardin du Palais Royal GARDENS

6 Map p58, E3

The Jardin du Palais Royal is a perfect spot to sit, contemplate, and picnic between boxed hedges or shop in the trio of arcades that frame the garden so beautifully: the Galerie de Valois (east), Galerie de Montpensier (west) and Galerie Beaujolais. However, it's the southern end of the complex, polka-dotted with sculptor Daniel Buren's 260 black-and-white striped columns, that has become the garden's signature feature.
(2 place Colette, 1er; admission free; 7am-10.15pm Apr & May, to 11pm Jun-Aug, shorter hours rest of year; M Palais Royal–Musée du Louvre)

Église St-Eustache CHURCH

7 Map p58, F4

Just north of the gardens snuggling up to the city's old marketplace, now the bustling Forum des Halles, is one of the most beautiful churches in Paris. Majestic, architecturally

magnificent and musically outstanding, St-Eustache has made spirits soar for centuries.
(www.st-eustache.org; 2 impasse St-Eustache, 1er; 9.30am-7pm Mon-Fri, 9am-7pm Sat & Sun; M Les Halles)

Palais Garnier

OPERA HOUSE

8 Map p58, C1

The fabled 'phantom of the opera' lurked in this opulent opera house designed in 1860 by Charles Garnier (then an unknown 35-year-old architect). You can reserve a spot on an English-language guided tour or take an unguided tour of the attached museum, with posters, costumes, backdrops, original scores and other memorabilia, which includes a behind-the scenes peek (except during matinees and rehearsals). Highlights include the Grand Staircase and horseshoe-shaped, gilded auditorium with red velvet seats, a massive chandelier and Chagall's gorgeous ceiling mural.
(08 25 05 44 05; www.operadeparis.fr; cnr rues Scribe & Auber, 9e; adult/child €10/6, guided tour adult/child €14/12.50; 10am-5pm, to 1pm on matinee performance days, guided tour by reservation; M Opéra)

La Pinacothèque

ART MUSEUM

9 Map p58, B2

The top private museum in Paris, La Pinacothèque organises three to four major exhibits per year. Its nonlinear approach to art history, with exhibits that range from Mayan masks to retrospectives covering the work of artists such as Edvard Munch, has shaken up the otherwise rigid Paris art world and won over residents used to more formal presentations.
(www.pinacotheque.com; 28 place de la Madeleine, 8e; adult/child from €12.30/10.80; 10.30am-6pm Sat-Tue & Thu, to 9pm Wed & Fri; M Madeleine)

Musée du Parfum

MUSEUM

10 Map p58, C2

If the art of perfume-making entices, stop by this collection of copper distillery vats and antique flacons and test your nose on a few basic scents. Run by the parfumerie Fragonard, it's located in a beautiful old *hôtel particulier* (private mansion); free guided visits are available in multiple languages. A short distance south, a separate wing in a 20th-century theatre, the **Théâtre-Musée des Capucines** (39 blvd des Capucines, 2e; 9am-6pm Mon-Sat; M Opéra), concentrates largely on the bottling and packaging side of perfume production.
(www.fragonard.com; 9 rue Scribe, 9e; admission free; 9am-6pm Mon-Sat, to 5pm Sun; M Opéra)

Eating

Pirouette

NEOBISTRO €€

11 Map p58, G4

In one of the best restaurants in the vicinity of the old 'belly of Paris', chef Tomy Gousset's kitchen crew is working wonders at this cool loft-like space, serving up tantalising creations

Understand

Flâneurie

Parisian writer Charles Baudelaire (1821–67) came up with the whimsical term *flâneur* to describe a 'gentleman stroller of city streets' or a 'detached pedestrian observer of a metropolis'.

Paris' ornate arcades were closely tied to the concept of *flâneurie* in philosopher Walter Benjamin's *Arcades Project* (written between 1927 and 1940, and published posthumously). Known as *passages couverts* (covered passages), these marble-floored, iron-and-glass-roofed shopping arcades, streaming with natural light, were the elegant forerunners of department stores and malls.

The term *flâneurie* is now widely used, especially in the context of architecture and town planning. But Paris – with its village-like backstreets, riverbank paths, parks and gardens and its passages – remains the ultimate place for a *flâneur* to meander without any particular destination in mind.

Discover Paris' finest remaining passages on a walking tour (p176).

that range from seared duck, asparagus and Buddha's hand fruit to rum baba with Chantilly and lime. Some unique ingredients and a new spin for French cuisine.
(☎01 40 26 47 81; 5 rue Mondétour, 1er; lunch menus €18, 3-/6-course dinner menus €40/60; ⏰noon-2.30pm & 7.30-10.30pm Mon-Sat; Ⓜ Les Halles)

Richer — NEOBISTRO €€

12 Map p58, G1

Run by the same team as across-the-street neighbour **L'Office** (☎01 47 70 67 31; 3 rue Richer, 9e; 2-/3-course lunch menus €22/27, dinner menus €28/34; ⏰noon-2.30pm & 7.30-10.30pm Mon-Fri; Ⓜ Poissonière or Bonne Nouvelle), Richer's pared-back, exposed-brick decor is a smart setting for genius creations like trout tartare with cauliflower and tomato and citrus mousse, and quince and lime cheesecake for dessert. It doesn't take reservations, but if it's full, Richer posts a list of recommended local addresses outside. Fantastic value.
(2 rue Richer, 9e; mains €16-25; ⏰kitchen noon-2.30pm & 7.30-10.30pm; Ⓜ Poissonière or Bonne Nouvelle)

Frenchie — BISTRO €€€

13 Map p58, G3

Tucked down an alley you wouldn't venture down otherwise, this bijou bistro with wooden tables and old stone walls is iconic. Frenchie is always packed and for good reason: excellent-value dishes are modern, market-driven (the menu changes daily with a choice of two dishes) and

prepared with just the right dose of unpretentious creative flair by French chef Gregory Marchand.
(01 40 39 96 19; www.frenchie-restaurant.com; 5-6 rue du Nil, 2e; prix fixe menus €48; 7-11pm Mon-Fri; M Sentier)

Verjus
MODERN AMERICAN €€€

14 Map p58, E3

Opened by American duo Braden Perkins and Laura Adrian, Verjus was born out of a wildly successful clandestine supper club known as the Hidden Kitchen. The restaurant builds on that tradition, offering a chance to sample some excellent, creative cuisine (gnocchi with shiitake relish and parmesan, wild-boar confit with cherry compote) in a casual space. The tasting menu is a series of small plates, using ingredients sourced straight from producers.
(01 42 97 54 40; www.verjusparis.com; 52 rue de Richelieu, 1er; prixe-fixe menus €60; 7-10pm Mon-Fri; M Bourse or Palais Royal–Musée du Louvre)

Floquifil
TRADITIONAL FRENCH €€

15 Map p58, F1

If you were to envision the ultimate backstreet Parisian wine bar, it would probably look a lot like Floquifil: table-strewn terrace, dark timber furniture, aquamarine-painted walls and bottles galore. But while the by-the-glass wines are superb, you're missing out if you don't dine here (on rosemary-roasted lamb with ratatouille, or at the very least, a chacuterie platter).
(01 84 19 42 12; www.floquifil.fr; 17 rue de Montyon, 9e; mains €14-25; 11am-midnight Mon-Fri, from 6.30pm Sat; M Grands Boulevards)

L'Ardoise
BISTRO €€

16 Map p58, B3

This is a lovely bistro with no menu as such (*ardoise* means 'blackboard', which is all there is), but who cares? The food – fricassée of corn-fed chicken with morels, pork cheeks in ginger, hare in black pepper, prepared by chef Pierre Jay (ex-Tour d'Argent) – is superb.
(01 42 96 28 18; www.lardoise-paris.com; 28 rue du Mont Thabor, 1er; menus €38; noon-2.30pm Mon-Sat, 7.30-10.30pm Mon-Sun; M Concorde or Tuileries)

La Tour de Montlhéry – Chez Denise
TRADITIONAL FRENCH €€

17 Map p58, F4

The most traditional eatery near the former Les Halles market-place, this boisterous old bistro with red-chequered tablecloths has been run by the same team for some 30 years. If you've just arrived and are ready to feast on all the French classics – snails in garlic sauce, veal liver, steak tartare, braised beef cheeks and housemade pâtés – reservations are in order. Open till dawn.
(01 42 36 21 82; 5 rue des Prouvaires, 1er; mains €23-28; noon-2.30pm & 7.30pm-5am Mon-Fri; M Châtelet)

Palais Garnier (p68)

Yam'Tcha

FUSION €€€

18 Map p58, F4

Adeline Grattard's ingeniously fused French and Cantonese flavours (fried squid with sweet-potato noodles) has earned the female chef no shortage of critical praise. Pair dishes on the frequently changing menu with wine or tea, or sample the special lunch menu (€60) offered Wednesday through Friday. Reserve up to two months in advance.
(01 40 26 08 07; www.yamtcha.com; 4 rue Sauval, 1er; prix-fixe menus €100; noon-2.30pm Wed-Sat, 7.30-10.30pm Tue-Sat; M Louvre Rivoli)

Passage 53

MODERN FRENCH €€€

19 Map p58, F2

No address inside Passage des Panoramas contrasts more dramatically with the outside hustle and bustle than this restaurant at No 53. An oasis of calm and tranquillity (with window blinds pulled firmly down when closed), this gastronomic address is an ode to the best French produce – worked to perfection in a series of tasting courses by Japanese chef Shinichi Sato. Reserve.
(01 42 33 04 35; www.passage53.com; 53 Passage des Panoramas, 2e; lunch/dinner menus €60/130; noon-2.30pm & 7.30-10.30pm Tue-Sat; M Grands Boulevards or Bourse)

Blend

BURGERS €

20 Map p58, F3

A burger cannot simply be a burger in gourmet Paris, where burger buffs dissolve into raptures of ecstacy over gourmet creations at Blend. Think homemade brioche buns and ketchup, hand-cut meat and the most inventive of toppings that transforms the humble burger into something rather special. Fries cost extra.
(www.blendhamburger.com; 44 rue d'Argout, 2e; burger & fries €14; noon-11pm daily; M Sentier)

Local Life

Moveable Feasts

Street food is taking the city by storm as food trucks specialising in everything from French favourites such as *tartiflette* (potatoes, cheese and bacon baked in a casserole) to gourmet burgers and wildly flavoured ice creams roll out across Paris.

Top picks include: **Camion Qui Fume** (www.lecamionquifume.com; burger & fries €10.50), which sizzles up gourmet burgers; **Cantine California** (www.cantinecalifornia.com; burger & fries €11), for its tacos and homemade desserts; and **Mes Bocaux** (www.mesbocaux.fr; 37 rue Marceau, 8e; 2-/3-course menu €11/13.50; M Alma-Marceau), with its French organic fare by chef Marc Veyrat served in jars (preorder before noon then pick up).

Le Soufflé

TRADITIONAL FRENCH €€

21 Map p58, B3

The faintly vintage, aqua-blue façade of this concept kitchen is reassuringly befitting of the timeless French classic it serves inside – the soufflé. The light fluffy dish served in white ramekins comes in dozens of different flavours, both savoury and sweet; *andouillette* (pig intestine sausage) is the top choice for fearless gourmets.
(01 42 60 27 19; www.lesouffle.fr; 36 rue du Mont Thabor, 1er; soufflés €13-19, menus €37 & €44; lunch & dinner Mon-Sat; M Concorde or Tuileries)

Frenchie To Go

FAST FOOD €

22 Map p58, G3

Despite the drawbacks – limited seating, eye-poppingly expensive donuts – the fast-food outpost of the burgeoning Frenchie (p63) empire is a wildly popular destination. Bilingual staff transform choice ingredients (eg cuts of meat from the Ginger Pig in Yorkshire) into American classics like pulled-pork and pastrami sandwiches, accompanied by cornets of fries, coleslaw and pickled veggies.
(www.frenchietogo.com; 9 rue du Nil, 2e; sandwiches €8-14; 8.30am-4.30pm Mon-Fri, 9.30am-5.30pm Sat & Sun; ; M Sentier)

Le Grand Véfour

TRADITIONAL FRENCH €€€

23  Map p58, E3

This 18th-century jewel on the northern edge of the Jardin du Palais Royal has been a dining favourite of the

Parisian elite since 1784; just look at who gets their names ascribed to each table – from Napoléon and Victor Hugo to Colette (who lived next door). The food is tip-top; expect a voyage of discovery in one of the most beautiful restaurants in the world.
(☎01 42 96 56 27; www.grand-vefour.com; 17 rue de Beaujolais, 1er; lunch/dinner menus €98/298; ⏰noon-2.30pm & 7.30-10.30pm Mon-Fri; M Pyramides)

Drinking

Harry's New York Bar — COCKTAIL BAR

24 Map p58, C2

One of the most popular American-style bars in the prewar years, Harry's once welcomed writers like F Scott Fitzgerald and Ernest Hemingway, who no doubt sampled the bar's unique cocktail and creation: the Bloody Mary. The Cuban mahogany interior dates from the mid-19th century and was brought over from a Manhattan bar in 1911.
(www.harrysbar.fr; 5 rue Daunou, 2e; ⏰noon-2am; M Opéra)

Social Club — CLUB

25  Map p58, F2

These subterranean rooms showcasing electro, hip hop, funk and live acts are a magnet for clubbers who take their music seriously. Across the street at No 146 is the cafe where French socialist Jean Jaurès was assassinated in 1914.
(www.parissocialclub.com; 142 rue Montmartre, 2e; ⏰11pm-6am Tue-Sat; M Grands Boulevards)

Angelina — TEAHOUSE

26  Map p58, C3

Clink china with lunching ladies, their posturing poodles and half the students from Tokyo University at Angelina, a grand dame of a tearoom dating to 1903. Decadent pastries are served here, against a fresco backdrop of belle époque Nice, but it is the superthick, decadently sickening 'African' hot chocolate (€8.20), which comes with a pot of whipped cream and a carafe of water, that prompts the constant queue for a table at Angelina.
(226 rue de Rivoli, 1er; ⏰8am-7pm Mon-Fri, 9am-7pm Sat & Sun; M Tuileries)

Le Garde Robe — WINE BAR

27  Map p58, F5

The Garde Robe may be the only bar in the world to serve alcohol with a 'Detox' menu. While you probably shouldn't come here for the full-on cleansing experience, you can expect excellent, affordable natural wines, a casual atmosphere and a good selection of eats, ranging from the standard cheese and charcuterie plates to more adventurous veg-friendly options.
(41 rue de l'Arbre Sec, 1er; ⏰12.30-2.30pm & 7.30-11pm Mon-Fri; M Louvre Rivoli)

Lockwood

CAFE

28 Map p58, G3

Hip coffee lovers can savour beans from the Belleville Brûlerie during the day and well-mixed cocktails in the subterranean candle-lit *cave* (wine cellar) at night.

(73 rue d'Aboukir, 2e; 8am-2am Mon-Sat; M Sentier)

Le Rex Club

CLUB

Attached to the Grand Rex cinema (see 35 Map p58, G2), this is Paris' premier house and techno venue where some of the world's best DJs play on a 70-speaker, multidiffusion sound system.

(www.rexclub.com; 5 bd Poissonnière, 2e; midnight-7am Thu-Sat; M Bonne Nouvelle)

Experimental Cocktail Club

COCKTAIL BAR

29 Map p58, G3

Called ECC by trendies, this speakeasy with grey façade and old-beamed ceiling is effortlessly hip. Oozing spirit and soul, the cocktail bar – with retro-chic decor by American interior designer Cuoco Black and sister bars in London and New York – is a flashback to those *années folles* (crazy years) of Prohibition New York.

(www.experimentalcocktailclub.com; 37 rue St-Saveur, 2e; 7pm-2am daily; M Réaumur-Sébastopol)

Telescope

CAFE

30 Map p58, D3

The barista delivers at this minimalist coffee shop, which brews frothy cappuccinos and serves sweet pastries.

(www.telescopecafe.com; 5 rue Villedo, 1er; 8.30am-5pm Mon-Fri, 9.30am-6.30pm Sat; M Pyramides)

Entertainment

Palais Garnier

OPERA

31 Map p58, C1

The city's original opera house is smaller than its Bastille counterpart, but has perfect acoustics. Due to its odd shape, some seats have limited or no visibility – book carefully. Ticket prices and conditions (including last-minute discounts) are available from the **box office** (cnr rues Scribe & Auber; 11am-6.30pm Mon-Sat).

(08 92 89 90 90; www.operadeparis.fr; place de l'Opéra, 9e; M Opéra)

Au Limonaire

LIVE MUSIC

32 Map p58, F1

This perfect little wine bar is one of the best places to listen to traditional French *chansons* and local singer-songwriters. Performances begin at 10pm Tuesday to Saturday and 7pm on Sunday. Entry is free; reservations are recommended if you plan on dining.

(01 45 23 33 33; http://limonaire.free.fr; 18 cité Bergère, 9e; 6pm-2am Tue-Sat, from 7pm Sun & Mon; M Grands Boulevards)

Comédie Française

THEATRE

33 Map p58, D4

Founded in 1680 under Louis XIV, this state-run theatre bases its repertoire around the works of classic French playwrights. The theatre has its roots in an earlier company directed by Molière at the Palais Royal – the French playwright and actor was seized by a convulsion on stage during the fourth performance of the *Imaginary Invalid* in 1673 and died later at his home on nearby rue de Richelieu. (www.comedie-francaise.fr; place Colette, 1er; M Palais Royal–Musée du Louvre)

Forum des Images

CINEMA

34 Map p58, F4

Cinemas showing films set in Paris are the centrepiece of the city's film archive, the Forum des Images. Created in 1988 to establish 'an audiovisual memory bank of Paris', and renovated in dramatic shades of pink, grey and black, the five-screen centre has a new library and resear ch centre with newsreels, documentaries and advertising. Check its program online for thematic series and frequent festivals and events. (www.forumdesimages.fr; 1 Grande Galerie, Porte St-Eustache, Forum des Halles, 1er; 1-10pm Tue-Fri, from 2pm Sat & Sun; M Les Halles)

Le Grand Rex

CINEMA

35 Map p58, G2

A trip to 1932 art-deco cinematic icon Le Grand Rex is like no other trip to the flicks. Screenings aside, the cinema runs 50-minute behind-the-scene tours (English soundtracks available) during which visitors – tracked by a sensor slung around their neck – are whisked right up (via a lift) behind the giant screen, tour a soundstage and get to have fun in a recording studio. Whizz-bang special effects along the way will stun adults and kids alike. (www.legrandrex.com; 1 bd Poissonnière, 2e; tour adult/child €11/9; tours 10am-7pm Wed-Sun; M Bonne Nouvelle)

Folies-Bergère

LIVE MUSIC

36 Map p58, F1

This is the legendary club where Charlie Chaplin, WC Fields and Stan Laurel appeared on stage together one night in 1911, and where Josephine Baker, accompanied by her diamond-collared pet cheetah and wearing only stilettos and a skirt made from bananas, bewitched audience members including Hemingway. Today, shows range from solo acts such as Ben Harper to musicals. (www.foliesbergere.com; 32 rue Richer, 9e; M Cadet)

Top Tip

Discount Theatre Tickets

Pick up half-price tickets for same-day performances at the free-standing **Kiosque Théâtre Madeleine** (Map p58, B2; opposite 15 place de la Madeleine, 8e; 12.30-8pm Tue-Sat, to 4pm Sun; M Madeleine).

Shopping

Didier Ludot

FASHION

37 Map p58, E3

In the rag trade since 1975, collector Didier Ludot sells the city's finest couture creations of yesteryear in his exclusive twinset of boutiques, hosts exhibitions, and has published a book portraying the evolution of the little black dress, brilliantly brought to life in his shop, **La Petite Robe Noire** (125 Galerie de Valois, 1er; 11am-7pm Mon-Sat; M Palais Royal–Musée du Louvre), which sells just that. (www.didierludot.fr; 19-20 & 23-24 Galerie de Montpensier, 1er; 10.30am-7pm Mon-Sat; M Palais Royal–Musée du Louvre)

Local Life

Place de la Madeleine

Ultragourmet food shops garland **Place de la Madeleine** (Map p58, B2; 8e; M Madeleine); many have in-house dining options too. Notable names include truffle dealers **La Maison de la Truffe** (01 42 65 53 22; www.maison-de-la-truffe.com; No 19; 10am-10pm Mon-Sat; M Madeleine); luxury food shop **Hédiard** (www.hediard.fr; No 2; 9am-8pm Mon-Sat; M Madeleine); mustard specialist **Boutique Maille** (01 40 15 06 00; www.maille.com; No 6; 10am-7pm Mon-Sat; M Madeleine); and Paris' most famous caterer, **Fauchon** (01 70 39 38 00; www.fauchon.fr; No 26 & 30; 8.30am-8.30pm Mon-Sat; M Madeleine), selling incredibly mouth-watering delicacies, from foie gras to jams, chocolates and pastries. Nearby is 'honey house' **La Maison du Miel** (01 47 42 26 70; www.maisondumiel.com; 24 rue Vignon, 9e; 9.30am-7pm Mon-Sat; M Madeleine).

Galeries Lafayette

DEPARTMENT STORE

38 Map p58, D1

Grande dame department store Galeries Lafayette is spread across the main store (whose magnificent stained-glass dome is over a century old), **men's store** and **homewares** store, and includes a gourmet emporium. Catch modern art in the **gallery** (www.galeriedesgaleries.com; 1st fl; admission free; 11am-7pm Tue-Sat), or take in a **fashion show** (bookings 01 42 82 30 25; 3pm Fri Mar-Jul & Sep-Dec by reservation); a free, rooftop panorama; or a break at one of its 19 restaurants and cafes. (http://haussmann.galerieslafayette.com; 40 bd Haussmann, 9e; 9.30am-8pm Mon-Sat, to 9pm Thu; M Auber or Chaussée d'Antin)

Le Printemps

DEPARTMENT STORE

39 Map p58, C1

Famous department store Le Printemps encompasses **Le Printemps de la Mode** (women's fashion), **Le Printemps de l'Homme** (men's fashion), both with established and up-and-coming designer wear, and Le Printemps de la Beauté et Maison (beauty and homewares), offering a staggering display of perfume, cosmetics and accessories. There's a free panoramic rooftop terrace and luxury eateries including Ladurée.

(www.printemps.com; 64 bd Haussmann, 9e; 9.35am-8pm Mon-Wed, Fri & Sat, to 10pm Thu; ; M Havre Caumartin)

Kiliwatch

FASHION

40 Map p58, F3

A Parisian institution, Kiliwatch gets packed with hip guys and gals rummaging through racks of new and used streetwear. Startling vintage range of hats and boots plus art and photography books, eyewear and the latest sneakers. (http://espacekiliwatch.fr; 64 rue Tiquetonne, 2e; 10.30am-7pm Mon, to 7.30pm Tue-Sat; M Étienne Marcel)

Legrand Filles & Fils

FOOD, DRINK

41 Map p58, E3

Tucked inside Galerie Vivienne since 1880, Legrand sells fine wine and all the accoutrements: corkscrews, decanters etc. It also has a fancy wine bar, *école du vin* (wine school) and *éspace dégustation* with several tastings a month; check its website for details. (www.caves-legrand.com; 1 rue de la Banque, 2e; noon-7.30pm Mon-Sat; M Pyramides)

Colette

CONCEPT STORE

42 Map p58, C3

Uber-hip is an understatement. Ogle designer fashion on the 1st floor, and streetwear, limited-edition sneakers, art books, music, gadgets and other high-tech, inventive and/or plain unusual items on the ground floor. End with a drink in the basement 'water bar' and pick up free design magazines and flyers for some of the city's hippest happenings by the door upon leaving. (www.colette.fr; 213 rue St-Honoré, 1er; 11am-7pm Mon-Sat; M Tuileries)

Top Tip

Forum des Halles Overhaul

On the site of Paris' old wholesale markets, a rainforest-inspired giant golden-hued translucent canopy and meadow-like gardens, atop the rejuvenated subterranean shopping mall **Forum des Halles** (Map p58, G4; www.forumdeshalles.com; 1 rue Pierre Lescot, 1er; shops 10am-8pm Mon-Sat; M Châtelet–Les Halles), will reach final completion in 2016. Check developments at www.parisleshalles.fr.

Antoine

FASHION

43 Map p58, D3

The Parisian master of canes, umbrellas, fans and gloves since 1745. (10 av de l'Opéra, 1er; 10.30am-1pm & 2-6.30pm Mon-Sat; M Pyramides or Palais Royal–Musée du Louvre)

Galignani

BOOKS

44 Map p58, C3

Proudly claiming to be the 'first English bookshop established on the continent', this shop stocks French and English books and is the best spot in Paris for picking up just-published titles. (http://galignani.com; 224 rue de Rivoli, 1er; 10am-7pm Mon-Sat; M Concorde)

Explore

Sacré-Cœur & Montmartre

Montmartre's slinking streets, lined with crooked ivy-clad buildings, retain a fairy-tale charm, despite the area's popularity. Crowned by the Sacré-Cœur Basilica, Montmartre is the city's steepest quarter (*mont* means hill; the martyr was St Denis, beheaded here in about AD 250). The lofty views, wine-producing vines and hidden village squares have lured painters since the 19th century.

The Sights in a Day

Montmartre makes for an enchanting stroll, especially early morning when tourists are few. Start at the top of the Butte de Montmartre at the striking **Sacré-Cœur** (p74) basilica for exceptional views (especially from inside its dome), then drop by the **Dalí Espace Montmartre** (p79).

After lunch at **Le Relais Gascon** (p82), wander through the peaceful **Cimetière de Montmartre** (p79), before visiting one of Paris' loveliest small museums, the **Musée de la Vie Romantique** (p79), dedicated to author George Sand. For a romantic museum of an altogether different kind, you might want to check out the **Musée de l'Érotisme** (p79) in Montmartre's southern neighbour, Pigalle – a (tame) red-light district fast becoming better known for its foodie scene. Follow it up with an *apéro* (predinner drink) at **La Fourmi** (p83).

Continue down **rue des Martyrs** (p85) to neighbourhood bistro **Le Miroir** (p85) for dinner, then catch a cabaret at the **Moulin Rouge** (p85) or a concert at **La Cigale** (p84).

For a local's day in Montmartre, see p76.

Top Sights

Sacré-Cœur (p74)

Local Life

Art in Montmartre (p76)

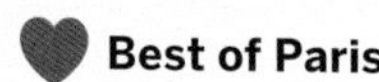

Best of Paris

Museums

Dalí Espace Montmartre (p79)

Eating

Le Pantruche (p80)

Le Miroir (p85)

Drinking

Le Progrès (p83)

Fashion

La Citadelle (p85)

Nights Out

Moulin Rouge (p85)

Au Lapin Agile (p77)

Getting There

M Metro Anvers (line 2) is the most convenient for Sacré-Cœur and its funicular.

M Metro Abbesses and Lamarck–Caulaincourt (line 12) are in Montmartre's heart.

M Metro Blanche and Pigalle (line 2) are your best bet for the restaurants and nightlife around Pigalle.

Top Sights
Sacré-Cœur

Visible from across the city, the dove-white domes of the Basilique du Sacré-Cœur (Sacred Heart Basilica) crown the 130m-high Butte de Montmartre (Montmartre Hill). The basilica's travertine stone exudes calcite, ensuring that it remains white despite weathering and pollution, while its lofty vantage point offers dizzying Parisian vistas from its steep surrounding streets, steps, and above all, its main dome.

Map p78, D2

www.sacre-coeur-montmartre.com

place du Parvis du Sacré-Cœur

dome adult/child €6/4, cash only

6am-10.30pm, dome 9am-7pm Apr-Sep, to 5.30pm Oct-Mar

M Anvers

Don't Miss

The History

Initiated in 1873 to atone for the bloodshed and controversy during the Franco-Prussian War (1870–71), designed by architect Paul Abadie and begun in 1875, the Roman-Byzantine basilica was funded largely by private, often small, donations. It was completed in 1914 but wasn't consecrated until after WWI in 1919.

The Blessed Sacrament

In a sense atonement here has never stopped: a prayer 'cycle' that began in 1835 continues around the clock, with perpetual adoration of the Blessed Sacrament that's on display above the high altar.

The Dome

The sublime views from Sacré-Cœur get even better when you climb the 234 steps spiralling inside its 83m-high main dome. From here, you can see up to 30km on a clear day.

The Crypt

In conjunction with the dome, for an extra €2 you can visit the enormous chapel-lined crypt.

France's Largest Bell

'La Savoyarde' in the basilica's huge square bell tower is the largest in France, weighing in at 19 tonnes. It can be heard ringing out across the neighbourhood and beyond.

The Christ in Majesty Mosaic

The magnificent apse mosaic *Christ in Majesty,* designed by Luc-Olivier Merson in 1922, is one of the largest of its kind in the world. Its golden hues lighten Sacré-Cœur's otherwise dark interior.

Top Tips

- To save you some of the climb, a scenic **funicular railway** shuttles up and down a 36m-long hillside track; journey time is 90 seconds. Metro tickets are valid; there are also ticket booths at the funicular's upper and lower stations.
- Keep one eye on the mesmerising views and the other on your belongings: the base of the basilica notoriously attracts pickpockets, scammers and touts.

Take a Break

The area has more than its fair share of tourist traps, but you'll find good value at **Chez Plumeau** (Map p78, D2; ☎01 46 06 26 29; 4 place du Calvaire, 18e; mains €15-26; ⏰11am-midnight Apr-Sep, noon-2.30pm & 7-10.30pm Thu-Mon Oct-Mar; ; M Abbesses), which opens to a great terrace.

Local Life
Art in Montmartre

For centuries Montmartre was a bucolic country village filled with *moulins* (mills) that supplied Paris with flour. Incorporated into the capital in 1860, its picturesque – and affordable – charm attracted painters including Manet, Degas, Renoir, Van Gogh, Toulouse-Lautrec, Dufy, Picasso, Utrillo, Modigliani and Dalí in its late 19th- and early 20th-century heyday. Although much frequented by tourists, its local village atmosphere endures.

1 Amélie's Cafe

Start with a coffee at this arty cafe, where Amélie worked as a waitress in the quirky film of the same name. **Café des Deux Moulins** (15 rue Lepic, 18e; 7.30am-1am; M Blanche) hangs on as a down-to-earth local where you can watch Montmartre go by.

2 Van Gogh's House

Théo Van Gogh owned the house at **54 rue Lepic**; his brother, the artist

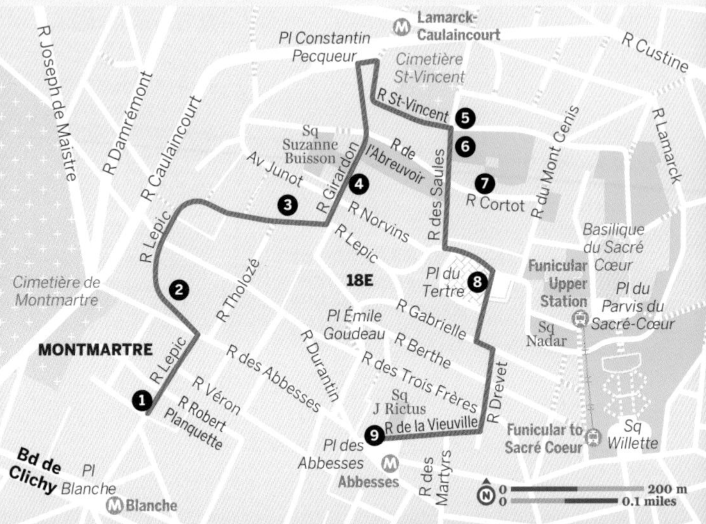

Vincent, stayed with him on the 3rd floor for two years from 1886.

❸ Renoir's Dance Hall

Montmartre's two surviving windmills are the **Moulin Blute-Fin** and, 100m east, the **Moulin Radet** (now a restaurant). In the 19th century, the windmills were turned into the open-air dance hall Le Moulin de la Galette, immortalised by Renoir in his 1876 tableau *Le Bal du Moulin de la Galette* (now displayed in the Musée d'Orsay).

❹ Aymé's Walker Through Walls

Crossing place Marcel Aymé you'll see a man emerging from a stone wall. The **Passe-Muraille statue** portrays Dutilleul, the hero of Marcel Aymé's short story *Le Passe-Muraille* (*The Walker through Walls*). Aymé lived in the adjacent building from 1902 to 1967.

❺ Gill's Rabbit

Look for caricaturist André Gill's mural *Le Lapin à Gill*. It shows a rabbit jumping out of a cooking pot on the facade of long-running local cabaret **Au Lapin Agile** (☎01 46 06 85 87; www.au-lapin-agile.com; 22 rue des Saules, 18e; adult €28, student except Sat €20; ⏰9pm-1am Tue-Sun; Ⓜ Lamarck-Caulaincourt).

❻ Montmartre's Vineyard

The only vineyard in central Paris, **Clos Montmartre** dates from 1933. Its 2000 vines produce an average 800 bottles of wine each October, celebrated by the five-day Fête des Vendanges de Montmartre, with festivities including a parade.

❼ Local History Lessons

Local history comes to life through paintings and documents at the **Musée de Montmartre** (www.museedemontmartre.fr; 12 rue Cortot, 18e; adult/child €9/5; ⏰10am-6pm; Ⓜ Lamarck–Caulaincourt), housed in Montmartre's oldest building – a 17th-century garden-set manor where Renoir, Utrillo and Dufy once lived. Suzanne Valadon's restored studio is set to open here.

❽ Artists at Work

The main square of the original village, **place du Tertre** (Ⓜ Abbesses) has drawn countless painters in its time. While it's awash with visitors, local, often very talented, artists paint, sketch and sell their creations at stalls here, and the portraitists, buskers and crowds create an unmissable carnival-like atmosphere.

❾ The Art of Travel

With its original glass canopy and twin wrought-iron lamp posts illuminating the dark-green-on-lemon-yellow *Metropolitain* sign still intact, Abbesses has the finest remaining example of art nouveau designer Hector Guimard's metro entrances.

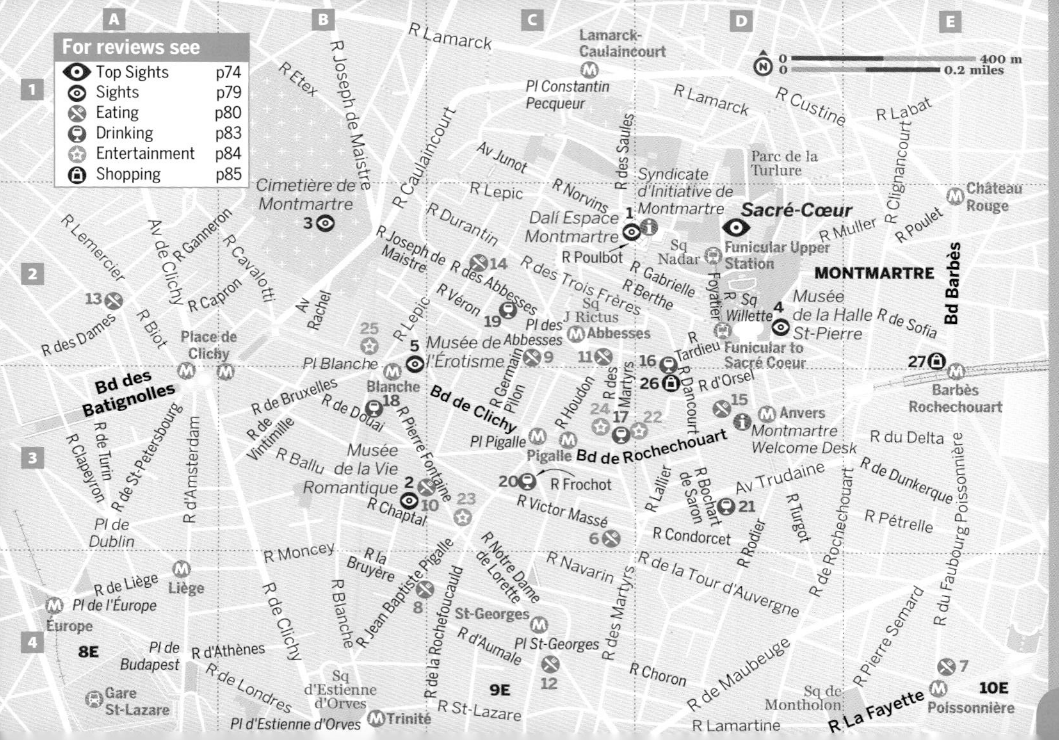
For reviews see
Top Sights p74
Sights p79
Eating p80
Drinking p83
Entertainment p84
Shopping p85
0 400 m
0 0.2 miles
Sacré-Cœur
MONTMARTRE
Bd Barbès
Château Rouge
Barbès Rochechouart
Lamarck-Caulaincourt
Abbesses
Anvers
Pigalle
Blanche
Place de Clichy
St-Georges
Liège
Europe
Trinité
Poissonnière
Gare St-Lazare
Cimetière de Montmartre
Parc de la Turlure
Syndicate d'Initiative de Montmartre
Dalí Espace Montmartre
Funicular Upper Station
Funicular to Sacré Coeur
Musée de la Halle St-Pierre
Montmartre Welcome Desk
Musée de l'Érotisme
Musée de la Vie Romantique
Sq Nadar
Sq Willette
Sq J Rictus
Sq de Montholon
Sq d'Estienne d'Orves
Bd de Rochechouart
Bd de Clichy
Bd des Batignolles
R La Fayette
R Lamarck
R Custine
R Caulaincourt
R Joseph de Maistre
R Lepic
Av Junot
R des Abbesses
R des Martyrs
R de Clichy
R d'Amsterdam
R de Londres
R St-Lazare
R Blanche
R Pierre Fontaine
R de Rochechouart
R du Faubourg Poissonnière
R de Maubeuge
R Condorcet
R Victor Massé
R Notre Dame de Lorette
R de la Tour d'Auvergne
R Turgot
Av Trudaine
Pl Pigalle
Pl Blanche
Pl des Abbesses
Pl St-Georges
Pl Constantin Pecqueur
Pl de Dublin
Pl de l'Europe
Pl de Budapest
Pl d'Estienne d'Orves
8E
9E
10E

Sights

Dalí Espace Montmartre

ART MUSEUM

1 Map p78, C2

More than 300 works by Salvador Dalí (1904–89), the flamboyant Catalan surrealist printmaker, painter, sculptor and self-promoter, are on display at this surrealist-style basement museum located just west of place du Tertre. The collection includes Dalí's strange sculptures (most in reproduction), lithographs, and many of his illustrations and furniture, including the famous Mae West lips sofa.

(www.daliparis.com; 11 rue Poulbot, 18e; adult/8-25yr €11.50/6.50; 10am-6pm, to 8pm Jul & Aug; M Abbesses)

Musée de la Vie Romantique

MUSEUM

2 Map p78, B3

This small museum is dedicated to two artists active during the Romantic era: the writer George Sand and the painter Ary Scheffer. Located at the end of a film-worthy cobbled lane, the villa housing the museum originally belonged to Scheffer and was the setting for popular salons of the day, attended by such notable figures as Delacroix, Liszt and Chopin (Sand's lover).

(www.vie-romantique.paris.fr; 16 rue Chaptal, 9e; admission free; 10am-6pm Tue-Sun; M Blanche or St-Georges)

Cimetière de Montmartre

CEMETERY

3 Map p78, B2

Established in 1798, this 11-hectare cemetery is perhaps the most celebrated necropolis in Paris after Père Lachaise. It contains the graves of writers Émile Zola (whose ashes are now in the Panthéon), Alexandre Dumas (fils) and Stendhal, composers Jacques Offenbach and Hector Berlioz, artist Edgar Degas, film director François Truffaut and dancer Vaslav Nijinsky, among others.

(8am-5.30pm Mon-Fri, from 8.30am Sat, from 9am Sun; M Place de Clichy)

Musée de la Halle St-Pierre

ART MUSEUM

4 Map p78, D2

Founded in 1986, this museum and gallery is in the lovely old covered St Peter's Market. It focuses on the primitive and Art Brut schools; there is no permanent collection, but the museum stages three temporary exhibitions a year. There's a lovely cafe on site.

(www.hallesaintpierre.org; 2 rue Ronsard, 18e; adult/senior & under 26yr €8/6.50; 11am-6pm Mon-Fri, 11am-7pm Sat, noon-6pm Sun; M Anvers)

Musée de l'Érotisme

ART MUSEUM

5 Map p78, B2

The Museum of Erotic Art attempts to raise around 2000 titillating statuary, stimulating sexual aids and fetishist items to a loftier plane, with antique and modern erotic art from four continents spread out across several floors. Some of the exhibits are, well, breathtaking, to say the least. (www.musee-erotisme.com; 72 bd de Clichy, 18e; admission €10; 10am-2am; M Blanche)

Eating

Le Pantruche
BISTRO €€

6 Map p78, C3

Named after a nearby 19th-century theatre, classy Pantruche has been making waves in the already crowded dining hotspot of South Pigalle. No surprise, then, that it hits all the right notes: seasonal bistro fare, reasonable prices and an intimate setting. The menu runs from classics (steak with béarnaise sauce) to more daring creations (scallops served in a parmesan broth with cauliflower mousseline). (01 48 78 55 60; www.lepantruche.com; 3 rue Victor Massé, 9e; lunch/dinner menus €19/35; 12.30-2.30pm & 7.30-10.30pm Mon-Fri; M Pigalle)

> **Local Life**
> **Behind the Butte**
> For a more typically residential Montmartre neighbourhood, head to the backside of the hill. There's plenty to discover here, such as **Soul Kitchen** (Map p78, D1; 33 Rue Lamarck, 18e; menu €13.50; 8.30am-6.30pm Tue-Fri, 10am-7pm Sat & Sun; M Lamarck–Caulaincourt), an inviting vegetarian eatery housed in an old cafe, where you can pick up market-driven dishes that change daily, including scrumptious soups, quiches and lasagna.

Abri
NEOBISTRO €€

7 Map p78, E4

It's no bigger than a shoebox and the decor is borderline nonexistent, but converts will tell you that's all part of the charm. The reason everyone's raving? Katsuaki Okiyama is a seriously talented chef with artistic flair, and his tasting menus (three courses at lunch, six at dinner) are exceptionally good value. (01 83 97 00 00; 92 rue du Faubourg Poissonnière, 9e; lunch/dinner menus €25/43; noon-2.30pm Mon, noon-2.30pm & 7.30-10pm Tue-Sat; M Poissonnière)

Bistrot La Bruyère
BISTRO €€

8 Map p78, B4

Young-gun chef Loïc Buisson is the wunderkind behind winning dishes like tomato gazpacho, pigs-trotter pancakes with apple chips, tuna with fried leeks, and beef from celebrated butcher Hugo Desnoyer at this unassuming but brilliant little bistro. One to watch. (09 81 22 20 56; 31 rue la Bruyère, 9e; 2-/3-course lunch menus €18/21, dinner menus €28/35; noon-2.30pm & 7.30-10.30pm Mon-Sat; M St-Georges)

Cimetière de Montmartre (p79)

Chez Toinette TRADITIONAL FRENCH €€

9 Map p78, C2

The atmosphere of this convivial restaurant is rivalled only by its fine cuisine (seared duck with honey, venison with foie gras). In the heart of one of the capital's most touristy neighbourhoods, Chez Toinette has kept alive the tradition of old Montmartre with its simplicity and culinary expertise. An excellent choice for a traditional French meal.

(☎01 42 54 44 36; 20 rue Germain Pilon, 18e; mains €19-24; ⏰7-11.30pm Mon-Sat; M Abbesses)

Le Garde Temps MODERN FRENCH €€

10 Map p78, B3

The chalkboard menus at this contemporary bistro are framed and hung on the walls, and thankfully the promise of gastronomic art does not disappoint. Old bistro standards have been swept away in favour of more imaginative creations (fondant of red cabbage topped with quail confit) and the dinner prices aren't much more than that ho-hum cafe down the street.

(☎01 83 76 04 66; www.restaurant-legardetemps.fr; 19bis rue Pierre Fontaine, 9e; lunch menus €17, 2-/3-course dinner menus €26/33; ⏰noon-2pm & 7-10.30pm Mon-Fri, 7-10.30pm Sat; M Pigalle)

Understand

Belle Époque Paris

La Belle Époque saw creativity flourish from the advent of France's Third Republic in 1870.

This 'Beautiful Era' launched art nouveau architecture, a whole field of artistic 'isms' from impressionism onwards, and advances in science and engineering, including the first metro line (1900). World Exhibitions were held in the capital in 1889 (showcased by the Eiffel Tower) and again in 1900 (by the Grand Palais and Petit Palais).

The Paris of nightclubs and artistic cafes made its first appearance around this time, and Montmartre became a magnet for artists, writers, pimps and prostitutes, with artists such as Toulouse-Lautrec creating caberet posters of the Moulin Rouge's can-can dancers.

Other glamorous hotspots still operating include the restaurant Maxim's, now with an art nouveau museum (p44) upstairs, and the newly renovated Ritz Paris. The Musée d'Orsay (p148) contains a wealth of artistic expression from this era, from paintings through to exquisite furniture.

This inspired time lasted until the onset of WWI in 1914 – it was named in retrospect, recalling a peaceful 'golden age'.

Le Relais Gascon GASCON €

Situated just a short stroll from the place des Abbesses, Relais Gascon has a relaxed atmosphere and authentic regional cuisine at very reasonable prices. The giant salads and *confit de canard* will satisfy big eaters, while the traditional *cassoulet* and *tartiflette* are equally delicious.

Another **branch** (01 42 52 11 11; 13 rue Joseph de Maistre; M Abbesses) is just down the street. No credit cards at the main restaurant.

(01 42 58 58 22; www.lerelaisgascon.fr; 6 rue des Abbesses, 18e; mains €11.50-16.50, lunch/dinner menus €17.50/27.50; 10am-2am; M Abbesses)

Les Coulisses Vintage BISTRO €€

12 Map p78, C4

Framed by red curtains tied back with gold tassels, Les Coulisses Vintage has a loyal local following for its excellent value-for-money dishes that straddle the divide between traditional and modern – foie gras in gingerbread crumbs, roast cod with porcini mushrooms, and chocolate soufflé or sublime cheeses for dessert.

(01 45 26 46 46; www.restolescoulisses.fr; 19 rue Notre Dame de Lorette, 9e; 2-course lunch menus €16, 2-/3-course dinner menus €32.50/39.50; noon-2.30pm Mon-Fri, 7-11pm Mon-Sat; M St-Georges)

Bistro des Dames

BISTRO €€

13 Map p78, A2

This charming little bistro will appeal to lovers of simple, authentic cuisine, with hearty salads, tortillas and glorious charcuterie platters of *pâté de campagne* and paper-thin Serrano ham. The dining room, which looks out onto the street, is lovely, but in summer it's the cool and tranquillity of the small back garden that pulls in the punters.

(☎01 45 22 13 42; 18 rue des Dames, 17e; mains €15-21; ⏰noon-2pm & 7-10.30pm; M Place de Clichy)

La Mascotte

SEAFOOD, CAFE €€€

14 Map p78, C2

Founded in 1889, this unassuming bar is about as authentic as it gets in Montmartre. It specialises in quality seafood – oysters, lobster, scallops – and regional dishes (Auvergne sausage), but you can also pull up a seat at the bar for a simple glass of wine and a plate of charcuterie.

(☎01 46 06 28 15; www.la-mascotte-montmartre.com; 52 rue des Abbesses, 18e; lunch/dinner menus €29/45, mains €23-39; ⏰8am-11.30pm; M Abbesses)

Le Petit Trianon

CAFE €

15 Map p78, D3

With its large windows and a few carefully chosen antiques, this recently revived belle époque cafe at the foot of Montmartre feels about as timeless as the Butte itself. Dating back to 1894 and attached to the century-old Le Trianon theatre, it's no stretch to imagine artists like Toulouse-Lautrec and crowds of showgoers who once filled the place in the evening.

(☎01 44 92 78 08; 80 bd de Rochechouart, 18e; mains €7.50-13.50; ⏰8am-2pm; M Anvers)

Drinking

Le Progrès

BAR

16 Map p78, D2

A real live *café du quartier* perched in the heart of Abbesses, the 'Progress' occupies a corner site with huge windows and simple seating and attracts a relaxed mix of local artists, shop staff, writers and hangers-on. It's great for convivial evenings, but it's also a good place to come for inexpensive meals and cups of coffee.

(7 rue des Trois Frères, 18e; ⏰9am-2am; M Abbesses)

La Fourmi

BAR

17 Map p78, C3

A Pigalle institution, La Fourmi hits the mark with its high ceilings, long zinc bar and unpretentious vibe. Get up to speed on live music and club nights or sit down for a reasonably priced meal and drinks.

(74 rue des Martyrs, 18e; ⏰8am-1am Mon-Thu, to 3am Fri & Sat, 10am-1am Sun; M Pigalle)

Au P'tit Douai

BAR

18 Map p78, B3

This neighbourhood cafe is just down the street from the Moulin Rouge, but it might as well be light years away. Trade in the mayhem for some tranquillity over coffee, wines by the glass or traditional French fare at meal times. (92 rue Blanche, 9e; 8am-2am Sat, 11am-8pm Sun; ; MBlanche)

La Machine du Moulin Rouge

CLUB

Part of the original Moulin Rouge (see 25 Map p78, B2) – well, the boiler room, anyway – this club packs 'em in on weekends with a dance floor, concert hall, Champagne bar and outdoor terrace. (90 bd de Clichy, 18e; hours vary; MBlanche)

Cave des Abbesses

WINE BAR

19 Map p78, C2

Pass through the door at the back of the Cave des Abbesses wine shop and you'll discover a quirky little bar. It feels like one of those places only regulars know about, but don't be intimidated; sit down, order a plate of cheese and a glass of Corbières, and you'll blend right in. (43 rue des Abbesses, 18e; cheese & charcuterie €7-13; 5-9.30pm Tue-Sun; MAbbesses)

Glass

BAR

20 Map p78, C3

Pop into this old girly bar, tinted windows and all, for Brooklyn Brewery and Demury beers on tap, beef hot dogs and punk rock on the stereo. With €4 half pints it's certainly no dive bar, however much it may look the part. (7 rue Frochot, 9e; 7pm-2am; MPigalle)

Artisan

COCKTAIL BAR

21 Map p78, D3

Pigalle doesn't have many sophisticated drinking options, but the white-walled Artisan fits the bill nicely, with delicious small plates, wines by the glass and well-mixed cocktails. (14 rue Bochart de Saron, 9e; 7pm-2am Tue-Sat, noon-4pm Sun; MAnvers)

Entertainment

La Cigale

LIVE MUSIC

22 Map p78, D3

Now classed as a historical monument, this music hall dates from 1887 but was redecorated 100 years later by Philippe Starck. Artists who have performed here recently include Rufus Wainwright, Ryan Adams and Ibrahim Maalouf. (01 49 25 89 99; www.lacigale.fr; 120 bd de Rochechouart, 18e; admission €25-60; MAnvers or Pigalle)

Bus Palladium

LIVE MUSIC

23 Map p78, C3

Once the place to be, back in the 1960s, the Bus is now back in business 50 years later, with funky DJs and performances by indie and pop groups. (www.lebuspalladium.com; 6 rue Pierre Fontaine, 9e; hours vary; MBlanche)

Le Divan du Monde

LIVE MUSIC

24  Map p78, C3

Take some cinematographic events, Gypsy gatherings, *nouvelles chansons françaises* (new French songs). Add in soul/funk fiestas, air-guitar face-offs and rock parties of the Arctic Monkeys/Killers/Libertines persuasion and stir with an Amy Winehouse swizzle stick. You may now be getting some idea of the inventived approach at this excellent cross-cultural venue in Pigalle. (☎01 40 05 06 99; www.divandumonde.com; 75 rue des Martyrs, 18e; ⏰hours vary; Ⓜ Pigalle)

Moulin Rouge

CABARET

25  Map p78, B2

Immortalised in the posters of Toulouse-Lautrec and later on screen by Baz Luhrmann, the Moulin Rouge twinkles beneath a 1925 replica of its original red windmill. Yes, it's rife with bus-tour crowds. But from the opening bars of music to the last high kick it's a whirl of fantastical costumes, sets, choreography and Champagne. Booking advised. (☎01 53 09 82 82; www.moulinrouge.fr; 82 bd de Clichy, 18e; Ⓜ Blanche)

Shopping

La Citadelle

FASHION, ACCESSORIES

26 Map p78, D3

This designer discount shop hidden away in Montmartre has some real finds from new French, Italian and Japanese designers. Look out for such labels as Les Chemins Blancs and Yoshi Kondo. (1 rue des Trois Frères, 18e; ⏰10am-7pm; Ⓜ Abbesses)

Local Life

Rue des Martyrs

Gourmet shops along foodie strip rue des Martyrs include *boulangerie* **Arnaud Delmontel** (Map p78, C4; 39 rue des Martyrs, 9e; ⏰7am-8.30pm Wed-Mon; Ⓜ Pigalle), known for its award-winning baguettes. For a sit-down meal, unassuming bistro **Le Miroir** (Map p78, C4; ☎01 46 06 50 73; http://restaurantmiroir.com; 94 rue des Martyrs, 18e; lunch menus €19.50, dinner menus €27-34; ⏰noon-2.30pm & 7.30-11pm Tue-Sat; Ⓜ Abbesses) serves delightful pâtés and rillettes and well-prepared standards, and has its own wine shop across the street. Or try edgy neobistro fare at **Cul de Poule** (Map p78, C3; ☎01 53 16 13 07; 53 rue des Martyrs, 9e; 2-/3-course menus lunch €16/19, dinner €24/29; ⏰noon-2.30pm & 8-11pm Mon-Sat; Ⓜ Pigalle).

Tati

DEPARTMENT STORE

27 Map p78, E2

This bargain-filled, rough-and-tumble, frill-free department store is every fashionable Parisian's guilty secret. (4 bd de Rochechouart, 18e; ⏰10am-7pm Mon-Fri, 9.30-7pm Sat; Ⓜ Barbès Rochechouart)

Local Life
Canal St-Martin & Around

Getting There

Canal St-Martin is about 4km north of Notre Dame.

Ⓜ **Metro** République (lines 3, 5, 8, 9 and 11) is centrally located.

Ⓜ **Metro** Château d'Eau, Jacques Bonsergent, Gare de l'Est and Parmentier are useful stations.

Bordered by shaded towpaths and criss-crossed with iron footbridges, Canal St-Martin wends through the city's northern *quartiers* (quarters). You can float past them on a canal cruise, but strolling among this rejuvenated neighbourhood's cool cafes, offbeat boutiques and hip bars and clubs lets you see why it's beloved by Parisian *bobos* (bourgeois bohemians).

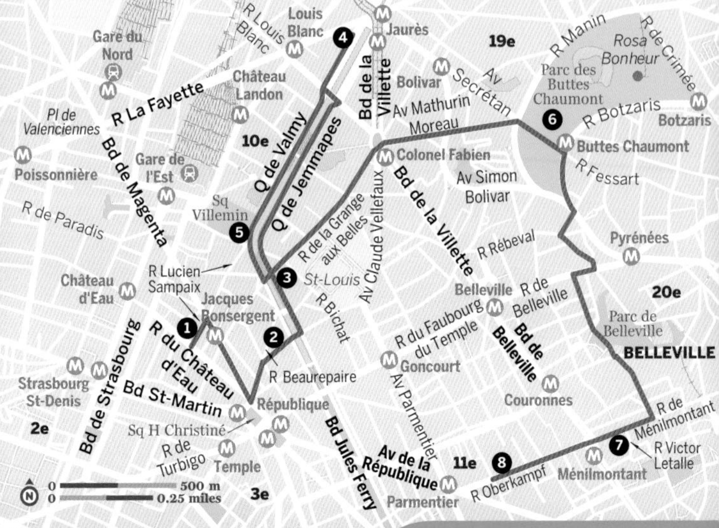

❶ Coffee with the Locals

Kick off at **Le Petit Château d'Eau** (34 rue du Château d'Eau, 10e; 8am-2am Mon-Fri, 9am-5pm Sat; M Jacques Bonsergent or Château d'Eau), an unchanged-in-decades neighbourhood cafe (with cracked lemon-and-lime tiles, oversized mirrors and time-worn maroon-leather booths), where locals chat with staff over the zinc bar.

❷ Retro Clothes Shopping

Flip through colour-coded racks of vintage cast-offs at **Frivoli** (26 rue Beaurepaire, 10e; 11am-7pm Mon-Fri, 2-7pm Sat & Sun; M Jacques Bonsergent), on boutique-lined rue Beaurepaire.

❸ Pizza Picnic

Order a Poulidor (duck, apple and goats cheese) or Basquiat (gorgonzola, figs and cured ham) pizza from **Pink Flamingo** (01 42 02 31 70; www.pinkflamingopizza.com; 67 rue Bichat, 10e; pizzas €11.50-17; 7-11.30pm Mon-Thu, noon-3pm & 7-11.30pm Fri-Sun; M Jacques Bonsergent) and receive a pink helium balloon; it's used to locate you and your perfect canal-side picnic spot when the pizza is delivered.

❹ Cultural Cool

Within a converted warehouse, alternative cultural centre **Point Éphémère** (www.pointephemere.org; 200 quai de Valmy, 10e; 12.30pm-2am Mon-Sat, 12.30-11pm Sun; M Louis Blanc) has resident artists and musicians, exhibitions and a chilled, bar-restaurant. Pop back at night for live music, DJs and clubbing events.

❺ Cafe Culture

Watch the boats from spirited **L'Atmosphere** (49 rue Lucien Sampaix, 10e; 9.30am-1.45am Mon-Sat, to midnight Sun; M Jacques Bonsergent or Gare de l'Est), hit barista-run **Holybelly** (http://holybel.ly; 19 rue Lucien Sampaix, 10e; 9am-6pm Thu-Mon, from 10am Sat & Sun; M Jacques Bonsergent) or head to original *bobo* hangout **Chez Prune** (71 quai de Valmy, 10e; 8am-2am Mon-Sat, 10am-2am Sun; M République).

❻ Hilltop Haven

A far cry from its former incarnation as a rubbish tip and quarry for Baron Haussmann's 19th-century reformation, hilly, forested **Parc des Buttes Chaumont** (rue Manin & rue Botzaris, 19e; 7am-10pm May-Sep, to 8pm Oct-Apr; M Buttes-Chaumont or Botzaris) conceals grottoes, artificial waterfalls and a temple-topped island reached by footbridges, as well as the cafe-dance hall, **Rosa Bonheur**.

❼ Post-Industrial Dining

Book ahead to dine on contemporary bistro fare at white-walled shop-turned-restaurant **Chatomat** (01 47 97 25 77; 6 rue Victor Letalle, 20e; mains €15-20; 7.30-10.30pm Tue-Sat & 1st Sun of month; M Ménilmontant, Couronnes or Père Lachaise).

❽ Nightcap, Nightlife

Finish with a drink at the belle époque **Café Charbon** (www.lecafecharbon.com; 109 rue Oberkampf, 11e; 9am-2am; M Parmentier) or kick on at its live music and DJ venue, **Le Nouveau Casino** (www.nouveaucasino.net; 109 rue Oberkampf, 11e; Tue-Sun; M Parmentier).

Explore

Centre Pompidou & Le Marais

Paris' *marais* (marsh) was cleared in the 12th century but Haussmann's reformations left its tangle of medieval laneways largely intact. Hip bars and restaurants, emerging designers' boutiques and the city's thriving gay and Jewish communities all squeeze into this vibrant neighbourhood and its equally buzzing eastern neighbour, Bastille.

The Sights in a Day

The twice-weekly **Marché Bastille** (p103) is one of the largest, liveliest street markets in Paris – catch it if you can before visiting Paris' fascinating history museum, the **Musée Carnavalet** (p96), and the **Maison de Victor Hugo** (p96), the author's former home on elegant **place des Vosges** (p98).

Join the locals queuing at the takeaway window of **L'As du Fallafel** (p99). After lunch, stroll along the leafy **Promenade Plantée** (p99) walkway above an old railway viaduct, or simply spend the afternoon browsing the Marais' trove of colourful and quirky shops, stopping for afternoon tea at enchanting **Le Loir dans la Théière** (p105).

The **Centre Pompidou** (p90) stays open until 9pm, so head here in the late afternoon to see its amazing collection of modern and contemporary art and the awesome views from its roof. After dinner at **Le 6 Paul Bert** (p101), begin a bar-hop at **Le Cap Horn** (p104).

For a local's day in the Haut Marais, see p92.

Top Sights

Centre Pompidou (p90)

Local Life

A Heads-Up on the Haut Marais (p92)

Best of Paris

Eating

Le 6 Paul Bert (p101)

Bones (p102)

CheZaline (p104)

Drinking

Le Pure Café (p104)

La Fée Verte (p105)

La Caféothèque (p106)

Le Baron Rouge (p102)

Le Mary Céleste (p93)

Getting There

M Metro Rambuteau (line 11) is the most convenient for the Centre Pompidou.

M Metro Other central metro stations include Hôtel de Ville (lines 1 and 11), St-Paul (line 1) and Bastille (lines 1, 5 and 8).

Boat The hop-on, hop-off Batobus stops outside the Hôtel de Ville.

Top Sights
Centre Pompidou

The building housing Paris' premier cultural centre is so iconic that you could spend hours looking at it without ever going inside. But you should! As well as containing France's national modern and contemporary art museum, the Musée National d'Art Moderne, the centre's cutting-edge cultural offerings include temporary exhibition spaces, a public library, cinemas and entertainment venues.

Map p94, A2

www.centrepompidou.fr

place Georges Pompidou, 4e

museum, exhibitions & panorama adult/child €13/free

11am-9pm Wed-Mon

M Rambuteau

Don't Miss

The Architecture

Former French President Georges Pompidou wanted an ultra-contemporary artistic hub and he got it. Competition-winning architects Renzo Piano and Richard Rogers effectively designed the building inside out, with utilitarian features such as plumbing, pipes, air vents and electrical cables forming part of the external façade, freeing up the interior space for exhibitions and events.

The then-controversial, now much-loved centre opened in 1977. Viewed from a distance (such as from Sacré-Cœur) its primary-coloured, box-like form amid a sea of muted-grey Parisian rooftops makes it look like a child's Meccano set abandoned on someone's elegant living-room rug.

Musée National d'Art Moderne

Europe's largest collection of modern art fills the airy, well-lit galleries of the National Museum of Modern Art. On a par with the permanent collection are the two temporary exhibition halls (on the ground floor/basement and the top floor) which host memorable blockbuster exhibits. There's a wonderful children's gallery on the 1st floor.

The permanent collection changes every two years, but incorporates artists such as Picasso, Matisse, Chagall, Kandinsky, Kahlo, Warhol, Pollock and many more. The 5th floor showcases artists active between 1905 and 1970 (give or take a decade); the 4th floor focuses on more contemporary creations, roughly from the 1980s onward.

The Rooftop

Although just six storeys high, Paris' low-rise cityscape means sweeping views extend from the rooftop, reached by external escalators enclosed in tubes.

Top Tips

- The Centre Pompidou opens late every night (except Tuesday, when the centre's closed), so head here around 5pm to avoid the daytime crowds.
- Skip the queues by buying museum and events tickets online.
- Rooftop admission is included in museum and exhibition admission; alternatively, buy a **panorama ticket** (admission €3; 11am-10pm Wed-Mon) just for the roof.

Take a Break

Outside the main entrance, **place Georges Pompidou** is a hub for busking musicians, mime artists and street artists, while the mechanical fountains on adjacent **place Igor Stravinsky** are a riot of skeletons, dragons and other outlandish creations.

For a drink or delicious meal, head to nearby **Café La Fusée** (Map p94, A1; 168 rue St-Martin, 3e; 8am-2am daily; M Rambuteau or Étienne Marcel).

Local Life
A Heads-Up on the Haut Marais

The lower Marais has long been fashionable but the real buzz these days is in the haut Marais (upper, ie northern Marais). Its warren of narrow streets is a hub for up-and-coming fashion designers, art galleries, vintage, accessories and homewares boutiques, all sitting alongside long-established enterprises enjoying a renaissance. Look out for new openings, exhibitions, events and pop-up shops.

1 Charitable Fashion

Fronted by a Fiat Cinquecento, unique concept store **Merci** (www.merci-merci.com; 111 bd Beaumarchais, 3e; ⌚10am-7pm Mon-Sat; Ⓜ St-Sébastien Froissart) donates all profits from its cutting-edge fashions, homewares, gifts, cafe and canteen to a children's charity in Madagascar.

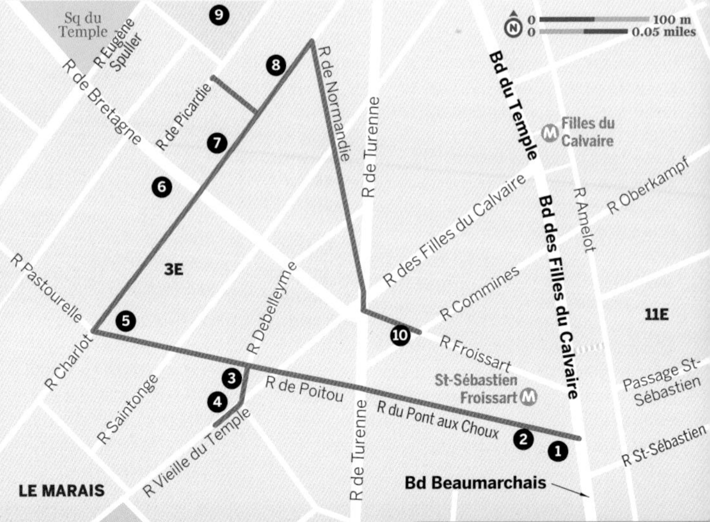

2 Coffee Fix

Reboot with a Parisian-roasted coffee at **Boot Café** (19 rue du Pont aux Choux, 3e; ⏲8.30am-7.30pm Tue-Fri, 10am-6pm Sat; Ⓜ Filles du Calvaire). Set inside an old cobbler's shop, whose original washed-blue façade and 'Cordonnerie' lettering have been beautifully preserved.

3 Groundbreaking Fashion

Among the first boutiques to put the haut Marais on the fashion map, **Shine** (15 rue de Poitou, 3e; ⏲11am-7.30pm Mon-Sat; Ⓜ Filles du Calvaire) stocks hand-picked pieces from young designers.

4 Arty Fashion

In addition to edgy, up-to-the-minute clothing, **Surface to Air** (www.surfacetoair.com; 108 rue Vieille du Temple, 3e; ⏲11.30am-7.30pm Mon-Sat, 1.30-7.30pm Sun; Ⓜ St-Sébastien Froissart or Filles du Calvaire) has arty books and accessories. It also welcomes regular installations and collaborative events with artists.

5 Discounted Fashion

Savvy Parisians grab last season's designer wear (for both men and women) at up to 70% off original prices at **L'Habilleur** (www.lhabilleur.fr; 44 rue de Poitou, 4e; ⏲noon-7.30pm Mon-Sat; Ⓜ St-Sébastien Froissart).

6 Market Lunch

Hidden behind an inconspicuous green metal gate, **Marché aux Enfants Rouges** (39 rue de Bretagne, 3e; ⏲8.30am-1pm & 4-7.30pm Tue-Fri, 4-8pm Sat, 8.30am-2pm Sun; Ⓜ Filles du Calvaire) has produce stalls and dishes that range from bento boxes to crêpes, which you can eat at communal tables.

7 Handbag Heaven

Super-soft, super-stylish **Pauline Pin** (www.paulinepin.com; 51 rue Charlot, 3e; ⏲11am-7.30pm Tue-Sat; Ⓜ Filles du Calvaire) handbags are made here at founder-designer Clarisse's flagship store and workshop.

8 Fibre Fashion

Clothing and textile artworks crafted from natural and rare animal fibres are exhibited and sold at **La Boutique Extraordinaire.** (67 rue Charlot, 3e; ⏲11am-8pm Tue-Sat, 3-7pm Sun; Ⓜ Filles du Calvaire)

9 Cultural Happenings

The quarter's old covered market with magnificent art nouveau ironwork, **Le Carreau du Temple** (☎01 83 81 93 30; www.lecarreaudutemple.eu; 4 rue Eugène Spuller, 3e; ⏲ticket office 2-6pm Mon-Sat; Ⓜ Temple) is now a vast stage for exhibitions, concerts, sports classes and theatre.

10 Cocktail Hour

Snag a stool at the central circular bar of ubercool **Le Mary Céleste** (www.lemaryceleste.com; 1 rue Commines, 3e; cocktails €12-13, tapas €8-12; ⏲6pm-2am; Ⓜ Filles du Calvaire) for creative cocktails and tapas-style 'small plates'.

A
B
C
D
1
2
3
4
5
R de Turbigo
Étienne Marcel
R des Gravilliers
28
R au Maire
3
Sq du Temple
R Chapon
R de Montmorency
R aux Ours
1ER
RIGHT BANK
R St-Martin
Rambuteau
Bd de Sébastopol
R Michel le Comte
R du Temple
16
R Pastourelle
3E
R de Bretagne
R Charlot
R Saintonge
15
Filles du Calvaire
Bd des Filles du Calvaire
R des Archives
R de Poitou
R Froissart
St-Sébastien Froissart
5
Musée d'Art et d'Histoire du Judaïsme
R Rambuteau
Pl Georges Pompidou
Centre Pompidou
R des Coutures St-Gervais
R des Fils
Jardin de l'Hôtel Salé
10
R St-Claude
R St-Merri
Pl Igor Stravinsky
Pl E Michelet
LE MARAIS
33
Musée Picasso
R de Thorigny
R des Blancs Manteaux
R de la Verrerie
R Ste-Croix de la Bretonnerie
R du Renard
R Vieille du Temple
R Barbette
R du Parc Royal
Tour St-Jacques
29
R Elzévir
6
Musée Cognacq-Jay
Sq de la Tour St-Jacques
12
Châtelet
R de Moussy
32
R des Hospitalières St-Gervais
17
R Payenne
Musée Carnavalet
R St-Gilles
1
36
Hôtel de Ville
R de Rivoli
21
R des Écouffes
31
R des Rosiers
R des Francs Bourgeois
R de Béarn
R des Tournelles
Q des Gesvres
Hôtel de Ville
7
Pl St-Gervais
Pl Baudoyer
R du Roi de Sicile
26
R Pavée
R Malher
R de Sévigné
R de Turenne
R du Pas de la Mule
Pl des Vosges
Q de l'Hôtel de Ville
Pont d'Arcole
R François Miron
Mémorial de la Shoah
St-Paul
4
Maison Européenne de la Photographie
Maison de Victor Hugo
2
Hôtel Dieu
R d'Arcole
Q aux Fleurs
Batobus Stop
8
30
R Geoffroy l'Asnier
R de l'Hôtel de Ville
Sq A Schweitzer
R Charlemagne
24
R de Birague
R St-Antoine
Île de la Cité
Pont Louis-Philippe
R de Fourcy
R du Cloître Notre Dame
Pont Marie
Q des Célestins
R St-Paul
R Charles V
R du Petit Musc
Q de Bourbon
Cathédrale de Notre Dame de Paris
Pont St-Louis
Pont Marie
4E
Sq Jean XXIII
Île St-Louis
Q d'Anjou
Sully Morland
Bd Henri IV
Pont de l'Archevêché
Q d'Orléans
R St-Louis en l'Île
Sq H Galli
Pont de Sully
Seine
R de l'Arsenal
Q de la Tournelle
Q de Béthune
Bd Morland
Pl Maubert
R des Bernardins
Pont de la Tournelle
Sq Barve
R Mornay
Bd Bourdon
Bd St-Germain
R du Cardinal Lemoine
Q St-Bernard
Q Henri IV
R de Schomberg
5E
LATIN QUARTER
Universités Paris VI & VII
Port de Plaisance de Paris Arsenal

E
F
G
H
1
2
3
4
5
0 400 m
0 0.2 miles
For reviews see
Top Sights p90
Sights p96
Eating p101
Drinking p104
Entertainment p107
Shopping p107
Oberkampf
R Oberkampf
R St-Sébastien
St-Ambroise
R St-Ambroise
R St-Maur
Sq Maurice Gardette
Av Parmentier
Bd Voltaire
Richard Lenoir
Bd Richard Lenoir
R Pelée
R Moufle
R du Chemin Vert
11E
R Duranti
R Merlin
Sq de la Roquette
R Amelot
Sq Denis Poulot
R de la Roquette
Voltaire
Pl Léon Blum
Chemin Vert
Bd Beaumarchais
Sq Bréguet Sabin
Bréguet Sabin
R Froment
R Bréguet
R Popincourt
R Sedaine
R Léon Frot
R de Belfort
R Godefroy Cavaignac
R Cadet Lamy
R du
R de la Roquette
Passage Charles Dallery
R Basfroi
R St-Sabin
R Daval
R Keller
R des Taillandiers
Passage Thiéré
R de Lappe
R de la Bastille
Place de la Bastille
Bastille
Charonne
R Jules Vallès
R de Charonne
R Jean Macé
R Faidherbe
R Chanzy
R Charles Delescluze
R Trousseau
R du Faubourg St-Antoine
Ledru-Rollin
R de Charenton
R Paul Bert
R Titon
Bd de la Bastille
R de Lyon
Sq Trousseau
Pl Dr Antoine Béclère
R de Montreuil
Faidherbe Chaligny
Av Ledru-Rollin
R de Prague
R de Cotte
R d'Aligre
R Crozatier
R de Cîteaux
R de Chaligny
R de Reuilly
R Moreau
12E
R Émilio Castelar
Pl d'Aligre
St-Antoine
R Jules César
Av Daumesnil
Promenade Plantée

Sights

Musée Carnavalet

MUSEUM

1 Map p94, D3

This engaging history museum, spanning from Gallo-Roman times to modern day, is in two *hôtels particuliers:* mid-16th-century Renaissance-style Hôtel Carnavalet and late-17th-century Hôtel Le Peletier de St-Fargeau. Some of the nation's most important documents, paintings and other objects from the French Revolution are here.

Don't miss Georges Fouquet's stunning art nouveau jewellery shop from rue Royale, and Marcel Proust's cork-lined bedroom from his bd Haussmann apartment where he wrote his 7350-page literary cycle *À la Recherche de Temps Perdu (*Remembrance of Things Past).

(www.carnavalet.paris.fr; 23 rue de Sévigné, 3e; admission free; 10am-6pm Tue-Sun; M St-Paul, Chemin Vert or Rambuteau)

Maison de Victor Hugo

HOUSE MUSEUM

2 Map p94, D3

Between 1832 and 1848 writer Victor Hugo lived in an apartment on the 3rd floor of Hôtel de Rohan-Guéménée, overlooking one of Paris' most elegant squares. He moved here a year after the publication of *Notre Dame de Paris* (The Hunchback of Notre Dame), completing *Ruy Blas* while living here. His house is now a small museum devoted to the life and times of the celebrated novelist and poet, with an impressive collection of his personal drawings and portraits.

(www.musee-hugo.paris.fr; 6 place des Vosges, 4e; admission free; 10am-6pm Tue-Sun; M St-Paul or Bastille)

Musée des Arts et Métiers

MUSEUM

3 Map p94, C1

The Arts & Crafts Museum, dating to 1794 and Europe's oldest science and technology museum, is a must for anyone with kids – or an interest in how things tick or work. Housed inside the sublime 18th-century priory of St-Martin des Champs, some 3000 instruments, machines and working models from the 18th to 20th centuries are displayed across three floors. In the attached church of St-Martin des Champs is Foucault's original pendulum, introduced to the world at the Universal Exhibition in Paris 1855.

(www.arts-et-metiers.net; 60 rue de Réaumur, 3e; adult/child €6.50/free; 10am-6pm Tue, Wed & Fri-Sun, to 9.30pm Thu; M Arts et Métiers)

Maison Européenne de la Photographie

MUSEUM

4 Map p94, C3

The European House of Photography, housed in the overly renovated Hôtel Hénault de Cantorbe (dating – believe it or not – from the early 18th century), has cutting-edge temporary exhibits (usually retrospectives on single photographers), as well as an

Musée Carnavalet

enormous permanent collection on the history of photography and its connections with France.

There are frequent showings of short films and documentaries on weekend afternoons. The Japanese garden at the entrance is a delight. (www.mep-fr.org; 5-7 rue de Fourcy, 4e; adult/child €8/4.50; ⌚11am-7.45pm Wed-Sun; M St-Paul or Pont Marie)

Musée d'Art et d'Histoire du Judaïsme MUSEUM

5 ◎ Map p94, B2

To delve into the historic heart of the Marais' long-established Jewish community in Pletzl (from the Yiddish for 'little square'), visit this fascinating museum inside Hôtel de St-Aignan, dating from 1650. The museum traces the evolution of Jewish communities from the Middle Ages to the present, with particular emphasis on French Jewish history. Highlights include documents relating to the Dreyfus Affair, and works by Chagall, Modigliani and Soutine. Creative workshops for children, adults and families complement excellent temporary exhibitions. (www.mahj.org; 71 rue du Temple, 4e; adult/child €8/free; ⌚11am-6pm Mon-Fri, 10am-6pm Sun; M Rambuteau)

Local Life

Place des Vosges

Inaugurated in 1612 as place Royale, Paris' oldest square **place des Vosges** (Map p94, D3; 4e; MSt-Paul or Bastille) is an elegant ensemble of 36 symmetrical houses with steep slate roofs, large dormer windows and ground-floor arcades. It houses galleries, boutiques and busking violinists and cellists, arranged around a leafy square. In 1800 its name was changed to honour the Vosges *département* (administrative division) for being the first in France to pay its taxes. Pop around the corner for a drink at wood-panelled **Café Martini** (www.cafemartini.fr; 9 rue du Pas de la Mule, 4e; 6pm-midnight; MChemin Vert).

Musée Cognacq-Jay ART MUSEUM

6 Map p94, C2

This museum inside Hôtel de Donon displays oil paintings, pastels, sculpture, *objets d'art*, jewellery, porcelain and furniture from the 18th century assembled by Ernest Cognacq (1839–1928), founder of La Samaritaine department store, and his wife Louise Jay.

Although Cognacq appreciated little of his collection, boasting that he had never visited the Louvre and was only acquiring collections for the status, the artwork and *objets d'art* give a good idea of upper-class tastes during the Age of Enlightenment.

(www.cognacq-jay.paris.fr; 8 rue Elzévir, 3e; admission free; 10am-6pm Tue-Sun; MSt-Paul or Chemin Vert)

Hôtel de Ville CITY HALL

7 Map p94, A3

Paris' beautiful neo-Renaissance town hall was gutted during the Paris Commune of 1871 and rebuilt in luxurious neo-Renaissance style between 1874 and 1882. The ornate facade is decorated with 108 statues of illustrious Parisians, and the outstanding temporary exhibitions (admission free) held inside in its **Salle St-Jean** almost always have a Parisian theme.

From December to early March, an ice-skating rink sets up outside this beautiful building, creating a real picture-book experience.

(www.paris.fr; place de l'Hôtel de Ville, 4e; admission free; MHôtel de Ville)

Mémorial de la Shoah MUSEUM

8 Map p94, B3

Established in 1956, the Memorial to the Unknown Jewish Martyr has metamorphosed into the Memorial of the Shoah – a Hebrew word meaning 'catastrophe' and synonymous with the Holocaust. Exhibitions relate to the Holocaust and German occupation of parts of France and Paris during WWII. The actual memorial to the victims of the Shoah stands at the entrance.

(www.memorialdelashoah.org; 17 rue Geoffroy l'Asnier, 4e; admission free; 10am-6pm Sun-Wed & Fri, to 10pm Thu; MSt-Paul)

Promenade Plantée

PARK

9 Map p94, F5

The disused 19th-century Vincennes railway viaduct was successfully reborn as the world's first elevated park, planted with a fragrant profusion of cherry trees, maples, rose trellises, bamboo corridors and lavender. Three storeys above ground, it provides a unique aerial vantage point of the surrounding architecture. Access is via a staircase – usually at least one per city block – and lift (elevator; although they're invariably out of service). At street level, the **Viaduc des Arts** (www.viaducdesarts.fr; 1-129 av Daumesnil, 12e; vary; M Bastille or Gare de Lyon) gallery-workshops run along av Daumesnil. (12e; 8am-9.30pm May-Aug, to 5.30pm Sep-Apr; M Bastille or Gare de Lyon)

Musée Picasso

ART MUSEUM

10 Map p94, C2

One of Paris' most beloved art collections reopened its doors after a huge renovation and much controversy in late 2014. Housed in the mid-17th-century Hôtel Salé, the Musée Picasso woos art lovers with 5000 drawings, engravings, paintings, ceramic works and sculptures by the *grand maître* (great master) Pablo Picasso (1881–1973). The extraordinary collection was donated to the French government by the artist's heirs in lieu of paying inheritance tax. (01 42 71 25 21; www.museepicassoparis.fr; 5 rue de Thorigny, 3e; admission €11; 11.30am-6pm Tue-Sun, to 9pm 3rd Sat of month; M St-Paul or Chemin Vert)

Place de la Bastille

SQUARE

11 Map p94, E4

The Bastille, a 14th-century fortress built to protect the city gates, is the most famous monument in Paris that no longer exists. Nothing remains of the prison it became under Cardinal Richelieu, which was mobbed on 14 July 1789, igniting the French Revolution, but you can't miss the 52m-high green-bronze column topped by a gilded, winged Liberty. Revolutionaries from the uprising of 1830 are buried beneath. Now a skirmishly busy roundabout, it's still Paris' most symbolic destination for political protests. (M Bastille)

Local Life

Pletzl

The Jewish area around Le Marais' rue des Rosiers and rue des Écouffes was traditionally known as the Pletzl, and it's still filled with kosher delis and takeaway felafel windows such as Parisian favourite **L'As du Fallafel** (Map p94, C3; 34 rue des Rosiers, 4e; takeaway dishes €5.50-8.50; noon-midnight Sun-Thu, to 5pm Fri; M St-Paul) – the inevitable queue is worth the wait. The Pletzl's **art nouveau synagogue** (Map p94, C3; 10 rue Pavée, 4e) was designed in 1913 by Hector Guimard (who also designed Paris' iconic metro entrances).

Understand

Village Life

Within the Walls

Paris is defined by its walls (that is, the *Périphérique* or ring road). Intramuros (Latin for 'within the walls'), the 105 sq km interior has a population of just under 2.2 million, while the greater metropolitan area (the Île de France *région*, encircled by rivers) has some 12 million inhabitants, about 19% of France's total population. This makes Paris – the capital of both the *région* and the highly centralised nation – in effect an 'island within an island' (or, as residents elsewhere might say, a bubble).

Communal Living

Paris isn't merely a commuter destination, however – its dense inner-city population defines city life. Paris' shops, street markets, parks and other facets of day-to-day living evoke a village atmosphere, and its almost total absence of high-rises gives it a human scale.

Single-occupant dwellings make up around half of central Paris' households. And space shortages mean residential apartments are often minuscule. As a result, communal areas are the living and dining rooms and backyards of many Parisians, while neighbourhood shops are cornerstones of community life.

This high concentration of city dwellers is why there are few late-night bars and cafes or inner-city nightclubs, due to noise restrictions. It's also why so many pet dogs live in Paris. But hefty fines have meant the pavements (which are washed every day) are the cleanest they've ever been.

Beyond the Walls

Paris is on the brink of redefining its traditional boundaries by expanding into the surrounding suburbs as part of the Grand Paris (Greater Paris) redevelopment project. Its crux is a massive decentralised metro expansion – 72 new stations and six suburban lines – with a target completion date of 2025. The key goal is to connect the suburbs with one another, rather than the current central inner-city hub with lines radiating outwards. It's expected that autonomous suburbs such as Vincennes, Neuilly, Issy, St-Denis etc will eventually become part of a much larger Grand Paris, governed by the Hôtel de Ville. It is no done deal, however, as uniting the wildly diverse municipalities will be no easy feat.

Hôtel de Ville (p98)

Tour St-Jacques

TOWER

12 Map p94, A3

Just north of place du Châtelet, the Flamboyant Gothic, 54m-high St James Tower is all that remains of the Église St-Jacques la Boucherie, built by the powerful butchers guild in 1523 as a starting point for pilgrims setting out for the shrine of St James at Santiago de Compostela in Spain. Recently restored, it should open to the public in the near future, allowing visitors to climb 300 stairs up to an expansive panorama.
(39 rue de Rivoli, 4e; adult €6; MChâtelet)

Eating

Le 6 Paul Bert

BISTRO €€

13 Map p94, H4

Opened by Bertrand Auboyneau of neighbouring **Bistrot Paul Bert** (01 43 72 24 01; 18 rue Paul Bert, 11e; 3-course lunch/dinner menus €19/38; noon-2pm & 7.30-11pm Tue-Sat; MFaidherbe–Chaligny) and Québecois chef Louis-Philippe Riel, Le 6 serves mindblowing menus of small(ish) plates. The exquisitely presented creations from Riel's kitchen change daily, but invariably involve unexpected flavour combinations (quail and turnip, artichoke and white chocolate).
(01 43 79 14 32; 6 rue Paul Bert, 12e; 2-/3-course lunch menus €15/19, 4-course

dinner menus €44; noon-2pm Tue, noon-2pm & 7.30-11pm Wed-Sat; Faidherbe–Chaligny)

Bones

BISTRO €€

14 Map p94, G3

Even if you don't score a first-service reservation (7pm to 7.30pm) for red-hot Australian chef James Henry's stripped-back new premises, you have a couple of back-up options. The second service (9.30pm to 10.30pm) is walk-in only. Or you can order Henry's signature small plates (smoked oyster, beef heart, sea-bass carpaccio, house-cured charcuterie) at the lively bar. (09 80 75 32 08; www.bonesparis.com; 43 rue Godefroy Cavaignac, 11e; bar dishes €4-16, 4-/5-course menus €47/55; kitchen 7-11pm Tue-Sat; Voltaire)

Local Life

Marché d'Aligre

All the staples of French cuisine can be found at the chaotic **Marché d'Aligre** (Map p94, G5; http://marchedaligre.free.fr; rue d'Aligre, 12e; 8am-1pm & 4-7.30pm Tue-Sat, 8am-1.30pm Sun; Ledru-Rollin) – cheese, coffee, chocolate, wine, charcuterie. Offerings at the covered **Marché Beauvau**, in the centre of place d'Aligre, are a bit more gourmet. The morning **Marché aux Puces d'Aligre** (place d'Aligre, 12e; 8am-1pm Tue-Sun; Ledru-Rollin) flea market takes place here. Food shops, wine bars – such as the wonderful, barrel-lined **Le Baron Rouge** (1 rue Théophile Roussel, 12e; 10am-2pm & 5-10pm Tue-Fri, 10am-10pm Sat, 10am-4pm Sun; Ledru-Rollin) and a rapidly increasing number of restaurants fan out into the surrounding streets.

Candelaria

TAQUERIA €

15 Map p94, D1

You need to know about this terribly cool taqueria to find it. Made of pure, unadulterated hipness in that brazenly nonchalant manner Paris does so well, clandestine Candelaria serves delicious homemade tacos, quesadillas and tostadas in a laid-back setting – squat at the bar in the front or lounge out back around a shared table with bar stools or at low coffee tables. (www.candelariaparis.com; 52 rue Saintonge; tacos €3.20-3.75, quesadillas & tostadas €3.50, lunch menus €11.50; noon-midnight Thu-Sat, to 11pm Sun-Wed; ; Filles du Calvaire)

Dessance

DESSERTS €€

16 Map p94, C1

Dining at Dessance is unique. Only desserts are served – with an astonishing eye for detail and creative zeal for marrying unexpected ingredients (yes, broccoli, beetroot and roquette with chocolate and caramel). Whether you opt for the four-dessert menu or à la carte, a sweet *amuse-bouche* kicks off the experience and a plate of mini *gourmandises* (sweet things) ends it. (01 42 77 23 62; www.dessance.fr; 74 rue des Archives, 3e; desserts à la carte €19, 4-course dessert menu €36-44; 3-11pm

Wed-Fri, noon-midnight Sat & Sun; ; Arts et Métiers)

Chez Marianne JEWISH €€

17 Map p94, C3

Heaving at lunchtime, Chez Marianne translates as elbow-to-elbow eating beneath age-old beams on copious portions of felafel, hummus, aubergine puree and 25-odd other *zakouski* (hors d'œuvres; €14/16/18 for plate of four/five/six). Fare is Sephardic rather than Ashkenazi (the norm at most Pletzl eateries), ans not Beth Din kosher. A hole-in-the-wall window sells felafel in pita (€7) to munch on the move.
(2 rue des Hospitalières St-Gervais, 4e; mains €18-25; noon-midnight; St-Paul)

Marché Bastille MARKET €

18 Map p94, E3

If you only get to one open-air street market in Paris, this one, stretching between the Bastille and Richard Lenoir metro stations, is among the very best.
(bd Richard Lenoir, 11e; 7am-2.30pm Thu & Sun; Bastille or Richard Lenoir)

À la Biche au Bois TRADITIONAL FRENCH €€

19 Map p94, E5

Game, especially *la biche,* is the speciality of the convivial 'doe in the woods', but dishes such as foie gras and *coq au vin* also add to the ambience of being out in the countryside, as do the green awning and potted plants out front. The cheeses and wines are excellent, but top honours, game aside, go to the sensational *frites*.
(01 43 43 34 38; 45 av Ledru-Rollin, 12e; 7-10.45pm Mon, noon-2.30pm & 7-10.45pm Tue-Sat; 3-course lunch menu €29.80, mains €17-22.50; Gare de Lyon)

Clamato SEAFOOD €€

20 Map p94, G4

Arrive early: unlike its raved-about sister restaurant and next-door neighbour **Septime** (01 43 67 38 29; 80 rue de Charonne, 11e; lunch menus €28-55, dinner menus €58; 7-10pm Mon, 12.15-2pm & 7-10pm Tue-Fri; Charonne), Clamato doesn't take reservations, and you seriously don't want to miss out on Bertrand Grébaut and Théo Pourriat's seafood tapas. The menu changes daily but might include mussels with onion confit and saffron, baked razor clams with crushed peanuts and herb butter or octopus carpaccio with grapefruit pulp.
(www.septime-charonne.fr; 80 rue de Charonne, 11e; tapas €6-19; 7-11pm Mon-Fri, noon-11pm Sat & Sun; Charonne)

Pozzetto ICE CREAM €

21 Map p94, B3

Urban myth says this gelato maker opened when friends from northern Italy couldn't find their favourite ice cream in Paris so they imported the ingredients to make it themselves. Twelve flavours – served with a spatula, not scoop – include *gianduia* (hazelnut chocolate from Turin) and *zabaione*, made from egg yolks, sugar and sweet Marsala wine. Great Italian *caffè* too. (www.pozzetto.biz; 16 rue Vieille du Temple, 4e; cone or pot €4-5.90; 11.30am-9pm Mon-Thu, to 11.30pm Fri-Sun; M St-Paul)

CheZaline

DELICATESSEN €

22 Map p94, G3

A former horse-meat butcher's shop (*chevaline,* hence the spin on the name) is now a fabulous deli creating seasonally changing baguettes filled with ingredients like ham and house-made pesto. Other delicacies include salads and homemade terrines. There's a handful of seats (and plenty of parks nearby). Prepare to queue. (85 rue de la Roquette, 11e; dishes €6.50-9; 11am-5.30pm Mon-Fri; M Voltaire)

Local Life

Rue de Lappe

Quiet during the day, little rue de Lappe comes alive at night when its string of bars are in full swing. Catch music at the 1936-opened dance hall **Le Balajo** (Map p94, E4; www.balajo.fr; 9 rue de Lappe, 11e; vary; M Bastille), with everything from salsa to R&B, plus old-time tea dancing during *musettes* (accordion gigs) from 2pm to 7pm on Mondays. Or try **La Chapelle des Lombards** (Map p94, F4; www.la-chapelle-des-lombards.com; 19 rue de Lappe, 11e; 11pm-5am Sun & Wed-Thu, to 6am Fri & Sat; M Bastille), which usually has concerts on Friday and Saturday.

Bofinger

BRASSERIE €€

23 Map p94, E4

Founded in 1864, Bofinger is reputedly Paris' oldest brasserie, though its polished art nouveau brass, glass and mirrors suggests redecoration a few decades later. Specialities include Alsatian-inspired dishes such as *choucroute* (sauerkraut), oysters and seafood dishes. Ask for a seat downstairs and under the *coupole* (stained-glass dome) (01 42 72 87 82; www.bofingerparis.com; 5-7 rue de la Bastille, 4e; menus €36.50-59, mains €22.50-46; noon-3pm & 6.30pm-midnight; M Bastille)

Drinking

Le Cap Horn

BAR

24 Map p94, D4

On summer evenings the ambience at this laid-back, Chilean bar is electric. The crowd spills onto the pavement, parked cars doubling as table tops for well-shaken pina coladas, punch cocos and cocktails made with pisco, a fiery Chilean grape *eau-de-vie*. Find it steps from place des Vosges. (8 rue de Birague, 4e; 10-1am; M St-Paul or Chemin Vert)

Le Pure Café

CAFE

25 Map p94, H4

A classic Parisian haunt, this rustic, cherry-red corner cafe featured in the art-house film *Before Sunset,* but it's still a refreshingly unpretentious spot

ALEX SEGRE / ALAMY ©

Le Pure Café

for a drink, cheese or chacuterie platters, fusion cuisine or Sunday brunch. (www.purecafe.fr; 14 rue Jean Macé, 11e; 7am-2am Mon-Fri, 8am-2am Sat, 9am-midnight Sun; M Charonne)

Le Loir dans la Théière — CAFE

26  Map p94, C3

Its cutesy name (Dormouse in the Teapot) notwithstanding, this is a wonderful old space filled with retro toys, comfy couches and scenes of *Through the Looking Glass* on the walls. Its dozen different types of tea poured in the company of excellent savoury tarts and crumble-type desserts ensure a constant queue on the street outside. Breakfast and brunch too.

(3 rue des Rosiers, 4e; 9am-7.30pm; M St-Paul)

La Fée Verte — BAR

27  Map p94, G3

You guessed it, the 'Green Fairy' specialises in absinthe (served traditionally with spoons and sugar cubes), but this fabulously old-fashioned neighbourhood cafe and bar also serves terrific food.

(108 rue de la Roquette, 11e; 8am-2am Mon-Sat, 9am-2am Sun; ; M Voltaire)

Le Tango — CLUB

28  Map p94, B1

Billing itself as a *boîte à frissons* (club of thrills), Le Tango hosts a mixed and

cosmopolitan, gay and lesbian crowd in a historic 1930s dance hall. Its atmosphere and style is retro and festive, with waltzing, salsa and tango on from the moment it opens. From about 12.30am onwards DJs play. Sunday's gay tea dance is legendary.
(www.boiteafrissons.fr; 13 rue au Maire, 3e; admission €6-9; 10.30pm-5am Fri & Sat, 6-11pm Sun; M Arts et Métiers)

Open Café

CAFE

29 Map p94, B2

A gay venue for all types at all hours, this spacious bar-cafe with twinkling disco balls strung from the starry ceiling has bags of appeal – not least, a big buzzing pavement terrace, a kitchen serving breakfast (€8.70), all-day *tartines* (€6.70), and a four-hour happy hour kicking in daily at 6pm.
(www.opencafe.fr; 17 rue des Archives, 4e; 11am-2am; M Hôtel de Ville)

La Caféothèque

CAFE

30 Map p94, B4

From the industrial grinder to elaborate tasting notes, this maze of a coffee house is serious. Grab a pew, pick your bean, and get it served just the way you like it (espresso, ristretto, latte etc). The coffee of the day (€3) keeps well-travelled tastebuds on their toes, as does the €10 *dégustation* (tasting) of three different *crus*.
(www.lacafeotheque.com; 52 rue de l'Hôtel de Ville, 4e; 9.30am-7.30pm; ; M St-Paul or Hôtel de Ville)

3w Kafé

GAY BAR

31 Map p94, C3

The name of this flagship cocktail bar-pub on a street with several lesbian bars means 'women with women'. It's relaxed and there's no ban on men (they must be accompanied by a woman). On weekends there's dancing downstairs with a DJ and themed evenings take place regularly. Check its Facebook page for events.
(8 rue des Écouffes, 4e; 8pm-3am Wed & Thu, to 5.30am Fri & Sat; M St-Paul)

Quetzal

GAY BAR

32 Map p94, B3

This perennial favourite gay bar is opposite rue des Mauvais Garçons (Bad Boys' Street), a road named after the brigands who congregated here in 1540. It's always busy, with house and dance music playing at night, and cruisy at all hours; plate-glass windows allow you to check out the talent before it arrives.
(10 rue de la Verrerie, 4e; 5pm-2am; M Hôtel de Ville)

La Perle

CAFE, BAR

33 Map p94, C2

This party bar is where bobos (bohemian bourgeois) come to slum it over *un rouge* (glass of red wine) in the Marais until the DJ arrives to liven things up. Unique trademarks: the (for real) distressed look of the place and the model locomotive over the bar.
(http://cafelaperle.com; 78 rue Vieille du Temple, 3e; 9am-2am; M St-Paul or Chemin Vert)

Entertainment

Opéra Bastille

OPERA, BALLET

34 Map p94, E4

This 3400-seat venue is the city's main opera hall; it also occasionally stages ballet and classical concerts. Tickets go on sale online up to two weeks before they're available by telephone or at the **box office** (01 40 01 19 70; 130 rue de Lyon, 12e; 2.30-6.30pm Mon-Sat; M Bastille). Standing-only tickets (*places débouts;* €5) are available 90 minutes before performances begin. (08 92 89 90 90; www.operadeparis.fr; 2-6 place de la Bastille, 12e; M Bastille)

Badaboum

LIVE MUSIC

35 Map p94, F4

Formerly La Scène Bastille and freshly refitted, the onomatopoeically named Badaboum hosts a mixed bag of concerts on its up-close-and-personal stage but focuses on electro, funk and hip-hop. Great atmosphere, super cocktails and a secret room upstairs. (www.badaboum-paris.com; 2bis rue des Taillandiers, 11e; cocktail bar 7pm-2am Wed-Sat, club & concerts vary; M Bastille or Ledru-Rollin)

Shopping

Paris Rendez-Vous

CONCEPT STORE

36 Map p94, A3

Only the city of Paris could be so chic as to have its own designer line of souvenirs, sold in its own ubercool concept store inside the Hôtel de Ville. Shop here for everything from clothing and homeware to Paris-themed books, toy sailing boats and signature Jardin du Luxembourg's Fermob chairs. (29 rue de Rivoli, 4e; 10am-7pm Mon-Sat; M Hôtel de Ville)

La Manufacture de Chocolat

FOOD, DRINK

37 Map p94, E4

If you dine at superstar chef Alain Ducasse's restaurants, the chocolate will have been made here at Ducasse's own chocolate factory – the first in Paris to produce 'bean-to-bar' chocolate – which he set up with his former executive pastry chef Nicolas Berger. Deliberate over ganaches, pralines and truffles and no fewer than 44 flavours of chocolate bar. (www.lechocolat-alainducasse.com; 40 rue de la Roquette, 11e; 10.30am-7pm Tue-Sat; M Bastille)

My Crazy Pop

FOOD

38 Map p94, G5

Wasabi, Parmesan, barbecue and olive tapenade are among the amazing savoury flavours at this popcorn shop (a French first); sweet styles include gingerbread praline, salted-butter caramel, and orange and cinnamon. Wander through to the viewing window at the back to watch the kernels being popped using heat and pressure only (no oil). (15 rue Trousseau, 11e; 11am-7pm Tue-Fri, to 8pm Sat; M Ledru-Rollin)

Top Sights
Père Lachaise

Getting There

Père Lachaise is about 4.5km northeast of Notre Dame.

M Metro Philippe Auguste (line 2), Gambetta (lines 3 and 3b) and Père Lachaise (lines 2 and 3).

Paris is a collection of villages and these 44 hectares of cobbled lanes and elaborate tombs, with a population (as it were) of more than a million, certainly qualify as one. The world's most visited cemetery was founded in 1804, and initially attracted few funerals because of its distance from the city centre. The authorities responded by exhuming famous remains and resettling them here. Their marketing ploy worked and Cimetière du Père Lachaise has been Paris' most fashionable final address ever since.

Don't Miss

Molière & Fontaine's Graves

Division 25

The first of the famous graves moved to Père Lachaise when Parisians refused to leave their local *quartier* were popular playwright Molière (1622–73) and poet Jean de la Fontaine (1621–95), who arrived here in 1817.

Édith Piaf's Grave

Division 97

Songstress Édith Piaf (née Gassion) died in 1963, leaving behind a string of stirring classics like 'Non, je ne regrette rien' and 'La vie en rose'. Time-honoured tomb traditions at Père Lachaise include leaving red roses on Piaf's grave.

Jim Morrison's Grave

Division 6

Père Lachaise's most venerated tomb belongs to The Doors' Jim Morrison, who died in a Marais apartment in 1971. Prior to his family's complaints, 'traditions' included fans taking drugs and having sex on his grave. Security has since been increased and barricading has been added to the tomb.

Oscar Wilde's Grave

Division 89

Topped by a naked winged angel, the flamboyant grave of Irish playwright and humorist Oscar Wilde, who died in Paris in 1900, was plastered in lipstick kisses until a glass cover was installed in 2011.

Chopin's Grave

Division 11

Add a devotional note to the handwritten letters and flowers brightening the marble tomb

☎01 43 70 70 33

www.pere-lachaise.com

16 rue du Repos & bd de Ménilmontant, 20e

admission free

⏲8am-6pm Mon-Fri, 8.30am-6pm Sat, 9am-6pm Sun

Ⓜ Père Lachaise or Gambetta

☑ Top Tips

- Maps locating noteworthy graves are posted around the cemetery and online, or pick one up at the conservation office near the main bd de Ménilmontant entrance.
- Visiting Père Lachaise fits well with a stroll along Canal St-Martin.

✕ Take a Break

- Built on a former construction yard, bistro **Yard** (☎01 40 09 70 30; 6 rue de Mont Louis, 11e; 3-course lunch menus €18, mains €15-18; ⏲noon-2.30pm Mon, noon-2.30pm & 8-10.30pm Tue-Fri; Ⓜ Philippe Auguste) has been resurrected by chefs Shaun Kelly and Elenie Sapera, working the open kitchen and tapas bar.

of Polish composer-pianist Chopin (1810–49), who spent his short adult life in Paris. His heart is buried in Warsaw.

André Chabot's Grave-to-Be

Division 20

Contemporary photographer André Chabot (b 1941) shoots funerary art, hence the bijou 19th-century chapel he's equipped with a monumental granite camera in preparation for the day he departs – and QR code.

Mur des Fédérés

Division 76

This plain brick wall was where 147 Communard insurgents were lined up and shot in 1871. Equally emotive is the sculpted walkway of commemorative war memorials surrounding the mass grave.

BRAUNO DE HOGUES / GETTY IMAGES ©

Bronze statue adorns a tomb

Monsieur Noir

Division 92

Protests saw the removal of a fence around the grave of Monsieur Noir, aka journalist Yvan Salman (1848–70), who was shot at the age of 22 by Pierre Bonaparte, great-nephew of Napoléon. Legend says women who stroke the amply filled crotch of Monsieur Noir's bronze effigy will enjoy a better sex life and fertility.

Abélard & Héloïse's Graves

Division 7

Also re-interred in Père Lachaise in 1817 to increase the cemetery's profile were tragic 12th-century lovers Abélard and Héloïse, who were torn apart Romeo and Juliet style but continued to correspond via passionate, poetic letters. They were reunited here beneath a neo-Gothic tombstone, where romantics regularly leave love letters.

Balzac's Grave

Division 48

The great French writer Honoré de Balzac, author of *La Comédie Humaine* (depicting French life following the 1815 fall of Napoléon), was buried here in 1850. Among the literary elite who attended his funeral, Victor Hugo was a pallbearer and eulogist.

HUW JONES / GETTY IMAGES ©

Monsieur Noir

Delacroix' Grave

Division 49

Seminal French romantic artist Eugène Delacroix (1798–63) is among numerous artists buried here. Delacriox's works include frescoes in St-Sulpice, major works in the Louvre and more intimate ones at his former home, now the Musée National Eugène Delacroix.

Georges Seurat's Grave

Division 66

The tomb of pointillism pioneer Georges Seurat (1859–91) is one of many that resemble a small house, adding to Père Lachaise's village-like feel.

Marcel Proust's Grave

Division 85

Madeleine cakes are traditionally left on the tomb of Marcel Proust (1871–1922), author of *À la Recherche du Temps Perdu* (*Remembrance of Things Past*, also translated as *In Search of Lost Time*).

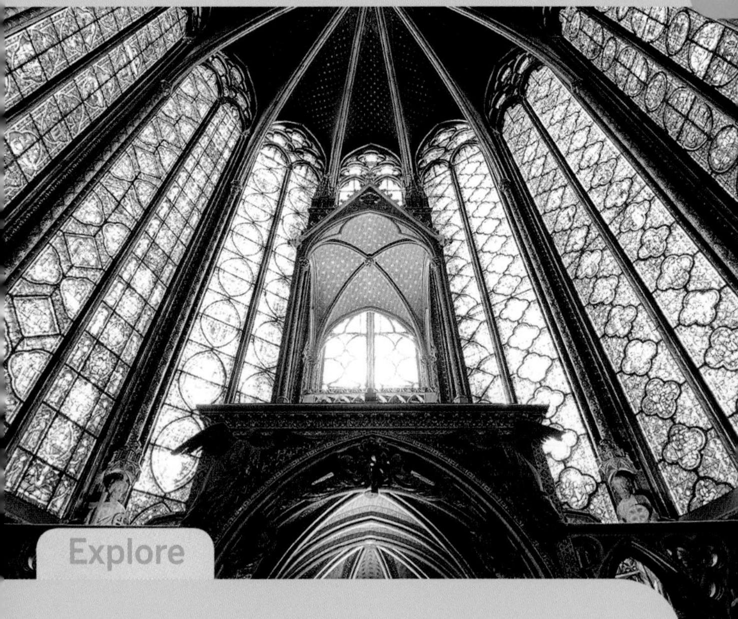

Explore

Notre Dame & the Islands

Paris' geographic, spiritual and historic heart is situated here in the Seine. The city's watery beginnings took place on the Île de la Cité, the larger of the two inner-city islands. To its east, the serene Île St-Louis is graced with elegant, exclusive apartments, along with a handful of intimate hotels and charming eateries and boutiques.

The Sights in a Day

The city's landmark cathedral, **Notre Dame,** (p114) dominates the Île de la Cité, so where better to start your explorations? (Heading here first also means you'll beat the crowds.) In addition to viewing its stained-glass interior, allow around an hour to visit the top and another to explore the archaeological crypt. For even more beautiful stained-glass, don't miss nearby **Sainte-Chapelle** (p122). From here it's a few footsteps to the intriguing French Revolution prison, the **Conciergerie** (p122).

Cross the **Pont St-Louis** (p126) to the enchanting little Île St-Louis. After lunch at deliciously Parisian hangout **Café Saint Régis** (p125), browse the island's **boutiques** and buy a **Berthillon** (p123) ice cream.

After a traditional French meal at **Le Tastevin** (p125), stroll back over the Pont St-Louis (where you're likely to catch buskers) for a nightcap at the Île de la Cité's venerable wine bar **Taverne Henri IV** (p126). If you're still going strong, cross the **Pont Neuf** (p122) for entertainment options on either side of the Seine.

Top Sights

Notre Dame (p114)

Best of Paris

History

Notre Dame (p114)

Sainte-Chapelle (p122)

Conciergerie (p122)

Drinking

Taverne Henri IV (p126)

Markets

Marché aux Fleurs Reine Elizabeth II (p127)

Churches

Notre Dame (p114)

Ste-Chapelle (p122)

Getting There

Ⓜ **Metro** Cité (line 4) on the Île de la Cité is the islands' only metro station, and the most convenient for Notre Dame.

Ⓜ **Metro** Pont Marie (line 7), on the Right Bank, is the Île St-Louis' closest station.

Boat The hop-on, hop-off Batobus stops opposite Notre Dame on the Left Bank.

Top Sights
Notre Dame

The mighty Cathédrale Notre Dame de Paris (Cathedral of Our Lady of Paris) is a masterpiece of French Gothic architecture. Built on the site of earlier churches and, a millennium before that, a Gallo-Roman temple, it was largely completed by the early 14th century. The cathedral was badly damaged during the French Revolution, and extensive restorations were finished in 1864. Today, it's the city's most visited un-ticketed site, with upwards of 14 million people crossing its threshold each year.

Map p120, D3

www.cathedraledeparis.com

6 place du Parvis Notre Dame, 4e

cathedral free, towers adult/child €8.50/free

cathedral 7.45am-6.45pm Mon-Sat, to 7.15pm Sun

M Cité

Don't Miss

The Scale

The single most impressive aspect of Notre Dame is its sheer size: the interior alone is 130m long, 48m wide and 35m high, and can accommodate more than 6000 worshippers.

The Rose Windows

Exceptional features of Notre Dame include three spectacular rose windows. The 10m-wide window over the western façade (partly obscured by the organ) and the window on the northern side of the transept (which has remained virtually unchanged since the 13th century), are the most renowned.

The Flying Buttresses

The little park behind the cathedral, Square Jean XXIII, has the best views of the forest of ornate flying buttresses. One of the world's first buildings to use them, Notre Dame wasn't originally designed to include flying buttresses around the choir and nave, but exterior supports were necessary after stress fractures occurred as the walls pushed outwards.

The Towers

The **Tours de Notre Dame** (Notre Dame Towers; rue du Cloître Notre Dame, 4e; adult/child €8.50/free; ⏲10am-6.30pm, to 11pm Fri & Sat Jul & Aug, to 5.30pm daily Oct-Mar; Ⓜ Cité) entrance is accessed via the North Tower. Limber up to climb the 400-odd spiralling steps – there's no lift (elevator) – to the top.

The Treasury

The **Trésor** (Treasury; adult/child €3/2; ⏲9.30am-6pm Mon-Fri, 9.30am-6.30pm Sat, 1.30-6.30pm Sun) contains relics such as the Ste-Couronne (Holy Crown), allegedly the wreath of thorns placed on Jesus'

☑ Top Tips

- Queues can be long and get longer throughout the day, especially during the summer months – arrive as early as possible to avoid the worst of the crowds.
- Pick up an audio guide (€5) from Notre Dame's information desk, just inside the entrance. Audio-guide rental includes admission to the treasury.
- Join a free 90-minute English-language tour. Tour times are posted on the website, or ask at the information desk.
- Admission to the towers is free on the first Sunday of the month from November to March.
- Remember that Notre Dame is an active place of worship.

✕ Take a Break

Pop across to the adjacent Île St-Louis for a Berthillon ice cream (p123), or for a drink, snack or meal at Café Saint Régis (p125).

NOTRE DAME

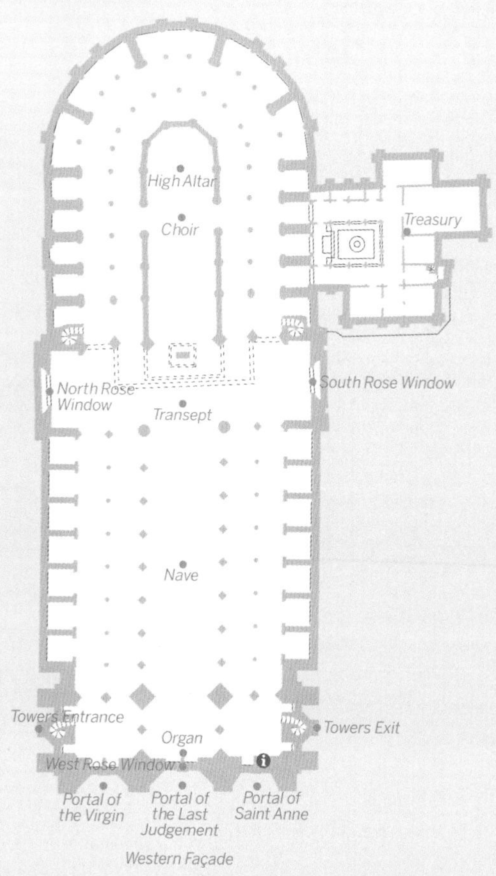
High Altar
Choir
Treasury
North Rose Window
South Rose Window
Transept
Nave
Towers Entrance
Towers Exit
Organ
West Rose Window
Portal of the Virgin
Portal of the Last Judgement
Portal of Saint Anne
Western Façade

Gargoyle

head before he was crucified. It's exhibited between 3pm and 4pm on the first Friday of each month, 3pm to 4pm every Friday during Lent, and 10am to 5pm on Good Friday.

The Gargoyles

Arriving at the top of the western façade brings you face to face with the cathedral's most frightening gargoyles. These grotesque statues divert rainwater from the roof to prevent masonry damage, with the water exiting through their elongated, open mouths, and, purportedly, ward off evil spirits. Although they appear medieval, they were installed by Eugène Viollet-le-Duc in the 19th century.

The Views

From the Galerie des Chimères (Chimera Gallery), named for Viollet-le-Duc's mythical creatures and monsters, at the top of the western façade, you will find a spectacular panorama of the Paris skyline, including the Latin Quarter's ancient streets and the Eiffel Tower.

The Bells

The top of the western façade offers an impressive view of the South Tower's 13-tonne bourdon bell, Emmanuel (all of the cathedral's bells are named). During the night of 24 August 1944, when the Île de la Cité was retaken by French, Allied and Resistance troops,

Understand

Notre Dame Timeline

1160 The Bishop of Paris, Maurice de Sully, ordered the demolition of the original cathedral, the 4th-century Saint-Étienne (St Stephen's).

1163 Notre Dame's cornerstone was laid and construction began on the new cathedral.

1182 The apse and choir were completed.

Early 1200s Work commenced on the western façade.

1225 The western façade was completed.

1250 Work finished on the western towers and north rose window.

Mid-1200s To 'modernise' the cathedral, the transepts were remodelled in the Rayonnant style.

1345 The cathedral was completed.

1548 Huguenots stormed and damaged the cathedral following the Council of Trent.

1793 Damage during the most radical phase of the French Revolution saw many of Notre Dame's treasures plundered or destroyed.

1845–64 Following petitions to save the, by then, derelict cathedral from demolition, architect Eugène Viollet-le-Duc carried out extensive repairs and architectural additions.

1991 A lengthy maintenance and restoration program was initiated.

2013 Notre Dame celebrated 850 years since construction began.

the tolling of the Emmanuel announced Paris' approaching liberation. Emmanuel's peal purity comes from precious gems and jewels Parisian women threw into the pot when it was recast from copper and bronze in 1631. Admire its original siblings in Square Jean XXII. As part of the 2013 celebrations for Notre Dame's 850th anniversary since construction began, nine new bells were installed, replicating the original medieval chimes.

The Bees

Since spring 2013 a beehive has been set up on the cathedral's roof near Square Jean XXIII, with the aim of preserving biodiversity and remembering 'the beauty of creation and the responsibility of Man towards her'.

The Portals

On the western façade, check out the exquisite detail of its three 13th-century portals: the Portal of the Virgin, on the left, depicting Mary's ascension to heaven; the Portal of the Last Judgement, in the centre, representing the Last Judgement according to the Gospel of Saint Matthew; and the oldest, the Portal of Saint Anne, on the right.

The Organ

Notre Dame's splendid organ is one of the largest in the world, with 7800 pipes (900 of which have historical classification), 111 stops, five 56-key manuals and a 32-key pedalboard. It's played during Sunday services and free recitals at 4.30pm on Sundays.

Services

All religious services are conducted in French except the 'international' mass held at 11.30am on Sunday, which includes some readings and prayer in English; there are no English-only services. Midnight mass on Christmas Eve is a particularly popular occasion. Service times are posted on the cathedral's website.

Evening Concerts

From October to June the cathedral stages evening concerts; check the program online at www.musique-sacree-notredamedeparis.fr.

Landmark Occasions

Historic events that have taken place at Notre Dame include Henry VI of England's 1431 coronation as King of France, the 1558 marriage of Mary, Queen of Scots, to the Dauphin Francis (later Francis II of France), the 1804 coronation of Napoléon I by Pope Pius VII and the 1909 beatification and 1920 canonisation of Joan of Arc.

Point Zéro

Notre Dame is the heart of Paris – so much so that distances from Paris to the rest of mainland France are measured from place du Parvis Notre Dame, the square in front of the cathedral. A bronze star marks the precise location of *point zéro des routes de France*.

Archaeological Crypt

The archaeological crypt beneath place du Parvis Notre Dame, the **Crypte Archéologique du Parvis Notre Dame** (http://crypte.paris.fr; 7 Parvis Notre Dame, 4e; adult/child €4/3; ⌚10am-6pm Tue-Sun; Ⓜ Cité), reveals layer by layer the Île de la Cité history, from the Gallo-Roman town of Lutetia to the 20th century, including a few of the original sewers sunk by Haussman.

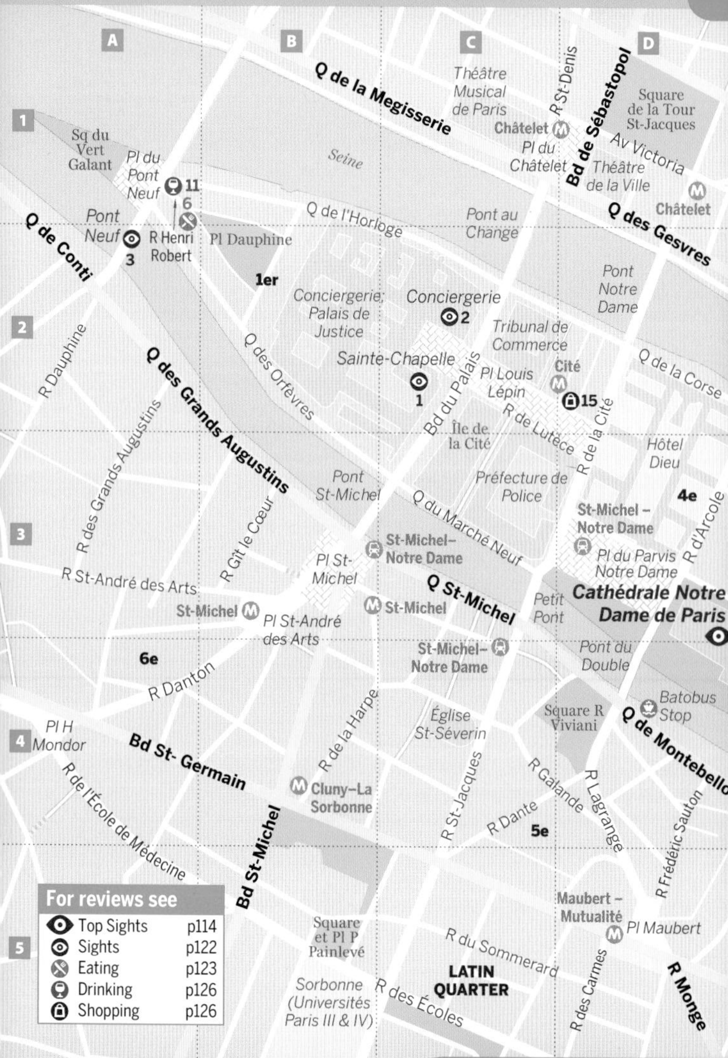

For reviews see

Top Sights	p114
Sights	p122
Eating	p123
Drinking	p126
Shopping	p126

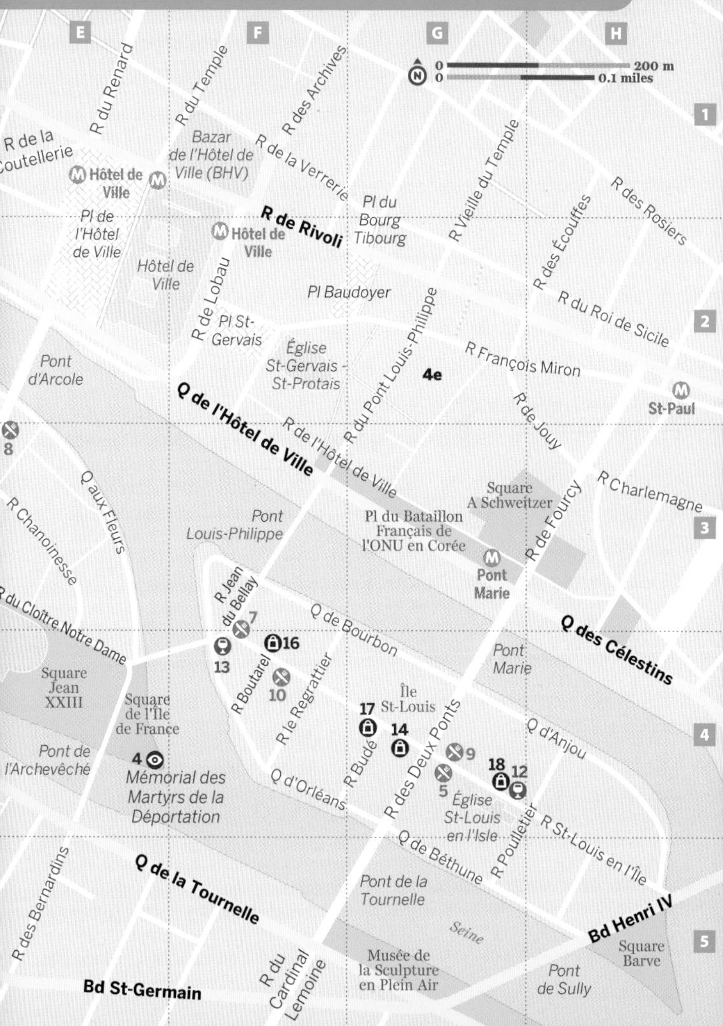
E
F
G
H
0 200 m
0 0.1 miles
1
2
3
4
5
R du Renard
R du Temple
R des Archives
R de la Coutellerie
Hôtel de Ville
Bazar de l'Hôtel de Ville (BHV)
R de la Verrerie
Pl de l'Hôtel de Ville
Hôtel de Ville
R de Rivoli
Pl du Bourg Tibourg
R Vieille du Temple
R des Écouffes
R des Rosiers
Hôtel de Ville
R de Lobau
Pl Baudoyer
R du Roi de Sicile
Pl St-Gervais
Église St-Gervais - St-Protais
R du Pont Louis-Philippe
4e
R François Miron
Pont d'Arcole
Q de l'Hôtel de Ville
R de l'Hôtel de Ville
R de Jouy
St-Paul
8
Q aux Fleurs
R Chanoinesse
Square A Schweitzer
R de Fourcy
R Charlemagne
Pont Louis-Philippe
Pl du Bataillon Français de l'ONU en Corée
Pont Marie
R Jean du Bellay
R du Cloître Notre Dame
7
Q de Bourbon
16
13
Q des Célestins
Pont Marie
Square Jean XXIII
R Boutarel
10
R le Regrattier
Île St-Louis
17
14
R des Deux Ponts
Q d'Anjou
Square de l'Île de France
Pont de l'Archevêché
4
Mémorial des Martyrs de la Déportation
R Budé
9
18
12
5
Église St-Louis en l'Isle
Q d'Orléans
R Poulletier
R St-Louis en l'Île
Q de Béthune
R des Bernardins
Q de la Tournelle
Pont de la Tournelle
Seine
Bd Henri IV
Square Barve
Musée de la Sculpture en Plein Air
Pont de Sully
R du Cardinal Lemoine
Bd St-Germain

Sights

Sainte-Chapelle

CHAPEL

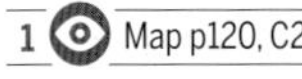

Try to save Sainte-Chapelle for a sunny day, when Paris' oldest, finest stained glass is at its dazzling best. Enshrined within the **Palais de Justice** (Law Courts), this gem-like Holy Chapel is Paris' most exquisite Gothic monument. Sainte-Chapelle was built in just six years (compared with nearly 200 years for Notre Dame) and consecrated in 1248.

The chapel was conceived by Louis IX to house his personal collection of holy relics, including the famous Holy Crown (now in Notre Dame).

(01 53 40 60 80, concerts 01 42 77 65 65; http://sainte-chapelle.monuments-nationaux.fr; 8 bd du Palais, 1er; adult/child €8.50/free, joint ticket with Conciergerie €12.50; 9.30am-6pm daily, to 9.30pm Wed mid-May–mid-Sep, 9am-5pm daily Nov-Feb; M Cité)

Understand

Île St-Louis: Two Islands in One

Today's Île St-Louis was actually two uninhabited islets called Île Notre Dame (Our Lady Isle) and Île aux Vaches (Cows Island) in the early 17th century. That was until building contractor Christophe Marie and two financiers worked out a deal with Louis XIII to create one island and build two stone bridges to the mainland. In exchange they could subdivide and sell the newly created real estate, and by 1664 the entire island was covered with fine houses facing the quays and the river, which remain today.

Conciergerie

MONUMENT

2 Map p120, C2

A royal palace in the 14th century, the Conciergerie later became a prison. During the Reign of Terror (1793–94) alleged enemies of the Revolution were incarcerated here before being brought before the Revolutionary Tribunal next door in the **Palais de Justice**. Top-billing exhibitions take place in the beautiful, Rayonnant Gothic **Salle des Gens d'Armes**, Europe's largest surviving medieval hall.

(www.monuments-nationaux.fr; 2 bd du Palais, 1er; adult/child €8.50/free, joint ticket with Sainte-Chapelle €12.50; 9.30am-6pm; M Cité)

Pont Neuf

BRIDGE

3 Map p120, A2

Paris' oldest bridge has linked the western end of Île de la Cité with both river banks since 1607, when the king inaugurated it by crossing the bridge on a white stallion. The occasion is commemorated by an equestrian **statue of Henry IV**, known to his subjects as the Vert Galant ('jolly rogue' or 'dirty old man', perspective depending).

Pont Neuf

View the bridge's seven arches, decorated with humorous and grotesque figures of barbers, dentists, pickpockets, loiterers etc, from a spot along the river or afloat.
(M Pont Neuf)

Mémorial des Martyrs de la Déportation MONUMENT

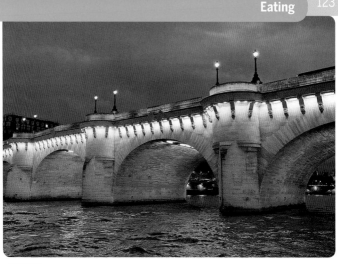
4 Map p120, E4

The Memorial to the Victims of the Deportation, erected in 1962, remembers the 160,000 residents of France (including 76,000 Jews, of whom 11,000 were children) deported to and murdered in Nazi concentration camps during WWII. A single barred 'window' separates the bleak, rough-concrete courtyard from the waters of the Seine. Inside lies the **Tomb of the Unknown Deportee**.
(square de l'Île de France, 4e; 10am-noon & 2-7pm Apr-Sep, to 5pm Oct-Mar; M St-Michel–Notre Dame)

Eating

Berthillon ICE CREAM €

5 Map p120, G4

Berthillon is to ice cream what Château Lafite Rothschild is to wine and Valrhona is to chocolate. Among its 70-odd flavours, the fruit-flavoured sorbets are renowned, as are its rich chocolate, coffee, *marrons glacés* (candied chestnuts) and Agenaise (Armagnac and prunes).

Understand

The French Revolution

By the late 1780s, the extravagance of Louis XVI and his queen, Marie-Antoinette, had alienated virtually every segment of society and the king became increasingly isolated as unrest and dissatisfaction reached boiling point. When he tried to neutralise the power of the more reform-minded delegates at a meeting of the États-Généraux (States-General), the masses took to the streets. On 14 July 1789, a mob raided the Hôtel des Invalides for rifles, seizing 32,000 muskets, and then stormed the prison at Bastille. The French Revolution had begun.

At first the Revolution was in the hands of moderate republicans called the Girondins. France was declared a constitutional monarchy and reforms were introduced, including the adoption of the Déclaration des Droits de l'Homme and du Citoyen (Declaration of the Rights of Man and of the Citizen). But as the masses armed themselves against the external threat to the new government by Austria, Prussia and the exiled French nobles, patriotism and nationalism combined with extreme fervour to both popularise and radicalise the Revolution. It was not long before the Girondins lost out to the extremist Jacobins, who abolished the monarchy and declared the First Republic in 1792. The Assemblée Nationale (National Assembly) was replaced by an elected Revolutionary Convention.

Louis XVI, who had unsuccessfully tried to flee the country, was convicted of 'conspiring against the liberty of the nation' and guillotined at today's place de la Concorde in January 1793. Marie-Antoinette was later executed in October 1793.

The Jacobins set up the notorious Committee of Public Safety to deal with national defence and to apprehend and try 'traitors'. This body had dictatorial control over the city and the country during the Reign of Terror (from September 1793 to July 1794), which saw thousands beheaded, most religious freedoms revoked and churches closed to worship and desecrated.

After the Reign of Terror faded, moderate republicans set themselves up to rule the republic. A group of royalists bent on overthrowing them were led by Napoléon, whose victories would soon turn him into an independent political force.

Watch for seasonal flavours like roasted pineapple and basil, or ginger and caramel. Eat in or take away.
(31 rue St-Louis en l'Île, 4e; 2-/3-/4-ball cones or tubs €2.50/5.50/7; ⏲10am-8pm Wed-Sun; Ⓜ Pont Marie)

Les Voyelles — MODERN FRENCH €€

6 Map p120, A1

This new kid on the block is worth the short walk from Notre Dame. The Vowels – spot the letters casually scattered between books and beautiful objects on the shelves lining the intimate 'library' dining room – is thoroughly contemporary, with a menu ranging from finger food to full-blown dinner to match. Its pavement terrace is Paris gold.
(☎01 46 33 69 75; www.les-voyelles.com; 74 quai des Orfèvres, 4e; plats du jour €12, 2-/3-course menus €17/22.50; ⏲8am-midnight Tue-Sat; Ⓜ Pont Neuf)

Café Saint Régis — CAFE €

7 Map p120, F3

Hip and historical, with an effortless dose of retro vintage thrown in, Le Saint Régis – as those in the know call it – is a deliciously Parisian hangout any time of the day. From pastries for breakfast to a mid-morning pancake, brasserie lunch or early-evening oyster platter, Café St-Regis gets it just right.
(http://cafesaintregisparis.com; 6 rue Jean du Bellay, 4e; salads & mains €14.50-28; ⏲7am-2am; 📶; Ⓜ Pont Marie)

Huré — BOULANGERIE €

8 Map p120, E3

Feisty savoury tarts and quiches, jumbo salads bursting with fresh veggies, giant cookies and cakes every colour and flavour of the rainbow: assuming it's a light lunch al fresco you're after, you'll be hard pushed to find a better *boulangerie* in spitting distance of Notre Dame than this. Simply look for the mountains of giant meringues piled high on the counter and the queue stretching halfway down the street.
(www.hure-createur.fr; 1 rue d'Arcole, 4e; takeaway lunch menus €8.50-9.30, sandwiches €4-6; ⏲6.30am-8pm Mon-Sat; Ⓜ St-Michel Notre Dame or Châtelet)

Le Tastevin — TRADITIONAL FRENCH €€€

9 Map p120, G4

With its old-fashioned lace curtains, wood panelling and beamed ceiling, this posh old-style address in a 17th-century building smacks of charm. Its excellent cuisine is equally traditional: think *escargots* (snails), foie gras, sole, or *ris de veau* (calf sweetbreads) with morels and tagliatelli.
(☎01 43 54 17 31; www.letastevin-paris.com; 46 rue St-Louis en l'Île, 4e; mains €27-34.50, menus from €33; ⏲noon-2pm & 7-11.15pm Tue-Sun; Ⓜ Pont Marie)

Mon Vieil Ami — TRADITIONAL FRENCH €€€

10 Map p120, F4

Alsatian chef Antoine Westermann is the creative talent behind this sleek black neobistro where guests are

treated like old friends (hence the name) and vegetables get royal treatment. The good-value lunchtime *plat du jour* (dish of the day) is a perfect reflection of the season. Dinner is served from 6.30pm – handy for those seeking an early meal.
(01 40 46 01 35; www.mon-vieil-ami.com; 69 rue St-Louis en l'Île, 4e; plats du jour €15.50, menus €47.50; noon-2.30pm & 7-11pm; M Pont Marie)

Drinking

Taverne Henri IV

WINE BAR

11  Map p120, A1

One of the few places to drink on Île de la Cité, this bar dates to 1885 and lures legal types from the Palais de Justice (as well as celeb writers and actors, as the autographed snaps testify). A choice of *tartines* (open sandwiches), *charcuterie* (cold cooked meats) and cheese platters complement its extensive wine list.
(13 place du Pont Neuf, 1er; 11.30am-11pm Mon-Sat, closed Aug; M Pont Neuf)

Local Life

Buskers

Paris' eclectic gaggle of clowns, mime artists, living statues, acrobats, roller-bladers, buskers and other street entertainers cost substantially less than a theatre ticket (a few coins in the hat is appreciated). Some excellent musicians audition to perform aboard the metro and in the corridors. Outside, you can be sure of a good show at countless spots around the city. Two of the best are **Pont St-Louis** (M Pont Marie), the bridge between the Île de la Cité and Île St-Louis, and **Pont au Double**, the pedestrian bridge linking the Île de la Cité near Notre Dame with the Left Bank.

La Charlotte de l'Isle

TEAROOM

12  Map p120, G4

This tiny place is a particularly lovely *salon de thé* (tearoom) with a quaint fairy-tale theme, old-fashioned glass sweet jars on the shelf and a fine collection of tea to taste *in situ* or buy to sip at home. Hot chocolate, chocolate sculptures, cakes and pastries are other sweet reasons to come here.
(www.lacharlottedelisle.fr; 24 rue St-Louis en l'Île, 4e; 11am-7pm Wed-Sun; M Pont Marie)

Le Flore en l'Île

CAFE

13  Map p120, F4

Tourists pile into this elegant old-world people-watching spot with prime views of the buskers on Pont St-Louis.
(42 quai d'Orléans, 4e; 8am-1am; M Pont Marie)

Shopping

Clair de Rêve

TOYS

14  Map p120, G4

This shop is all about wind-up toys, music boxes and puppets – mostly

marionettes, which sway and bob suspended from the ceiling.
(www.clairdereve.com; 35 rue St-Louis en l'Île, 4e; 11am-1pm & 2-7pm Mon-Sat; M Pont Marie)

Marché aux Fleurs Reine Elizabeth II

MARKET

15 Map p120, D2

Blooms have been sold at this flower market since 1808, making it the oldest market of any kind in Paris. On Sunday, between 9am and 7pm, it transforms into a twittering bird market, **Marché aux Oiseaux** (9am-7pm).
(place Louis Lépin, 4e; 8am-7.30pm Mon-Sat; M Cité)

Il Campiello

CRAFTS

16 Map p120, F4

Venetian carnival masks – intricately crafted from papier mâché, ceramics and leather – are the speciality of this exquisite shop, which also sells jewellery made from Murano glass beads. It was established by a native of Venice, to which the Île St-Louis bears more than a passing resemblance.
(www.ilcampiello.com; 88 rue St-Louis en l'Île, 4e; 11am-7pm; M Pont Marie)

Première Pression Provence

FOOD

17 Map p120, G4

Its name evokes the first pressing of olives to make olive oil in the south of France and that is precisely what this gourmet boutique sells – be it as oil or in any number of spreads and sauces (pesto, tapenade etc).
(51 rue St-Louis en l'Île, 4e; 11am-1pm & 2-7pm Mon-Sat; M Pont Marie)

Local Life

Bouquinistes

Lining both banks of the Seine through the centre of Paris (not on the islands themselves), the open-air *bouquiniste* stalls selling secondhand, often out-of-print, books, rare magazines, postcards and old advertising posters are a definitive Parisian sight. Trading here since the 16th century, the name comes from *bouquiner*, meaning 'to read with appreciation'. At night, *bouquinistes'* dark-green metal stalls are folded down and locked like suitcases. Many open only from spring to autumn (and many shut in August), but even in the depths of winter, you'll still find somewhere to unearth antiquarian treasures.

Librairie Ulysse

BOOKS

18 Map p120, G4

You can barely move in between this shop's antiquarian and new travel guides, *National Geographic* back editions and maps. Opened in 1971 by the intrepid Catherine Domaine, this was the world's first travel bookshop. Hours vary, but ring the bell and Catherine will open up if she's around.
(www.ulysse.fr; 26 rue St-Louis en l'Île, 4e; 2-8pm Tue-Fri; M Pont Marie)

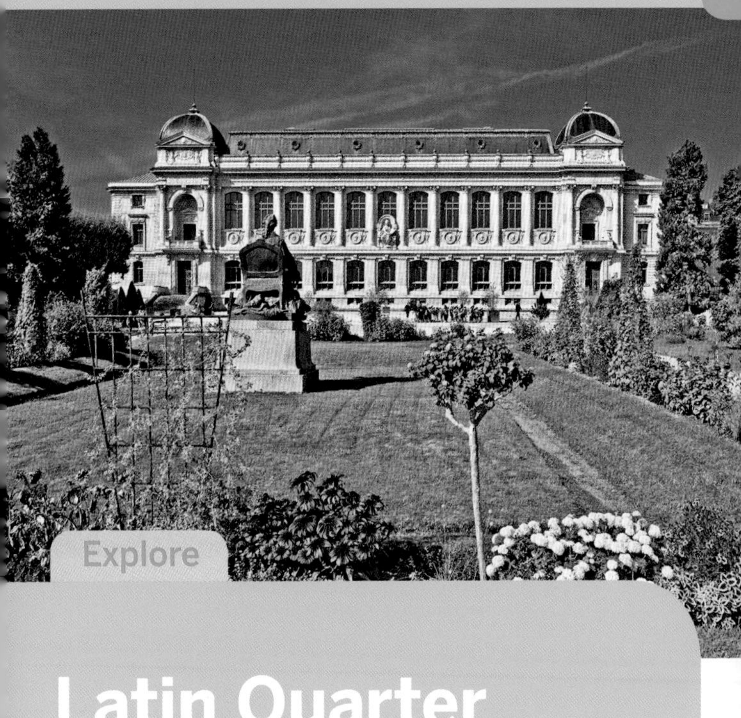

Explore

Latin Quarter

So named because international students communicated in Latin here until the French Revolution, the Latin Quarter remains the hub of academic life in Paris. Centred on the Sorbonne's main university campus, graced by fountains and lime trees, this lively area is also home to some outstanding museums and churches, along with Paris' beautiful art deco mosque and botanic gardens.

The Sights in a Day

The Batobus stops at Paris' botanic gardens, the **Jardin des Plantes** (p136), so consider cruising here first and exploring its **natural history museums** (p136) and **menagerie** (zoo). Then make your way to the **Mosquée de Paris** (p137) for a *hammam* (Turkish steambath). Enjoy sweet mint tea in its courtyard and delicious *tajines* for lunch.

Check out amazing Arab art and ingenious architecture at the **Institut du Monde Arabe** (p136) and pay your respects to some of France's most illustrious thinkers and innovators at the **Panthéon** (p136) mausoleum. For the ultimate medieval history lesson, visit the **Musée National du Moyen Âge** (p130).

After fusion cuisine at **Sola** (p139), browse late-night bookshops like the charming, cluttered **Shakespeare & Company** (p142), then catch jazz at **Caveau de la Huchette** (p142) or head to lively bars like **Le Pantalon** (p142).

For a local's day along Rue Mouffetard, see p132.

Top Sights

Musée National du Moyen Âge (p130)

Local Life

A Stroll along Rue Mouffetard (p132)

Best of Paris

Architecture

Institut du Monde Arabe (p136)

History

Musée National du Moyen Âge (p130)

Arènes de Lutèce (p138)

Sorbonne (p138)

Panthéon (p136)

Parks & Gardens

Jardin des Plantes (p136)

Getting There

Ⓜ **Metro** St-Michel (line 4) and the connected St-Michel–Notre Dame (RER B and C) is the neighbourhood's gateway.

Ⓜ **Metro** Other handy metro stations include Cluny–La Sorbonne (line 10) and Place Monge (line 7).

Boat The hop-on, hop-off Batobus stops in the Latin Quarter opposite Notre Dame and outside the Jardin des Plantes.

Top Sights
Musée National du Moyen Âge

Medieval history comes to life at France's Musée National du Moyen Âge. This national museum of the Middle Ages is often referred to as the Musée de Cluny (or just Cluny), due to the fact that it's partly – and atmospherically – housed in an ornate 15th-century mansion, the Hôtel de Cluny, Paris' finest civil medieval building. Sublime treasures here span medieval statuary, stained glass and *objets d'art* to the celebrated series of tapestries, *The Lady and the Unicorn* (1500).

Map p134, A2

www.musee-moyenage.fr

6 place Paul Painlevé, 5e

adult/child €8/free

9.15am-5.45pm Wed-Mon

Cluny–La Sorbonne

Gold artefact

Don't Miss

Roman Remains

The museum's northwestern corner is where you'll find the remains of the Gallo-Roman bathhouse, built around AD 200. Look for the display of the fragment of mosaic, *Love Riding a Dolphin,* as well as a gorgeous marble bathtub from Rome. Outside the museum, remnants of the other rooms – a *palestra* (exercise room), *tepidarium* (warm bath) and *calidarium* (hot bath) – are visible.

Hôtel de Cluny

Initially the residential quarters of the Cluny Abbots, the Hôtel de Cluny today holds some fascinating relics, not least of which is an entire room (No 8) dedicated to statuary from Notre Dame's façade, removed during the Revolution and later used to support the foundations of a private mansion.

The Lady & the Unicorn Tapestries

Upstairs on the 1st floor (room 13) are the unicorn tapestries, representing the five senses and an enigmatic sixth, perhaps the heart. It's believed that they were originally commissioned around 1500 by the Le Viste family in Paris. Discovered in 1814 in the Chateau de Boussac, they were acquired by the museum in 1882 and have since provided inspiration to many, from Prosper Mérimée and George Sand to, most recently, Tracy Chevalier.

The Gardens

Small gardens to the museum's northeast, including the Jardin Céleste (Celestial Garden) and the Jardin d'Amour (Garden of Love), are planted with flowers, herbs and shrubs that appear in works hanging throughout the museum.

☑ Top Tips

- Although it's a national museum, the Musée National du Moyen Âge doesn't attract the same volume of tourists as other major sights, so any time is generally good to visit. Tickets can't be purchased online, but the Paris Museum Pass and Paris City Passport are valid here.
- Audioguides are included in the admission price except on the first Sunday of the month year-round, when museum admission is free but audioguides cost €1.
- Medieval history buffs can visit the museum's document centre by appointment. There's also an excellent onsite bookshop.

Take a Break

For heritage-listed surrounds and outstanding French fare at reasonable prices, nearby brasserie Bouillon Racine (p159) is a treat.

Local Life
A Stroll along Rue Mouffetard

Originally a Roman road, rue Mouffetard acquired its name in the 18th century, when the now-underground River Bievre became the communal waste disposal for local tanners and wood-pulpers. The odours gave rise to the name Mouffettes ('skunks'), which evolved into Mouffetard. Today the aromas on 'La Mouffe', as it's nicknamed, are infinitely more enticing, particularly at its market stalls.

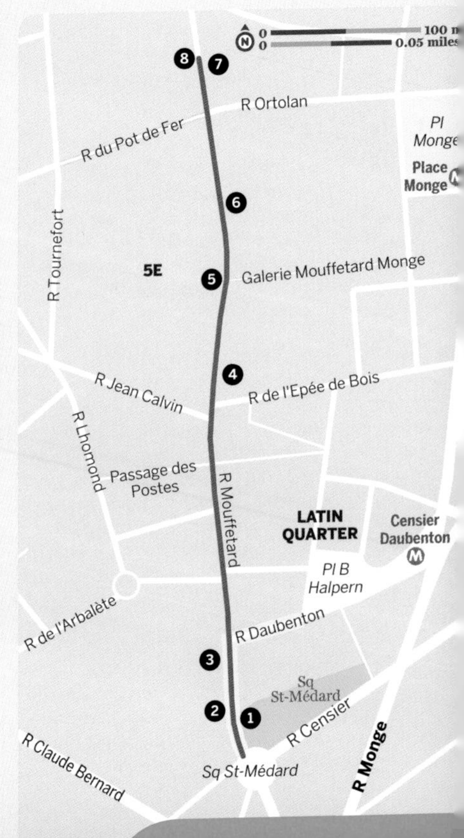

1 Market Shopping

Grocers, butchers, fishmongers and other food purveyors set their goods out on street stalls along this sloping, cobbled street during the **Marché Mouffetard** (8am-7.30pm Tue-Sat, to noon Sun; M Censier Daubenton)

❷ Fine Cheeses

You won't even have to worry about aromas if you're taking home something scrumptious from the *fromagerie* (cheese shop) **Androuet** (http://androuet.com; 134 rue Mouffetard, 5e; ⌚9.30am-1pm & 4-7.30pm Tue-Fri, 9.30am-7.30pm Sat, to 1.30pm Sun; Ⓜ Censier Daubenton); all of its cheeses can be vacuum-packed for free. (Be sure to look up to see the beautiful murals on the building's facade!)

❸ Delicious Deli

Stuffed olives and capsicums, and marinated eggplant are among the picnic goodies at gourmet Italian deli **Delizius** (134 rue Mouffetard, 5e; ⌚9.30am-8pm Tue-Sat, 9am-2pm Sun; Ⓜ Censier Daubenton), which also sells ready-to-eat hot meals, and fresh and dried pasta.

❹ Movie Time

Even locals find it easy to miss the small doorway leading to cinema **L'Epée de Bois** (100 rue Mouffetard, 5e; Ⓜ Censier Daubenton), which screens both art-house flicks and big-budget blockbusters.

❺ Sweet Treats

Light, luscious *macarons* in flavours such as jasmine, raspberry and black-currant, and a mouth-watering range of chocolates are laid out like jewels at **Chocolats Mococha** (www.chocolatsmococha.com; 89 rue Mouffetard, 5e; ⌚11am-8pm; Ⓜ Censier Daubenton). They are the creations of three *maîtres chocolatiers* (master chocolate-makers) – Fabrice Gillotte, Jacques Bellanger and Patrice Chapoare.

❻ Apéro at Le Vieux Chêne

Hosting revolutionary meetings in 1848 and believed to be Paris' oldest bar, **Le Vieux Chêne** (69 rue Mouffetard, 5e; ⌚4pm-2am Sun-Thu, to 5am Fri & Sat; Ⓜ Place Monge) is a student favourite these days, especially during happy hour (4pm to 9pm Tuesday to Sunday, and from 4pm until closing on Monday).

❼ Ice Cream

All that walking and peering in at gourmet food shops will no doubt leave you hungry, which means it's time for a stop at **Gelati d'Alberto** (45 rue Mouffetard, 5e; ⌚noon-midnight; Ⓜ Place Monge), where Italian ice-cream wizards shape your coned treat into a multiflavour flower.

❽ Crêpes at Chez Nicos

The signboard outside crêpe artist Nicos' unassuming little shop **Chez Nicos** (44 rue Mouffetard, 5e; crêpes €3-6; ⌚noon-2am; 👪; Ⓜ Place Monge), lists dozens of fillings. Ask by name for his masterpiece 'La Crêpe du Chef', stuffed with eggplant, feta, mozzarella, lettuce, tomatoes and onions. There's a handful of tables; otherwise, head to a nearby park.

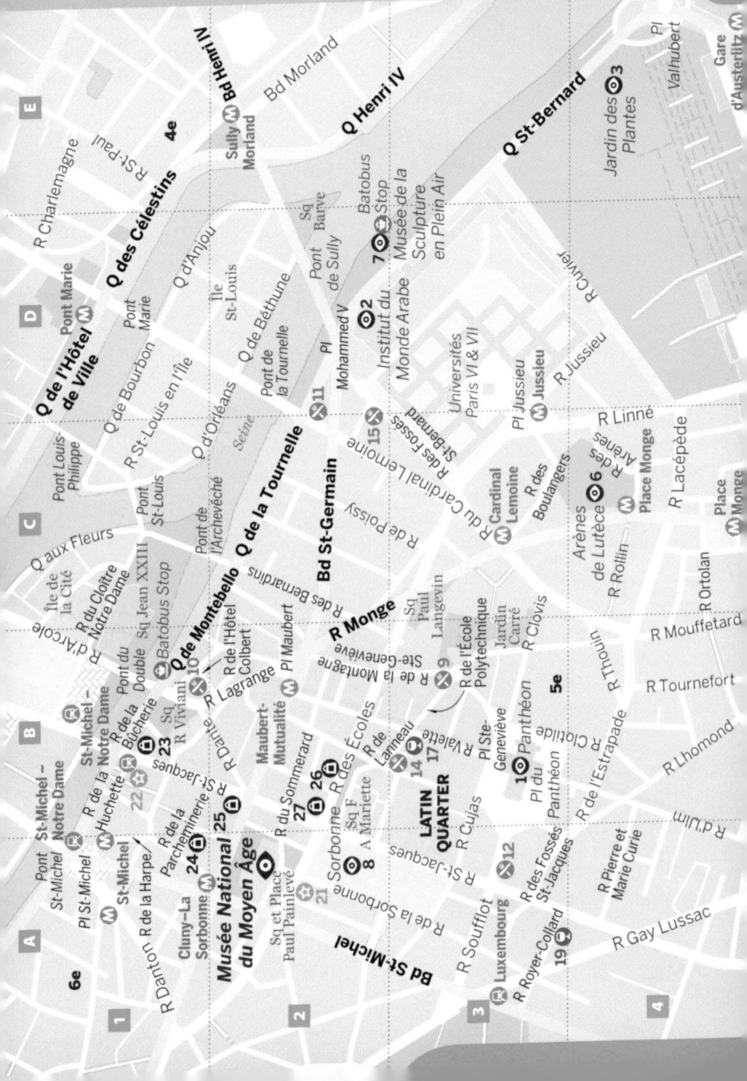

A B C D E
1 2 3 4

Musée National du Moyen Âge
Pont St-Michel
Pl St-Michel
St-Michel – Notre Dame
St-Michel
R de la Harpe
R Danton
6e
Cluny–La Sorbonne
R de la Parcheminerie
24
25
R St-Jacques
R de la Huchette
22
R de la Bûcherie
23
Sq R Viviani
R Dante
Pont du Double
Batobus Stop
Sq Jean XXIII
R d'Arcole
R du Cloître Notre Dame
Île de la Cité
Q aux Fleurs
Q de Montebello
10
R de l'Hôtel Colbert
R Lagrange
Pl Maubert
Maubert-Mutualité
R du Sommerard
27
26
R des Écoles
Sq F A Mariette
Sorbonne
8
21
Sq et Place Paul Painlevé
R de la Sorbonne
Bd St-Michel
R de Lanneau
14
17
R Valette
LATIN QUARTER
R Cujas
R St-Jacques
12
R Soufflot
Luxembourg
R Royer-Collard
19
R des Fossés St-Jacques
Pl du Panthéon
1
Panthéon
Pl Ste-Geneviève
R Clotilde
R de l'Estrapade
R d'Ulm
R Pierre et Marie Curie
R Gay Lussac
R Lhomond
R Tournefort
R Thouin
5e
R de l'École Polytechnique
9
R de la Montagne Ste-Geneviève
R Monge
Sq Paul Langevin
Jardin Carré
R Clovis
R Mouffetard
R Ortolan
R des Bernardins
Bd St-Germain
Q de la Tournelle
Pont de l'Archevêché
Pont St-Louis
Pont Louis-Philippe
R St-Louis en l'Île
Q de Bourbon
Q d'Orléans
Seine
Q de l'Hôtel de Ville
Pont Marie
Q des Célestins
R Charlemagne
R St-Paul
4e
Sully Morland
Bd Henri IV
Bd Morland
Q d'Anjou
Île St-Louis
Q de Béthune
Pont de la Tournelle
11
Pl Mohammed V
2
Institut du Monde Arabe
Pont de Sully
Sq Barye
7
Batobus Stop
Musée de la Sculpture en Plein Air
Q Henri IV
Q St-Bernard
3
Jardin des Plantes
Pl Valhubert
Gare d'Austerlitz
R Cuvier
R Jussieu
Jussieu
Pl Jussieu
Universités Paris VI & VII
15
R des Fossés St-Bernard
R du Cardinal Lemoine
R de Poissy
Cardinal Lemoine
R des Boulangers
R Linné
R des Arènes
6
Arènes de Lutèce
R Rollin
Place Monge
R Lacépède

Pl du Puits de l'Ermite
Mosquée de Paris
Muséum National d'Histoire Naturelle
R Buffon
R Monge
R Larrey
R Daubenton
R Mirbel
Pl B Halpern
Censier Daubenton
R Censier
R Mouffetard
R Erasme Brossolette
R des Feuillantines
R Rataud
R Vauquelin
R Claude Bernard
R St-Jacques
Val de Grâce
R de l'Arbalète
Sq St-Médard
Sq Marie Curie
R Poliveau
R Geoffroy St-Hilaire
R du Fer à Moulin
LATIN QUARTER
R Scipion
Bd St-Marcel
St-Marcel
R des Wallons
Bd de l'Hôpital
Hôpital de la Pitié–Salpêtrière
R Broca
R Pascal
Bd de Port Royal
Cochin
14e
R de la Santé
R de la Glacière
R St-Hippolyte
R Broca
Bd Arago
R Duméril
R Pirandello
R Lebrun
Les Gobelins
R du Banquier
Campo Formio
R Jeanne d'Arc
R Jenner
R Esquirol
R Berbier du Mets
R Léon Maurice Nordmann
R Corvisart
R Pascal
R de Cordelière
Av des Gobelins
R Rubens
13e
R Pinel
Sq René Le Gall
R Coypel
R de Croulebarbe
R Abel Hovelacque
R Vulpian
Bd Auguste Blanqui
Glacière
0 400 m
0 0.2 miles
Pl d'Italie
Place d'Italie
Bd Vincent Auriol
For reviews see
Top Sights p130
Sights p136
Eating p139
Drinking p141
Entertainment p142
Shopping p142

Sights

Panthéon
MAUSOLEUM

1 Map p134, B3

Overlooking the city from the Left Bank, the Panthéon's stately neoclassical dome stands out as one of the most recognisable icons in the Parisian skyline. Originally a church and now a mausoleum, it has served, since 1791, as the resting place of some of France's greatest thinkers, including Voltaire, Rousseau, Braille and Hugo. An architectural masterpiece, the interior is vast and certainly worth a wander. The dome is closed for renovations through to 2015 (other structural work will continue until 2022).

(www.monum.fr; place du Panthéon, 5e; adult/child €7.50/free; 10am-6.30pm Apr-Sep, to 6pm Oct-Mar; M Maubert-Mutualité, Cardinal Lemoine or RER Luxembourg)

Institut du Monde Arabe
MUSEUM

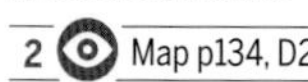

The Arab World Institute was jointly founded by France and 18 Middle Eastern and North African nations in 1980, with the aim of promoting cross-cultural dialogue. In addition to hosting concerts, film screenings and a research centre, the stunning landmark is also home to a new museum and temporary exhibition space.

(Arab World Institute; www.imarabe.org; 1 place Mohammed V, 5e; adult/child €8/4; 10am-6pm Tue-Thu, to 9.30pm Fri, to 7pm Sat & Sun; M Jussieu)

Jardin des Plantes
GARDENS

3  Map p134, E4

Founded in 1626 as a medicinal herb garden for Louis XIII, Paris' 24-hectare botanic gardens, visually defined by the double alley of plane trees that run the length of the park, are an idyllic spot to stroll around, break for a picnic – watch out for the automatic sprinklers! – and escape the city concrete for a spell. Upping its appeal are three museums from the Muséum National d'Histoire Naturelle (p136) and a small **zoo** (www.mnhn.fr; 57 rue Cuvier, 5e; adult/child €11/9; 9am-6.30pm Apr-Oct, shorter hours rest of year; M Gare d'Austerlitz, Censier Daubenton or Jussieu).

(www.jardindesplantes.net; place Valhubert & 36 rue Geoffroy-Saint-Hilaire, 5e; admission free; 7.30am-7.45pm Apr-Oct, 8am-5.15pm Nov-Mar; M Gare d'Austerlitz, Censier Daubenton or Jussieu)

Muséum National d'Histoire Naturelle
MUSEUM

4  Map p134, D5

Despite the name, the Natural History Museum is not a single building, but a collection of sites throughout France. Its historic home is in the Jardin des Plantes, and it's here you'll find the greatest number of branches: taxidermied animals in the excellent **Grande Galerie de l'Évolution** (adult/child €7/free; 10am-6pm Wed-Mon), fossils and dinosaur skeletons in the **Galeries d'Anatomie Comparée et de Paléontologie** (adult/child €7/free; 10am-5pm

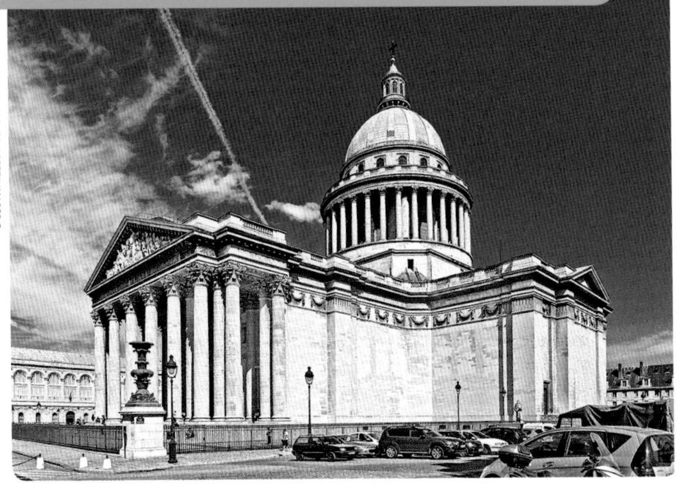

Panthéon

Wed-Mon) and meteorites and crystals in the **Galerie de Minéralogie et de Géologie**.

(www.mnhn.fr; place Valhubert & 36 rue Geoffroy St-Hilaire, 5e; Ⓜ Gare d'Austerlitz, Censier Daubenton or Jussieu)

Mosquée de Paris MOSQUE

5 Map p134, C5

Paris' central mosque, with striking 26m-high minaret, was completed in 1926 in an ornate art deco Moorish style. You can visit the interior to admire the intricate tile work and calligraphy. A separate entrance leads to the wonderful North African-style **hammam** (01 43 31 38 20; www.la-mosquee.com; 39 rue Geoffroy St-Hilaire, 5e; admission/spa package €18/from €43; 10am-9pm Wed-Mon; Ⓜ Censier Daubenton or Place Monge), **restaurant** (01 43 31 38 20; www.la-mosquee.com; 39 rue Geoffroy St-Hilaire, 5e; mains €15-26; noon-2.30pm & 7.30-10.30pm; Ⓜ Censier Daubenton or Place Monge) and *salon de thé* (tearoom), and a small *souk* (actually more of a gift shop). Visitors must be modestly dressed.

(01 45 35 97 33; www.la-mosquee.com; 2bis place du Puits de l'Ermite, 5e; adult/child €3/2; mosque 9am-noon & 2-6pm Sat-Thu; Ⓜ Censier Daubenton or Place Monge)

Understand

A Pivotal Year: 1968

The year 1968 was a watershed. In March a large demonstration in Paris against the Vietnam War gave impetus to protests by students of the University of Paris. In May police broke up yet another demonstration, prompting angry students to occupy the Sorbonne and erect barricades in the Latin Quarter. Workers quickly joined in, with six million people across France participating in a general strike that virtually paralysed the country.

But while workers wanted to reap greater benefits from the consumer market, the students supposedly wanted to destroy it. De Gaulle took advantage of this division and appealed to people's fear of anarchy. A 100,000-strong crowd of Gaullists marched in support for the government, quashing any idea of revolution.

Once stability was restored the re-elected government immediately decentralised the higher education system, and implemented a series of reforms (including lowering the voting age to 18 and enacting an abortion law) throughout the 1970s to create the modern society France is today.

Arènes de Lutèce RUINS

6 Map p134, C4

The 2nd-century Roman amphitheatre Lutetia Arena once sat 10,000 people for gladiatorial combats and other events. Found by accident in 1869 when rue Monge was under construction, it's now used by locals playing football and, especially, boules.

(www.arenesdelutece.com; 49 rue Monge, 5e; admission free; 9am-9.30pm Apr-Oct, 8am-5.30pm Nov-Mar; M Place Monge)

Musée de la Sculpture en Plein Air MUSEUM

7 Map p134, D2

Along quai St-Bernard, this open-air museum (also known as the Jardin Tino Rossi) has more than 50 late-20th-century sculptures, and makes a great picnic spot. A salad beneath a César or a baguette beside a Brancusi is a pretty classy way to see the Seine up close.

(quai St-Bernard, 5e; admission free; M Gare d'Austerlitz)

Sorbonne UNIVERSITY

8 Map p134, A2

The crème de la crème of academia flock to this distinguished university, one of the world's most famous. Today, 'La Sorbonne' embraces most of the 13 autonomous universities – 35,500-odd students in all – created when the University of Paris was reorganised after the student protests of 1968. Until 2015, when an ambitious, 10-year modernisation program costing €45 million reaches completion, parts of

the complex will be under renovation. Visitors are not permitted to enter.
(12 rue de la Sorbonne, 5e; M Cluny–La Sorbonne or RER Luxembourg)

Eating

Les Pipos WINE BAR €€

9 Map p134, B3

A feast for the eyes and the senses, this *bar à vins* is above all worth a visit for its food. The bistro standards *(boeuf bourguignon)* and *charcuteries de terroir* (regional cold meats and sausages) are mouth-watering, as is the cheese board, which includes all the gourmet names (bleu d'Auvergne, St-Félicien, St-Marcellin). No credit cards.
(☎01 43 54 11 40; www.les-pipos.com; 2 rue de l'École Polytechnique, 5e; mains €13.90-26.90; ⏲8am-2am Mon-Sat; M Maubert-Mutualité)

Sola FUSION €€€

10 Map p134, B1

For serious gourmands, Sola is arguably the Latin Quarter's proverbial brass ring. Pedigreed chef Hiroki Yoshitake combines French technique with Japanese sensibility, resulting in gorgeous signature creations (such as miso-marinated foie gras on *feuille de brick* served on a sli ce of tree trunk). The artful presentations and attentive service make this a great choice for a romantic meal – go for the full experience and reserve a table in the Japanese dining room downstairs.
(☎dinner 01 43 29 59 04, lunch 09 65 01 73 68; www.restaurant-sola.com; 12 rue de l'Hôtel Colbert, 5e; lunch/dinner €48/98; ⏲noon-2pm & 7-10pm Tue-Sat; M St-Michel)

La Tour d'Argent GASTRONOMIC €€€

11 Map p134, D2

The venerable 'Silver Tower' is famous for its *caneton* (duckling), rooftop garden with glimmering Notre Dame views and a fabulous history that hark back to 1582 – from Henry III's inauguration of the first fork in France to inspiration for the winsome animated film *Ratatouille*. Its wine cellar is one of Paris' best; dining is dressy and exceedingly fine.
(☎01 43 54 23 31; www.latourdargent.com; 15 quai de la Tournelle, 5e; lunch menus €65, dinner menus €170-190; ⏲noon-2.30pm & 7.30-10.30pm Tue-Sat; M Cardinal Lemoine or Pont Marie)

Le Comptoir du Panthéon CAFE, BRASSERIE €

12 Map p134, A3

Enormous, creative meal-size salads are the reason to pick this as a dining spot. Magnificently placed across from the domed Panthéon on the shady side of the street, its pavement terrace is big, busy and oh so Parisian – turn your head away from Voltaire's burial place and the Eiffel Tower pops into view.
(☎01 43 54 75 56; 5 rue Soufflot, 5e; salads €11-13, mains €12.40-15.40; ⏲7am-1.45am; 📶; M Cardinal Lemoine or RER Luxembourg)

L'Ourcine

NEOBISTRO €€

13 Map p134, B7

With wine corks in the window, this intimate place may be casual (no dress code) and affordable but it takes its food seriously. The superb menu ranges from starters like fish velouté or pig's head with mesclun to mains such as wild sea bream with semolina or free-range chicken with foie gras, and desserts like poached rhubarb with almond sorbet.

(01 47 07 13 65; www.restaurant-lourcine.fr; 92 rue Broca, 13e; menus €35; noon-2.30pm & 7-11pm Tue-Sat; M Les Gobelins)

Le Coupe-Chou

FRENCH €€

14 Map p134, B3

This maze of candlelit rooms inside a vine-clad 17th-century townhouse is overwhelmingly romantic. Ceilings are beamed, furnishings are antique, and background classical music mingles with the intimate chatter of diners. As in the days when Marlene Dietrich dined here, advance reservations are essential.

(01 46 33 68 69; www.lecoupechou.com; 9 & 11 rue de Lanneau, 5e; 2-/3-course menus €27/33; noon-2.30pm & 7.30-10.30pm; M Maubert-Mutualité)

Understand

Local Lingo

Parisians have long had a reputation for being unable or unwilling to speak English, but this has changed dramatically, particularly in the digital age. Signposts, menus, establishment names and buzzwords increasingly incorporate English.

Addressing people in French makes a *huge* difference, even simply '*Bonjour/bonsoir, parlez-vous anglais*?' (Good day/evening, do you speak English?). Often what is mistaken for Parisian arrogance is the equivalent of someone addressing you in a foreign language in your home country. On detecting an accent, many Parisians will switch to English to facilitate conversation (feel free to say if you prefer to converse in French).

Another potential cause for misunderstanding is the cut-to-the-chase directness of French communication. Whereas in English it's common to say, for example, 'Can I have a coffee, please?', the French '*Un café, s'il vous plaît.*' (A coffee, please.) can sound abrupt to an anglophone ear. Likewise, the French tendency to frame a question 'You would like a coffee?' rather than 'Would you like a coffee?' may seem forward, though it's unintentional.

L'AOC

TRADITIONAL FRENCH €€

15 Map p134, C2

'Bistrot carnivore' is the strapline of this ingenious restaurant concocted around France's most respected culinary products. The concept is Appellation d'Origine Contrôlée (AOC), meaning everything has been reared or produced according to strict guidelines. The result? Only the best! Choose between meaty favourites (steak tartare) or the rotisserie menu, ranging from roast chicken to suckling pig.

(☎01 43 54 22 52; www.restoaoc.com; 14 rue des Fossés St-Bernard, 5e; 2-/3-course lunch menus €21/29, mains €19-36; ⏰noon-2.30pm & 7.30-10.30pm Tue-Sat; M Cardinal Lemoine)

Restaurant Variations

BISTRO €€

16 Map p134, D6

In a pin-drop-quiet back street you'd never stumble on by chance, this light-filled restaurant is a diamond find. It's framed by huge glass windows and artfully decorated with large-scale photographs; square white plates showcase the colours and textures of brothers Philippe and Pierre Tondetta's Italian-accented offerings such as rack of lamb accompanied by polenta with olives and aged parmesan.

(☎01 43 31 36 04; www.restaurantvariations.com; 18 rue des Wallons, 13e; lunch menus €16.50-19, dinner menus €24-44; ⏰noon-2pm Mon-Fri, 7-10pm Mon-Sat; M St-Marcel)

Café de la Nouvelle Mairie

Hidden away in a small, fountained square just around the corner from the Panthéon, the narrow wine bar **Café de la Nouvelle** (Map p134, A3; 19 rue des Fossés St-Jacques, 5e; mains €14-16; ⏰8am-midnight Mon-Fri; M Cardinal–Lemoine) is a neighbourhood secret, serving blackboard-chalked natural wines by the glass and delicious seasonal bistro fare.

Drinking

Le Pub St-Hilaire

PUB

17 Map p134, B3

'Buzzing' fails to do justice to the pulsating vibe inside this student-loved pub. Generous happy hours last several hours and the place is kept packed with a trio of pool tables, board games, music on two floors, hearty bar food and various gimmicks to rev up the party crowd (a metre of cocktails, 'be your own barman' etc).

(2 rue Valette, 5e; ⏰3pm-2am Mon-Thu, 3pm-4am Fri, 4pm-4am Sat, 4pm-midnight Sun; M Maubert-Mutualité)

La Fût Gueuze

BAR

18 Map p134, D7

You won't find big-name, mass-market beers at this corner neighbourhood bar but you will find 74 bottled brews, mainly French, Belgian and German, and another 12 on tap, as well as a

good-time atmosphere. Happy 'hour' runs from 4pm to 9pm.
(24 rue Dumeril, 13e; 4pm-2am; M Campo-Formio)

Le Pantalon BAR

19  Map p134, A3

Ripped vinyl seats, coloured-glass light fittings and old stickers plastered on the walls make this rockin' little bar a favourite hang-out for those with little change but lots of heart.
(7 rue Royer-Collard, 5e; 5.30pm-2am; M Cluny–La Sorbonne or RER Luxembourg)

Entertainment

Café Universel JAZZ, BLUES

20 Map p134, A5

Café Universel hosts a brilliant array of live concerts with everything from bebop and Latin sounds to vocal jazz sessions. Plenty of freedom is given to young producers and artists, and its convivial relaxed atmosphere attracts a mix of students and jazz lovers. Concerts are free, but tip the artists when they pass the hat around.
(01 43 25 74 20; http://cafeuniversel.com; 267 rue St-Jacques, 5e; admission free; 9pm-2am Mon-Sat; ; M Censier Daubenton or RER Port Royal)

Le Champo CINEMA

21 Map p134, A2

This is one of the most popular of the many Latin Quarter cinemas, featuring classics and retrospectives looking at the films of such actors and directors as Alfred Hitchcock, Jacques Tati, Alain Resnais, Frank Capra, Tim Burton and Woody Allen. One of the two *salles* (cinemas) has wheelchair access.
(www.lechampo.com; 51 rue des Écoles, 5e; M St-Michel or Cluny–La Sorbonne)

Caveau de la Huchette JAZZ, BLUES

22  Map p134, B1

Housed in a medieval *caveau* (cellar) used as a courtroom and torture chamber during the Revolution, this club is where virtually all the jazz greats have played since the end of WWII. It attracts its fair share of tourists, but the atmosphere can be more electric than at the more serious jazz clubs. Sessions start at 10pm.
(01 43 26 65 05; www.caveaudelahuchette.fr; 5 rue de la Huchette, 5e; Sun-Thu €13, Fri & Sat €15, under 25yr €10; 9.30pm-2.30am Sun-Wed, to 4am Thu-Sat; M St-Michel)

Shopping

Shakespeare & Company BOOKS

23  Map p134, B1

This bookshop is the stuff of legends. A kind of spell descends as you enter, weaving between nooks and crannies overflowing with new and secondhand English-language books. The original shop (12 rue l'Odéon, 6e; closed by the Nazis in 1941) was run by Sylvia Beach and became the meeting point for Hemingway's 'Lost Generation'. Readings by emerging and illustri-

ous authors take place at 7pm most Mondays; it also hosts workshops and festivals.
(www.shakespeareandcompany.com; 37 rue de la Bûcherie, 5e; 10am-11pm Mon-Fri, from 11am Sat & Sun; M St-Michel)

Abbey Bookshop

BOOKS

24 Map p134, A1

In a heritage-listed townhouse, this welcoming Canadian-run bookshop serves free coffee (sweetened with maple syrup) to sip while you browse tens of thousands of new and used books, and organises literary events and countryside hikes.
(01 46 33 16 24; 29 rue de la Parcheminerie, 5e; 10am-7pm Mon-Sat; M St-Michel or Cluny–La Sorbonne)

Album

COMICS

25 Map p134, B2

Album specialises in *bandes dessinées* (comics and graphic novels), which have an enormous following in France, with everything from Tintin and Babar to erotic comics and the latest Japanese manga. Serious comic collectors – and anyone excited by Harry Potter wands, Star Wars, Superman and other superhero figurines and T-shirts (you know who you are!) – shouldn't miss it.
(www.album.fr; 67 bd St-Germain, 5e; 10am-8pm Mon-Sat, noon-7pm Sun; M Cluny–La Sorbonne)

Crocodisc

MUSIC

26 Map p134, B2

Music might be more accessible than ever before thanks to iPods, iPads and phones, but for many it will never replace rummaging through racks for treasures. New and secondhand CDs and vinyl discs at 40 rue des Écoles span world music, rap, reggae, salsa, soul and disco, while No 42 has pop, rock, punk, new wave, Electro and soundtracks.
(www.crocodisc.com; 40 & 42 rue des Écoles, 5e; 11am-7pm Tue-Sat; M Maubert-Mutualité)

Au Vieux Campeur

OUTDOOR EQUIPMENT

27 Map p134, B2

This outdoor store seems to have colonised the Latin Quarter, with some 25 different outlets scattered about, each devoted to your favourite sport: climbing, skiing, diving, camping, biking and so on. While it's a great resource if you need any gear, the many boutiques make shopping something of a treasure hunt – especially as many outlets change what they sell with the seasons.
(www.auvieuxcampeur.fr; 48 rue des Écoles, 5e; 11am-7.30pm Mon-Wed, Fri & Sat, to 9pm Thu; M Maubert-Mutualité or Cluny–La Sorbonne)

Local Life
Southeastern Discovery

Getting There

Southeastern Paris is about 3km southeast of Notre Dame.

Ⓜ **Metro** Gare de Lyon (lines 1 and 14) and Place d'Italie (lines 5, 6 and 7) are convenient start/end points.

Spanning both banks of the Seine, Paris' southeast is an eclectic mix of *quartiers* (quarters) that makes for a fascinating stroll if you've stood in one tourist queue too many. But while it's an authentic slice of local life, there are plenty of big-hitting attractions here too, including France's national cinema institute and national library.

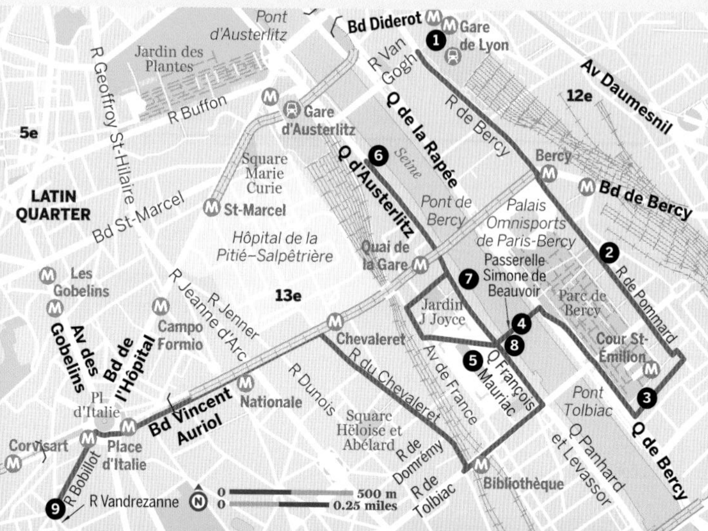

❶ Railway Station Splendour

Start your journey in style with a drink or classical fare like beef tartare prepared at your table at belle époque showpiece **Le Train Bleu** (☎01 43 43 09 06; www.le-train-bleu.com; 1st fl, Gare de Lyon, 26 place Louis Armand, 12e; menu €60-102, mains €27-46; ⏲kitchen 11.30am-3pm & 7-11pm, bar 7.30am-11pm Mon-Sat, 9am-11pm Sun; 📶👪; Ⓜ Gare de Lyon).

❷ Cinematic History

Cinephiles shouldn't miss **Cinémathèque Française** (www.cinematheque.fr; 51 rue de Bercy, 12e; exhibits adult/child €6/3; ⏲noon-7pm Mon & Wed-Sat, to 8pm Sun; Ⓜ Bercy), showcasing the history of French cinema at its museum, as well as screening classics and edgy new films.

❸ Village Spirit

There are more cinemas at **Bercy Village** (www.bercyvillage.com; cour St-Émilion, 12e; ⏲shops 11am-9pm Mon-Sat, restaurants & bars 11am-2am daily; Ⓜ Cour St-Émilion), but its main draw is its strip of former wine warehouses, sheltering shops, eateries and bars.

❹ Crossing the Bridge

Opened in 2006, Paris' 37th bridge, the oak-and-steel foot- and cycle bridge, **Passerelle Simone de Beauvoir**, links the Right and Left Banks.

❺ Hitting the Books

Topped by four sunlit glass towers shaped like open books, a rainforest wraps around the reading rooms of the **Bibliothèque Nationale de France** (☎01 53 79 59 59; www.bnf.fr; 11 quai François Mauriac, 13e; temporary exhibitions adult/child from €9/free; ⏲exhibitions 10am-7pm Tue-Sat, 1-7pm Sun, closed early-late Sep; Ⓜ Bibliothèque), which mounts exhibitions revolving around 'the word'.

❻ Dockside Fashion

Transformed warehouse **Docks en Seine** (Cité de la Mode et du Design; www.paris-docks-en-seine.fr; 36 quai d'Austerlitz, 13e; ⏲10am-midnight; Ⓜ Gare d'Austerlitz), aka the Cité de la Mode et du Design, is the French fashion institute's HQ, with exhibitions and events as well as hip restaurants, bars and clubs.

❼ Swimming on the Seine

Splash on (not in!) the Seine at the floating swimming pool **Piscine Joséphine Baker** (☎01 56 61 96 50; quai François Mauriac, 13e; pool adult/child €3/1.70, sauna €10/5; ⏲7-8.30am & 1-9pm Mon, Wed & Fri, 1-11pm Tue & Thu, 11am-8pm Sat, 10am-8pm Sun; Ⓜ Bibliothèque or Quai de la Gare).

❽ Drinking, Dining & Dancing on the Seine

Board floating bar-restaurant-clubs like the red tugboat **Le Batofar** (www.batofar.org; opp 11 quai François Mauriac, 13e; ⏲bar 12.30pm-midnight Tue, to 6am Wed-Fri, 6pm-6am Sat; Ⓜ Quai de la Gare or Bibliothèque).

❾ Heading to the 'Hood

To dine on terra firma, head to small bistro **Chez Nathalie** (☎01 45 80 20 42; www.cheznathalie.fr; 41 rue Vandrezanne, 13e; mains €21-28; ⏲noon-2.30pm Tue-Fri, 7-11pm Tue-Sat; Ⓜ Corvisart or Place d'Italie) in the bar-filled Butte aux Cailles neighbourhood.

Explore

Musée d'Orsay & St-Germain des Prés

Literary buffs, antique collectors and fashionistas flock to this mythological part of Paris. Legendary writers such as Sartre, de Beauvoir, Camus, Hemingway and Fitzgerald hung out here and further south at Montparnasse, where despite late 20th-century eyesores like the '70s smoked-glass Tour Montparnasse skyscraper you'll find surviving brasseries and re-energised backstreets.

The Sights in a Day

Get your bearings from the panoramic observation deck of **Tour Montparnasse** (p158), before paying homage to writers Sartre and de Beauvoir and singer Serge Gainsbourg in the **Cimetière du Montparnasse** (p158) and getting a contemporary-art fix at the **Fondation Cartier pour l'Art Contemporain** (p158).

After lunch at **Bouillon Racine** (p159) or a picnic in the **Jardin du Luxembourg** (p150), stroll through this beautiful park en route to viewing Delacroix' works in the **Église St-Sulpice** (p156) and **Musée National Eugène Delacroix** (p156). Stop by **Église St-Germain des Prés** (p156) before people-watching at famous literary cafes like **Les Deux Magots** (p162) and browsing designer boutiques.

Entry to the **Musée d'Orsay** (p148) is cheaper late afternoon, so it's an ideal time to check out its breathtaking collections. Dine nearby at **Les Climats** (p161), then return to one of Montparnasse's late-night cafes, such as **La Closerie des Lilas** (p162).

For a local's day in St Germain des Prés, see p152.

Top Sights

Musée d'Orsay (p148)

Jardin du Luxembourg (p150)

Local Life

St-Germain des Prés' Historic Shops (p152)

Best of Paris

Architecture

Musée d'Orsay (p148)

Bouillon Racine (p159)

Fondation Cartier pour l'Art Contemporain (p158)

Churches

Église St-Sulpice (p156)

Église St-Germain des Prés (p156)

For Kids

Jardin du Luxembourg (p150)

Getting There

Ⓜ **Metro** St-Germain des Prés (line 4), Mabillon (line 10) and Odéon (lines 4 and 10) are in the heart of the action.

Ⓜ **Metro** Montparnasse Bienvenüe (lines 4, 6, 12 and 13) is Montparnasse's hub.

Boat The hop-on, hop-off Batobus stops outside the Musée d'Orsay and at quai Malaquais in St-Germain des Prés.

Top Sights
Musée d'Orsay

Recently renovated to incorporate richly coloured walls, a reorganised layout and increased exhibition space, the home of France's national collection from the impressionist, postimpressionist and art nouveau movements is, appropriately, the glorious former Gare d'Orsay railway station, itself an art nouveau showpiece, where a roll-call of luminaries and their world-famous works are on display.

Map p154, B1

www.musee-orsay.fr

62 rue de Lille, 7e

adult/child €11/free

9.30am-6pm Tue, Wed & Fri-Sun, to 9.45pm Thu

M Assemblée Nationale or RER Musée d'Orsay

Don't Miss

The Building

Built for the 1900 Exposition Universelle, by 1939 the Gare d'Orsay's platforms were too short for trains, and in a few years all rail services ceased. In 1962 Orson Welles filmed Kafka's *The Trial* in the then-abandoned building before the government set about transforming it into the country's premier showcase for art from 1848 to 1914.

Don't miss the panorama through the station's giant glass clockface and from the adjacent terrace.

Painting Collections

Masterpieces include Manet's *On the Beach;* Monet's gardens at Giverny and *Rue Montorgueil, Paris, Festival of June 30, 1878;* Cézanne's card players, *Green Apples* and *Blue Vase;* Renoir's *Ball at the Moulin de la Galette* and *Girls at the Piano;* Degas' ballerinas; Toulouse-Lautrec's cabaret dancers; Pissarro's *The Harvest;* Sisley's *View of the Canal St-Martin;* and Van Gogh's *Starry Night.*

Decorative Arts Collections

Household items from 1848 to 1914, such as hat stands, desks, chairs, bookcases, vases, water pitchers, decorated plates, goblets, bowls – and even kettles and cutlery – are true works of art and incorporate exquisite design elements.

Sculptures

Sculptures by Degas, Gauguin, Camille Claudel, Renoir and Rodin are housed in the museum.

Graphic Arts Collections

Drawings and sketches from major artists are another of the Musée d'Orsay's highlights. Look for Georges Seurat's crayon on paper work *The Black Bow* (c 1882) and Paul Gauguin's poignant self-portrait (c 1902–03).

Top Tips

- Combined tickets are available with the Musée de l'Orangerie (€16 to visit both within four days) and the Musée Rodin (€15 to visit both on the same day).
- Musée d'Orsay admission drops to €8.50 for entry after 4.30pm (after 6pm on Thursday).
- Admission is free on the first Sunday of the month year round.
- Save time by purchasing tickets online.

Take a Break

Café Campana (dishes €9-18; 10am-5pm Tue, Wed & Fri-Sun, to 9pm Thu; M Assemblée Nationale or RER Musée d'Orsay) is designed like a fantasy underwater world, while time has scarcely changed the station's **Restaurant Musée d'Orsay** (01 45 49 47 03; 2-/3-course lunch menus €22/32, mains €16-25; 9.30am-5.45pm Tue-Wed & Fri-Sun, to 9.30pm Thu; M Assemblée Nationale or RER Musée d'Orsay).

Top Sights
Jardin du Luxembourg

An inner-city oasis of formal terraces, chestnut groves and lush lawns, the 23 gracefully laid-out hectares of the Luxembourg Gardens have a special place in the hearts of Parisians. Napoléon dedicated the park to the children of Paris, and many residents spent their childhoods enjoying old-fashioned activities that are still here today, in addition to the modern facilities.

Map p154, D5

numerous entrances

hours vary

M St-Sulpice, Rennes or Notre Dame des Champs, or RER Luxembourg

Don't Miss

Puppet Shows

You don't have to be a kid and you don't have to speak French to be delighted by marionette shows, which have entertained audiences in France since the Middle Ages. The lively puppets perform in the Jardin du Luxembourg's little **Théâtre du Luxembourg** (www.marionnettesduluxembourg.fr; tickets €4.80; ⌚usually 3.30pm Wed, 11am & 3.30pm Sat & Sun, daily during school holidays; Ⓜ Notre Dame des Champs).

Grand Bassin

All ages love the octagonal Grand Bassin, a serene ornamental pond that adults can lounge around while kids prod 1920s toy sailboats with long sticks. Nearby, littlies can ride ponies or the carousel (merry-go-round), or romp around the playgrounds. Small charges apply for all activities.

Musée du Luxembourg

Prestigious temporary art exhibitions, such as 'Cézanne et Paris', take place in the beautiful **Musée du Luxembourg** (www.museeduluxembourg.fr; 19 rue de Vaugirard, 6e; most exhibitions adult/child around €13.50/9; ⌚10am-7.30pm Tue-Thu, Sat & Sun, to 10pm Fri & Mon; Ⓜ Rennes or RER Luxembourg).

Around the back of the museum, lemon and orange trees, palms, grenadiers and oleanders shelter from the cold in the palace's **orangery**.

Palais du Luxembourg

The **Palais du Luxembourg** (rue de Vaugirard; Ⓜ Rennes or RER Luxembourg) was built in the 1620s for Marie de Médici. Since 1958 it's housed the **Sénat** (Senate; ☎01 44 54 19 49; www.senat.fr; rue de Vaugirard; adult/18-25yr €8/6) and can be visited by guided tour.

☑ Top Tips

▸ Park opening hours vary seasonally; times are posted at entrance gates.

▸ If you're picnicking, forget bringing a blanket – the elegantly manicured lawns are off-limits apart from a small wedge on the southern boundary. Instead, do as Parisians do: corral one of the 1923-designed sage-green metal chairs and find your own favourite part of the park.

▸ Arrive at least half an hour ahead of time for puppet shows.

☑ Take a Break

Kiosks and cafes are dotted throughout the park, including places selling fairy (candy) floss.

Polidor (☎01 43 26 95 34; www.polidor.com; 41 rue Monsieur le Prince, 6e; menus €22-35; ⌚noon-2.30pm & 7pm-12.30am Mon-Sat, noon-2.30pm & 7-11pm Sun; 👪; Ⓜ Odéon) and its decor date from 1845, and it still serves family-style French cuisine.

Local Life
St-Germain des Prés' Historic Shops

While St-Germain des Prés spills over with chic fashion and interior-design boutiques, it's also filled with locally patronised antique and vintage dealers, small shops specialising in everything from handmade umbrellas to tiny tin soldiers, and the city's oldest department store, the Gustave Eiffel–designed Le Bon Marché, which all provide an insight into the neighbourhood's soul.

❶ Arcade Exploration

Browse the shops in the 1735-built, glass-roofed passageway **Cour du Commerce St-André**, and have lunch at the world's oldest cafe, the 1686-founded **Le Procope** (www.procope.com; 13 rue de l'Ancienne Comédie, 6e; 2-/3-course menus from €29/36; ⌚11.30am-midnight Sun-Wed, to 1am Thu-Sat; 👪; Ⓜ Odéon).

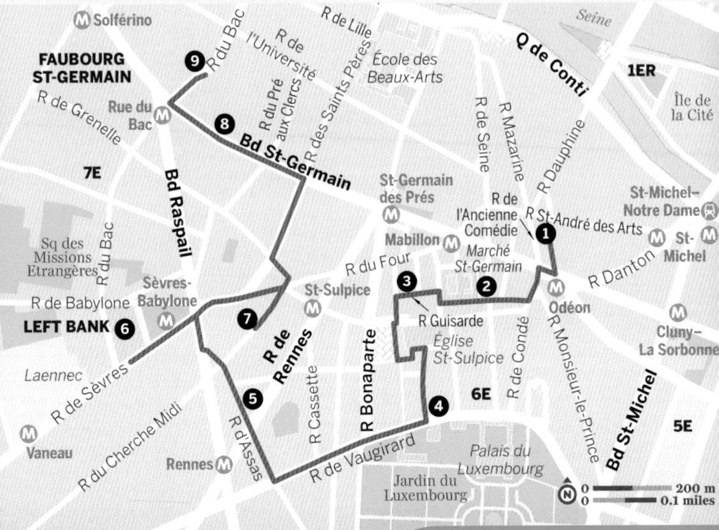

❷ Classic Candles

Claude Trudon began selling candles here in 1643, and **Cire Trudon** (www.ciretrudon.com; 78 rue de Seine, 6e; ⏲10am-7pm Tue-Sat; Ⓜ Odéon), which officially supplied Versailles and Napoléon with light, is now the world's oldest candle-maker (look for the plaque to the left of the awning).

❸ Soldiering On

Miniature tin and lead soldiers have been sold at the tiny **Au Plat d'Étain** (www.auplatdetain.sitew.com; 16 rue Guisarde, 6e; ⏲10.30am-6.30pm Tue-Sat; Ⓜ Odéon or Mabillon) since 1775.

❹ Doll's House

Opposite the residence of the French Senate's president, the teensy shop **La Maison de Poupée** (☎06 09 65 58 68; 40 rue de Vaugirard, 6e; ⏲2.30-7pm Mon-Sat, by appointment Sun; Ⓜ Odéon or RER Luxembourg) sells its namesake doll's houses as well as *poupées anciennes* (antique dolls).

❺ Bathroom Beauty

The antique and retro mirrors (hand-held and on stands), perfume spritzers, soap dishes and even basins and tapware at long-established shop **Le Bain Rose** (www.le-bain-rose.fr; 11 rue d'Assas, 6e; ⏲11.30am-7pm Mon-Sat, closed Aug; Ⓜ Rennes) can transform your bathroom into a belle époque sanctum.

❻ Department Store Decadence

The 1852-established department store **Le Bon Marché** (www.bonmarche.fr; 24 rue de Sèvres, 7e; ⏲10am-8pm Mon-Wed & Sat, to 9pm Thu & Fri; Ⓜ Sèvres Babylone) houses fashion, homewares and food hall **La Grande Épicerie de Paris** (www.lagrandeepicerie.fr; 36 rue de Sèvres, 7e; ⏲8.30am-9pm Mon-Sat; Ⓜ Sèvres Babylone), with displays of chocolates, pastries, biscuits, cheeses and more.

❼ Bakery Treats

Pierre Poilâne opened his *boulangerie* (bakery) **Poilâne** (www.poilane.fr; 8 rue du Cherche Midi, 6e; ⏲7.15am-8.15pm Mon-Sat; Ⓜ Sèvres-Babylone) upon arriving from Normandy in 1932. Today his granddaughter runs the company, which still turns out wood-fired, rounded sourdough loaves made with stone-milled flour and Guérande sea salt. The cafe next door uses Poilâne bread for gourmet *tartines* (open sandwiches).

❽ Rainy-Day Style

Pick up a *parapluie* (umbrella), parasol or walking cane handcrafted by **Alexandra Sojfer** (www.alexandrasojfer.com; 218 bd St-Germain, 7e; ⏲10am-7pm Mon-Sat; Ⓜ Rue du Bac) at this boutique, which has been in the trade since 1834.

❾ A Menagerie of Sorts

Overrun with creatures such as lions, tigers, zebras and storks, taxidermist **Deyrolle** (www.deyrolle.com; 46 rue du Bac, 7e; ⏲10am-1pm & 2-7pm Mon, 10am-7pm Tue-Sat; Ⓜ Rue du Bac) opened in 1831. In addition to stuffed animals (for rent and sale), it stocks minerals, shells, corals and crustaceans, stand-mounted ostrich eggs and pedagogical storyboards.

A
B
C
D
E
1
2
3
4
0
400 m
0.18 miles
Assemblée Nationale
Bd St-Germain
Pl du Palais Bourbon
Musée d'Orsay
Musée d'Orsay
Q Anatole France
Q des Tuileries
Pont Royal
Pont du Carroussel
Q Voltaire
Pl du Carrousel
Musée du Louvre
Louvre Rivoli
R de Rivoli
1er
Q du Louvre
Seine
Pont des Arts
Pont Neuf
Pont Neuf
Pl du Pont Neuf
R St-Dominique
Solférino
R de l'Université
R de Lille
R de Verneuil
18
R de Beaune
Q Malaquais
Pl de l'Institut
Q de Conti
5
FAUBOURG ST-GERMAIN
R de Bourgogne
R de Grenelle
R de Bellechasse
R du Bac
Musée des Lettres et Manuscrits
R Jacob
R des St-Pères
École des Beaux-Arts
R Bonaparte
Musée de la Monnaie de Paris
Pl Dauphine
Île de la Cité
Q des Orfèvres
Q des Grands Augustins
R de Varenne
Rue du Bac
4
LEFT BANK
17
R St-Benoît
Musée National Eugène Delacroix
R de Seine
R Mazarine
R Guénégaud
R Dauphine
7e
Bd St-Germain
Église St-Germain des Prés
23
21
2
R de Furstemberg
26
R de l'Abbaye
1
29
R des Grands Augustins
24
R Barbet de Jouy
R Vaneau
R de Varenne
R du Bac
Bd Raspail
R de Grenelle
31
14
Pl St-Germain des Prés
St-Germain des Prés
R de Buci
10
20
R St-André des Arts
St-Michel–Notre Dame
St-Michel
Pl St-Michel
Sq des Missions Etrangères
15
Sq Chaise Récamier
22
R du Dragon
R du Four
R des Canettes
R Princesse
Mabillon
Marché St-Germain
Pl H Mondor
12
R Danton
R de Babylone
Sq Boucicaut
St-Sulpice
R du Vieux Colombier
25
R St-Sulpice
Carrefour de l'Odéon
Odéon
R de l'École de Médecine
Cluny–La Sorbonne
Jardin Catherine Labouré
Sèvres-Babylone
3
R de Rennes
R de Mézières
Pl St-Sulpice
Église St-Sulpice
R Garancière
R de Condé
Sq et Pl P Painlevé
R Oudinot
Laennec
R Dupin
R de Sèvres
Vaneau
R Cassette
R Madame
R Bonaparte
Pl de l'Odéon
R Racine
11
R du Cherche Midi
R du Regard
30
R de Vaugirard
Pl Paul Claudel
R de Médicis
R Monsieur le Prince
Pl de la Sorbonne
Rennes
6e
Palais du Luxembourg

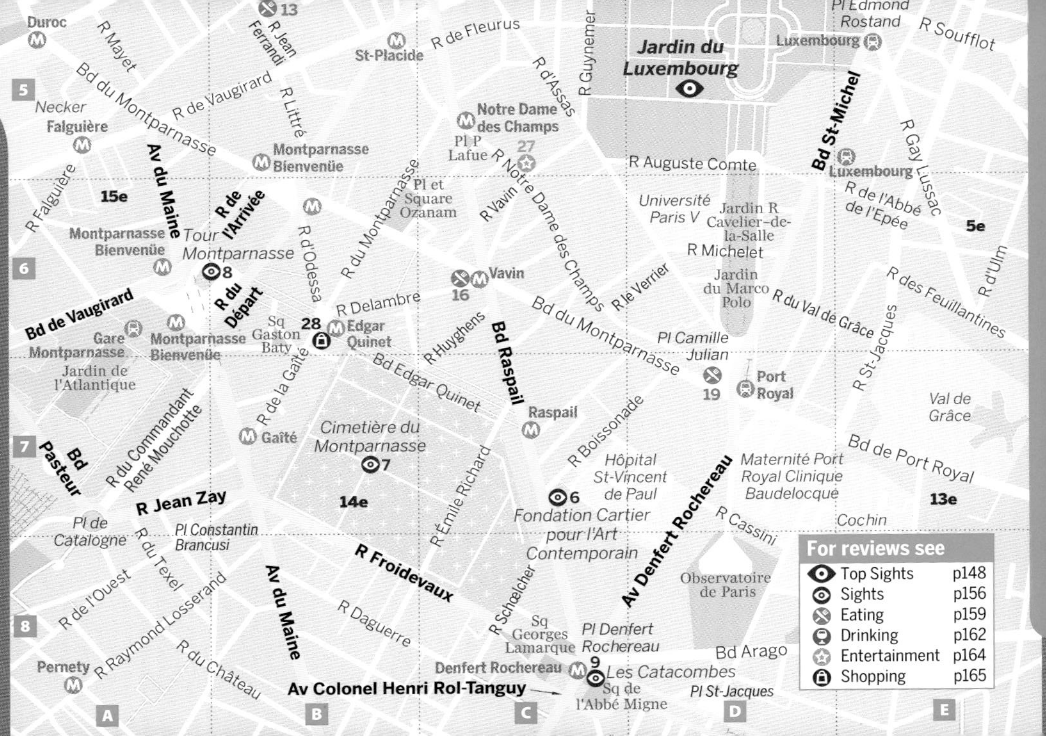

Duroc
R Mayet
13
R Jean Ferrandi
St-Placide
R de Fleurus
R Guynemer
Jardin du Luxembourg
Pl Edmond Rostand
Luxembourg
R Soufflot
5
Necker
Falguière
Bd du Montparnasse
R de Vaugirard
R Littré
R d'Assas
Notre Dame des Champs
Pl P Lafue
27
Montparnasse Bienvenüe
Av du Maine
R Auguste Comte
Bd St-Michel
Luxembourg
R Gay Lussac
R Falguière
15e
R de l'Arrivée
Pl et Square Ozanam
R du Montparnasse
R Vavin
R Notre Dame des Champs
Université Paris V
Jardin R Cavelier-de-la-Salle
R de l'Abbé de l'Epée
5e
Montparnasse Bienvenüe
Tour Montparnasse
R d'Odessa
R Michelet
6
8
Vavin
16
R le Verrier
Jardin du Marco Polo
R des Feuillantines
R d'Ulm
Bd de Vaugirard
R du Départ
R Delambre
R du Val de Grâce
Gare Montparnasse
Montparnasse Bienvenüe
Sq Gaston Baty
28
Edgar Quinet
R Huyghens
Bd Raspail
Bd du Montparnasse
Pl Camille Julian
R St-Jacques
Jardin de l'Atlantique
R de la Gaîté
Bd Edgar Quinet
19
Port Royal
Val de Grâce
Raspail
7
Bd Pasteur
R du Commandant René Mouchotte
Gaîté
Cimetière du Montparnasse
7
R Boissonade
Bd de Port Royal
Hôpital St-Vincent de Paul
Maternité Port Royal Clinique Baudelocque
R Jean Zay
14e
R Émile Richard
6
13e
Fondation Cartier pour l'Art Contemporain
Pl de Catalogne
Pl Constantin Brancusi
R Cassini
Cochin
R du Texel
R Froidevaux
Av Denfert Rochereau
R de l'Ouest
Av du Maine
R Schœlcher
Observatoire de Paris
8
R Raymond Losserand
R Daguerre
Sq Georges Lamarque
Pl Denfert Rochereau
Bd Arago
Pernety
R du Château
9
Denfert Rochereau
Les Catacombes
Av Colonel Henri Rol-Tanguy
Sq de l'Abbé Migne
Pl St-Jacques
A
B
C
D
E
For reviews see
Top Sights p148
Sights p156
Eating p159
Drinking p162
Entertainment p164
Shopping p165

Sights

Église St-Germain des Prés

CHURCH

1 Map p154, D3

Paris' oldest standing church, the Romanesque St Germanus of the Fields, was built in the 11th century on the site of a 6th-century abbey and was the dominant place of worship in Paris until the arrival of Notre Dame. It's since been altered many times, but the **Chapelle de St-Symphorien** (to the right as you enter) was part of the original abbey and is believed to be the resting place of St Germanus (AD 496–576), the first bishop of Paris. (www.eglise-sgp.org; 3 place St-Germain des Prés, 6e; 8am-7.45pm Mon-Sat, 9am-8pm Sun; M St-Germain des Prés)

Local Life

Les Berges de Seine

A breath of fresh air, this 2.3km-long riverside promenade is Parisians' latest spot to run, cycle, skate, play board games or take part in a packed program of events. Equally, it's simply a great place to hang out – in a Zzz shipping-container hut (free by reservation at the information point just west of the Musée d'Orsay), on the archipelago of floating gardens, or at the burgeoning restaurants and bars (some floating, too, aboard boats and barges).

Musée National Eugène Delacroix

MUSEUM

2 Map p154, D3

In a courtyard off a magnolia-shaded square, this was the romantic artist's home and studio at the time of his death in 1863, and contains a collection of his oil paintings, watercolours, pastels and drawings, including many of his more intimate works, such as *An Unmade Bed* (1828) and his paintings of Morocco.

A Musée du Louvre ticket allows entry to the museum on the same day (you can also buy tickets here and skip the Louvre's queues). (www.musee-delacroix.fr; 6 rue de Furstemberg, 6e; adult/child €6/free; 9.30am-5pm Wed-Mon; M Mabillon or St-Germain des Prés)

Église St-Sulpice

CHURCH

3  Map p154, D4

In 1646 work started on the twin-towered Church of St Sulpicius, lined inside with 21 side chapels, and it took six architects 150 years to finish. What draws most visitors isn't its Italianate facade with two rows of superimposed columns, its Counter-Reformation-influenced neoclassical decor or even its frescoes by Eugène Delecroix but its setting for a murder scene in Dan Brown's *The Da Vinci Code*.

You can hear the monumental, 1781-built organ during 10.30am Mass on Sunday or the occasional Sunday-afternoon concert. (http://pss75.fr/saint-sulpice-paris; place St-Sulpice, 6e; 7.30am-7.30pm; M St-Sulpice)

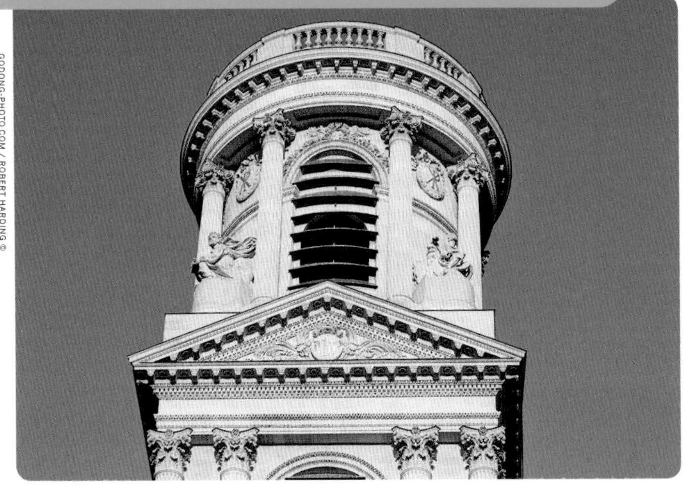

Église St-Sulpice

Musée des Lettres et Manuscrits

MUSEUM

4 Map p154, B2

Grouped into five themes (history, science, music, art and literature) the handwritten and annotated letters and works on display at this captivating museum provide a powerful emotional connection to their authors. They include Napoléon, Charles de Gaulle, Marie Curie, Albert Einstein, Mozart, Beethoven, Piaf, Monet, Toulouse-Lautrec, Van Gogh, Victor Hugo, Hemingway and F Scott Fitzgerald, and many, many more. It's thoroughly absorbing – allow at least a couple of hours. Temporary exhibitions also take place regularly. (MLM; www.museedeslettres.fr; 222 bd St-Germain, 7e; adult/child €7/5; 10am-7pm Tue-Wed & Fri-Sun, to 9.30pm Thu; M Rue du Bac)

Musée de la Monnaie de Paris

MUSEUM

5 Map p154, D2

Due to have reopened after extensive renovations by the time you're reading this, the Parisian Mint Museum traces the history of French coinage from antiquity onwards, with displays that help to bring to life this otherwise niche subject. It's housed in the 18th-century royal mint, the Monnaie de Paris, which is still used by the

Ministry of Finance to produce commemorative medals and coins.
(01 40 46 56 66; www.monnaiedeparis.fr; 11 quai de Conti, 6e; M Pont Neuf)

Fondation Cartier pour l'Art Contemporain MUSEUM

6 Map p154, C7

Designed by Jean Nouvel, this stunning glass-and-steel building is a work of art in itself. It hosts temporary exhibits on contemporary art (from the 1980s to today) in a diverse variety of media – from painting and photography to video and fashion, as well as performance art. Artist Lothar Baumgarten created the wonderfully rambling garden.
(www.fondation.cartier.com; 261 bd Raspail, 14e; adult/11-26yr €10.50/7; 11am-10pm Tue, to 8pm Wed-Sun; M Raspail)

Cimetière du Montparnasse CEMETERY

7 Map p154, B7

Opened in 1824, Montparnasse Cemetery, Paris' second largest after Père Lachaise, sprawls over 19 hectares shaded by 1200 trees, including maples, ash, lime trees and conifers. Among its illustrious 'residents' are poet Charles Baudelaire, writer Guy de Maupassant, playwright Samuel Beckett, sculptor Constantin Brancusi, painter Chaim Soutine, photographer Man Ray, industrialist André Citroën, Captain Alfred Dreyfus of the infamous affair, actress Jean Seberg, and philosopher-writer couple Jean-Paul Sartre and Simone de Beauvoir, as well as legendary singer Serge Gainsbourg.
(www.paris.fr; bd Edgar Quinet & rue Froidevaux, 14e; 8am-6pm Mon-Fri, 8.30am-6pm Sat, 9am-6pm Sun; M Edgar Quinet or Raspail)

Tour Montparnasse VIEWPOINT

8 Map p154, B6

Spectacular views unfold from this 210m-high smoked-glass and steel office block, built in 1973. (Bonus: it's about the only spot in the city where you can't see this startlingly ugly skyscraper, which dwarfs low-rise Paris.) Europe's fastest lift (elevator) whisks visitors up in 38 seconds to the indoor observatory on the 56th floor, with multimedia displays. Finish with a hike up the stairs to the 59th-floor open-air terrace (with a sheltered walkway) and bubbly at the terrace's Champagne bar.
(www.tourmontparnasse56.com; rue de l'Arrivée, 15e; adult/child €14.50/9; 9.30am-11.30pm daily Apr-Sep, to 10.30pm Sun-Thu, to 11pm Fri & Sat Oct-Mar; M Montparnasse Bienvenüe)

Les Catacombes CEMETERY

9 Map p154, C8

Paris' most macabre sight is its underground tunnels lined with skulls and bones. In 1785 it was decided to rectify the hygiene problems of Paris' overflowing cemeteries by exhuming the bones and storing them in disused quarry tunnels and the Catacombes were created in 1810.

After descending 20m (via 130 narrow, dizzying spiral steps) below street level, you follow the dark, subterranean passages to reach the ossuary itself (2km in all). Exit back up 83 steps onto rue Remy Dumoncel, 14e. (www.catacombes.paris.fr; 1 av Colonel Henri Roi-Tanguy, 14e; adult/child €8/free; 10am-5pm Tue-Sun; M Denfert Rochereau)

Eating

JSFP Traiteur DELICATESSEN €

10 Map p154, D3

Brimming with big bowls of salad, pâté and other delicacies, this deli is a brilliant bet for quality Parisian 'fast food' such as quiches in a variety of flavour combinations (courgette and chive, salmon and spinach) to take to a nearby park or stretch of riverfront. (http://jsfp-traiteur.com; 8 rue de Buci, 6e; dishes €3.40-5.70; 9.30am-8.30pm; ; M Mabillon)

Bouillon Racine BRASSERIE €€

11 Map p154, E4

Inconspicuously situated in a quiet street, this heritage-listed 1906 art-nouveau 'soup kitchen', with mirrored walls, floral motifs and ceramic tiling, was built in 1906 to feed market workers. Despite the magnificent interior, the food, inspired by age-old recipes, is by no means an afterthought. (01 44 32 15 60; www.bouillonracine.com; 3 rue Racine, 6e; weekday lunch menus €16, menus €31-42; noon-11pm; ; M Cluny–La Sorbonne)

L'Avant Comptoir FRENCH TAPAS €

12 Map p154, D3

Squeeze in around the zinc bar (there are no seats and it's tiny) and order from the menu suspended from the ceiling, to feast on amazing tapas dishes like Iberian ham or salmon tartare croquettes, duck-sausage hot dogs, blood-sausage *macarons,* and prosciutto and artichoke waffles, with wines by the glass in a chaotically sociable atmosphere. (www.hotel-paris-relais-saint-germain.com; 3 Carrefour de l'Odéon, 6e; tapas €3-7; noon-midnight; M Odéon)

Local Life

Rue Daguerre

Tucked just southwest of the Denfert Rochereau metro and RER stations near Les Catacombes, narrow **rue Daguerre** (Map p154, B8; 14e) – pedestrianised between av du Général-Leclerc and rue Boulard – is lined with florists, *fromageries*, *boulangeries*, patisseries, greengrocers, delis (including Greek, Asian and Italian) and classic cafes where you can watch the goings on.

Shops set up market stalls on the pavement; Sunday mornings are especially lively.

Café Trama

MODERN FRENCH €€

13 Map p154, B5

Cafe classics come with a contemporary twist at this black-awning-framed local with mellow lighting, chequered tiles, vintage furniture and pavement tables. Try the pan-fried squid with rocket and orange segments, croque monsieur with truffle salt on premium Poujauran bread, or ginger and basil beef tartare with meat from famed Parisian butcher Hugo Desnoyer, along with all-natural wines.

(01 45 48 33 71; 83 rue du Cherche Midi, 6e; mains €15-22; kitchen noon-2.45pm & 7.30-10pm Tue-Sat; M Vaneau or St-Placide)

Local Life

'Little Brittany'

Gare Montparnasse links Paris with Brittany, and the station's surrounding streets – especially rue du Montparnasse and rue d'Odessa, 14e – are lined with dozens of authentic crêperies. Breton savoury buckwheat-flour *galettes* and sweet crêpes, with traditional toppings such as *caramel au beurre salé* (salty caramel), are served flat on a plate and eaten using cutlery – and are best washed down with bowls of brut Breton cider. Try lace-curtain-screened **Crêperie Josselin** (Map p154, B6; 01 43 20 93 50; 67 rue du Montparnasse, 14e; crêpes €7-10; 11.30am-3pm & 5-11pm Tue-Fri, 11.30am-11pm Sat & Sun; ; M Edgar Quinet), filled with dark timber furniture and painted plates.

Brasserie Lipp

BRASSERIE €€

14 Map p154, C3

Waiters in black waistcoats, bow ties and long white aprons serve brasserie favourites such as *choucroute garnie* and *jarret de porc aux lentilles* (pork knuckle with lentils) at this illustrious wood-panelled establishment. (Arrive hungry: salads aren't allowed as meals.) Opened by Léonard Lipp in 1880, the brasserie achieved immortality when Hemingway sang its praises in *A Moveable Feast*.

(01 45 48 53 91; 151 bd St-Germain, 6e; mains €22-38; 11.45am-12.45am; M St-Germain des Prés)

Le Bac à Glaces

ICE CREAM €

15 Map p154, B3

Apricot and thyme, lemon and basil, strawberry and rose, and orange and sauvignon blanc are among the 60 flavours of all-natural ice creams at this luscious *glacière* (ice-cream maker).

(www.bacaglaces.com; 109 rue du Bac, 7e; ice cream from €3.50; 10.30am-7.30pm Mon-Sat; ; M Sèvres-Babylone)

Le Dôme

BRASSERIE €€€

16 Map p154, C6

A 1930s art deco extravaganza of the formal white-tablecloth and bow-tied-waiter variety, monumental Le Dôme is one of the swishest places around for shellfish platters piled high with fresh oysters, king prawns, crab claws and much more, followed by tradi-

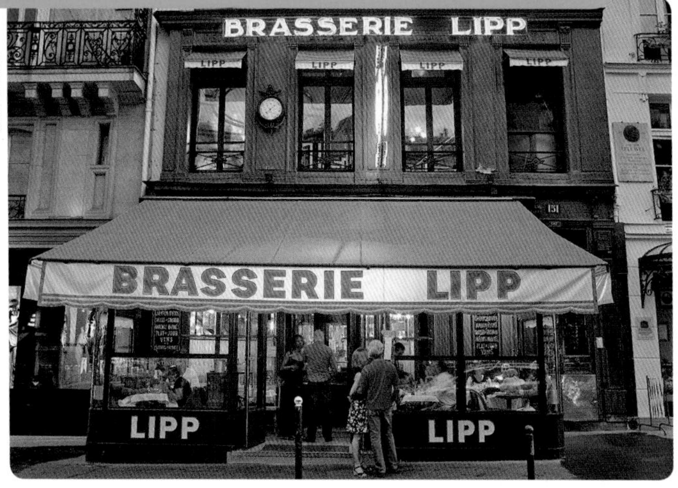

Brasserie Lipp

tional creamy homemade *millefeuille* for dessert, wheeled in on a trolley and cut in front of you.
(☎01 43 35 25 81; 108 bd du Montparnasse, 14e; mains €43-66.50, seafood platters €66; ⏲noon-3pm & 7-11pm; Ⓜ Vavin)

Au Pied de Fouet BISTRO €

17 Map p154, D2

Wholly classic bistro dishes such as *entrecôte* (steak), *confit de canard* (duck cooked slowly its own fat) and *foie de volailles sauté* (pan-fried chicken livers) at this busy bistro are astonishingly good value. Round off your meal with a *tarte Tatin,* wine-soaked prunes or bowl of *fromage blanc* (a cross between yoghurt, sour cream and cream cheese).
(☎01 43 54 87 83; www.aupieddefouet.com; 50 rue St-Benoît, 6e; mains €9-12.50; ⏲noon-2.30pm & 7-11pm Mon-Sat; Ⓜ St-Germain des Prés)

Les Climats TRADITIONAL FRENCH €€€

18 Map p154, C1

Like the neighbouring Musée d'Orsay, this is a magnficent art-nouveau treasure – a 1905-built former home for female telephone, telegram and postal workers – featuring soaring vaulted ceilings and original stained glass, as well as a garden for summer lunches and a glassed-in winter garden. Exquisite dishes complement its 150-page

list of wines, sparkling wines and whiskies purely from Burgundy.
(http://lesclimats.fr; 41 rue de Lille, 7e; 2-/3-course lunch menus €36/42, mains €32-44, bar snacks €7-22; restaurant noon-2.30pm & 7-10.30pm Tue-Sat, bar noon-2.30pm & 6-11pm; M Solférino)

La Closerie des Lilas — BRASSERIE **€€**

19 Map p154, D7

Brass plaques tell you exactly where Hemingway (who wrote much of *The Sun Also Rises* here) and luminaries like Picasso, Apollinaire, Man Ray, Jean-Paul Sartre and Samuel Beckett stood, sat or fell. The 'Lilac Enclosure' is split into a late-night piano bar, upmarket restaurant and more lovable (and cheaper) brasserie with a hedged-in pavement terrace.
(01 40 51 34 50; www.closeriedeslilas.fr; 171 bd du Montparnasse, 6e; restaurant mains €27.50-56.50, brasserie mains €25-33; restaurant noon-2.15pm & 7-11.30pm, brasserie noon-12.30am, piano bar 11am-1.30am; M Vavin or RER Port Royal)

Roger la Grenouille — TRADITIONAL FRENCH **€€**

20 Map p154, E3

Scattered with frog sculptures, B&W pictures of 1920s Paris and an array of old lamps, time-worn, sepia-coloured institution 'Roger the Frog' serves nine varieties of frogs' legs such as *à la Provençale* (with tomato) and *Normande* (cooked in cider and served with apple). If you're squeamish about devouring Roger, alternatives include dishes such as roast sea bass with braised fennel.
(01 56 24 24 34; 26-28 rue des Grands Augustins, 6e; lunch/dinner menus from €22/27; 7-11pm Mon, noon-2pm & 7-11pm Tue-Sat; M St-Michel)

Drinking

Les Deux Magots — CAFE

21  Map p154, C3

If ever there were a cafe that summed up St-Germain des Prés' early 20th-century literary scene, it's this former hangout of anyone who was anyone. You will spend *beaucoup* to sip a coffee in a wicker chair on the terrace, shaded by dark-green awnings and geraniums spilling from window boxes, but it's an undeniable piece of Parisian history.
(www.lesdeuxmagots.fr; 170 bd St-Germain, 6e; 7.30am-1am; M St-Germain des Prés)

Au Sauvignon — WINE BAR

22  Map p154, C3

Grab a table in the evening sun at this wonderfully authentic *bar à vin* or head to the quintessential bistro interior, with an original zinc bar, tightly packed tables and hand-painted ceiling celebrating French viticultural tradition. A plate of *casse-croûtes au pain Poilâne* – toast with ham, pâté, terrine, smoked salmon, foie gras – is the perfect accompaniment.
(80 rue des St-Pères, 7e; 8.30am-10pm Mon-Sat, to 9pm Sun; M Sèvres-Babylone)

Understand

Paris in Print & on Screen

Paris has been the inspiration for countless works of literature over the centuries, and is at least as much a star as the actors who compete with it on the big screen. Below is a selection of some of the best books and films set in the city.

Books

Les Misérables (Victor Hugo; 1862) Epic novel adapted to the stage and screen, tracing 20 years in the life of convict Jean Valjean through the battles and barricades of early-19th-century Paris.

Life: A User's Manual (Georges Perec; 1978) Intricately structured novel distilling Parisian life through a parade of characters inhabiting an apartment block between 1833 and 1975.

Down and Out in Paris and London (George Orwell; 1933) Eric Blair's (aka Orwell's) first published work is a no-holds-barred account of early-20th-century Paris, recounting his days as a dishwasher.

A Moveable Feast (Ernest Hemingway; 1964) Wry work recalling the author's early writing career in the 1920s with priceless vignettes depicting his contemporaries, including F Scott Fitzgerald and Gertrude Stein.

Films

Midnight in Paris (2011) Paris' timeless magic is palpable in Woody Allen's love letter to the city.

À Bout de Souffle (Breathless; 1960) Filmed with hand-held cameras, this new-wave story of a thief who kills a policeman revolutionised cinema.

La Haine (Hate; 1995) Raw, angst- and violence-ridden film shot in black and white. Three teenagers from Paris' *banlieues* (suburbs), trapped by crime, poverty and xenophobia, wait for a train overnight.

La Môme (La Vie en Rose; 2007) Acclaimed biopic of 'little sparrow' Édith Piaf, uncannily played by Marion Cotillard. Most songs on the soundtrack use Piaf's own voice.

Hugo (2011) A tribute to cinema and the legendary Georges Méliès.

Café de Flore

CAFE

23 Map p154, C3

The red upholstered benches, mirrors and marble walls at this art-deco landmark haven't changed much since the days when Jean-Paul Sartre and Simone de Beauvoir set up office here, writing during the Nazi occupation. (www.cafedeflore.fr; 172 bd St-Germain, 6e; 7am-2am; M St-Germain des Prés)

Bistro des Augustins

BAR, BISTRO

24 Map p154, E3

Plastered with old advertising posters from the *bouquiniste* (booksellers) stalls opposite, this bistro and bar manages to remain authentic and down-to-earth despite its epicentral Seine-side location. It's a cosy spot for a glass of red or a light meal like *gratin dauphinois* (potato bake). (39 quai des Grands Augustins, 6e; 10am-2am; M St-Michel)

On a Roll: Paris' Mass Skates

Mass skate **Pari Roller** (Map p154, A6; www.pari-roller.com; place Raoul Dautry, 14e; 10pm-1am Fri, arrive 9.30pm; M Montparnasse Bienvenüe) (aka 'Friday Night Fever') regularly attracts over 10,000 bladers and covers a different 30-odd-kilometre route each week. Routes incorporate cobblestones and downhill stretches, and are geared for experienced bladers only (for your safety and everyone else's).

Less feverish are the courses run by Rollers & Coquillages, organised through **Nomadeshop**, though you'll still need basic proficiency – that is, knowing how to brake!

Brasserie O'Neil

MICROBREWERY

25 Map p154, D3

Paris' first microbrewery was opened by a French restaurateur and French brewer over two decades ago, and still brews four fabulous beers (blond, amber, bitter brown and citrusy white) on the premises. Soak them up with thin *flammekueches* (Alsatian pizzas). (www.oneilbar.fr; 20 rue des Canettes, 6e; noon-2am; M St-Sulpice or Mabillon)

Jane Club

CLUB

26 Map p154, D3

Formerly Le Wagg and kitted out with a kickin' new sound system, Jane Club is a temple to golden '80s, golden '90s and timeless rock and roll. You can also catch live concerts here (Pete Doherty, for example). Salsa takes place every Sunday. Hours can vary. (www.wagg.fr; 62 rue Mazarine, 6e; 10.30pm-6am Fri & Sat, 3.30pm-2am Sun; ; M Odéon)

Entertainment

Le Lucernaire

CULTURAL CENTRE

27 Map p154, C5

Sunday-evening concerts are a fixture on the impressive repertoire of this dynamic Centre National d'Art et d'Essai (National Arts Centre). Be it classical guitar, baroque, French *chansons* or oriental music, these weekly concerts starting at 7.30pm are a real treat. Art and photography exhibitions, cinema, theatre, lectures, debates and guided walks round off the packed cultural agenda. (☎reservations 01 45 44 57 34; www.lucernaire.fr; 53 rue Notre Dame des Champs, 6e; ⏰bar 11am-10pm Mon, 11am-12.30am Fri, 4pm-12.30am Sat, 4-10pm Sun; Ⓜ Notre Dame des Champs)

Local Life

Antique Shopping

Art and antique dealers congregate within the **Carré Rive Gauche** (Map p154, C1; www.carrerivegauche.com; Ⓜ Rue du Bac or Solférino). Bounded by quai Voltaire and rues de l'Université, des St-Pères and du Bac, this 'Left Bank square' is home to more than 120 specialised merchants. Exhibitions take place throughout the year.

Shopping

Adam Montparnasse ART SUPPLIES

28 Map p154, B6

If Paris' art galleries have inspired you, pick up paint brushes, sketch-pads, watercolours, oils, acrylics, canvases and more at this historic shop. Picasso, Brancusi and Giacometti were among Édouard Adam's clients. Another seminal client was Yves Klein, with whom Adam developed the ultramarine 'Klein blue' – the VLB25 'Klein Blue' varnish is sold exclusively here. (www.adamparis.com; 11 bd Edgar Quinet, 14e; ⏰9.30am-7pm Mon-Sat; Ⓜ Edgar Quinet)

A La Recherche de Jane ACCESSORIES

29 Map p154, D3

This welcoming *chapelier* (milliner) has literally thousands of handcrafted hats on hand for both men and women, and can also make them to order. (http://alarecherchedejane.wordpress.com; 41 rue Dauphine, 6e; ⏰11.30am-7pm Wed-Sat, 1-7pm Sun; Ⓜ Odéon)

Plastiques HOMEWARES

30 Map p154, C4

Lollypop-coloured tableware (trays, dinner settings etc) and cookware (whisks, mixing bowls and much more) fill this original, inexpensive boutique. (www.plastiques-paris.fr; 103 rue de Rennes, 6e; ⏰10.15am-7pm Mon-Sat; Ⓜ Rennes)

Sonia Rykiel FASHION

31 Map p154, C3

In the heady days of May 1968, amid Paris' student uprisings, Sonia Rykiel opened her boutique here, and went on to revolutionise garments with inverted seams, 'no hems' and 'no lining'. Her diffusion labels are in separate boutiques nearby, with other outlets around Paris. (www.soniarykiel.com; 175 bd St-Germain, 6e; ⏰10.30am-7pm Mon-Sat; Ⓜ St-Germain des Prés)

Top Sights
Versailles

Getting There

Versailles is about 22km southwest of Notre Dame.

RER C5 (€3.25, 45 minutes, frequent) goes from Paris' Left Bank RER stations to Versailles-Château–Rive Gauche station.

The opulent-and-then-some Château de Versailles sits amid 900 hectares of fountain-graced gardens, pond-filled parks and woods. Louis XIV transformed his father's hunting lodge into the colossal Château de Versailles in the mid-17th century and the baroque palace was the kingdom's political capital and the seat of the royal court from 1682 until the fateful events of 1789, when revolutionaries massacred the palace guard. Louis XVI and Marie-Antoinette were ultimately dragged back to Paris and ingloriously guillotined.

Don't Miss

The Château de Versailles in Numbers

Louis XIV ordered 700 rooms, 2153 windows, 352 chimneys and 11 hectares of roof for the 580m-long main palace. It housed the entire court of 6000 (plus 5000 servants). The finest talent of the day installed some 6300 paintings, 2000 sculptures and statues, 15,000 engravings and 5000 furnishings and *objets d'art.*

The Hall of Mirrors

The palace's opulence peaks in its shimmering, sparkling Galerie des Glaces (Hall of Mirrors). This 75m-long ballroom with 17 giant mirrors on one side and an equal number of windows on the other has to be seen to be believed.

The King's and Queen's State Apartments

Luxurious, ostentatious appointments – frescoes, marble, gilt and woodcarvings, with themes and symbols drawn from Greek and Roman mythology – emanate from every last moulding, cornice, ceiling and door in the palace's Grands Appartements du Roi et de la Reine.

Guided Tours

To access areas that are otherwise off-limits and learn more about Versailles' history, take a 90-minute **guided tour** (☎01 30 83 77 88; www.chateauversailles.fr; tours €7 plus palace admission; ⏲English-language tours Tue-Sun, tour times vary) of the Private Apartments of Louis XV and Louis XVI and the Opera House or Royal Chapel. Tours include access to the most famous parts of the palace; book online.

The Gardens

Celebrated landscape artist André Le Nôtre was commissioned by Louis XIV to design the

☎01 30 83 78 00

www.chateauversailles.fr

passport ticket incl estate-wide access adult/child €18/free, with musical events €25/free, palace €15/free

⏲9am-6.30pm Tue-Sat, to 6pm Sun Apr-Oct, to 5.30pm Tue-Sun Nov-Mar

Ⓜ RER Versailles-Château–Rive Gauche

☑ Top Tips

- By noon queues for tickets and entering the château both spiral out of control: arrive early morning and avoid Tuesday and Sunday, the palace's busiest days.
- Prepurchase tickets online and head straight to Entrance A.
- Entry is free on the first Sunday of the month from November to March.

✕ Take a Break

Eateries around the estate include tearoom **Angelina** (www.angelina-versailles.fr; snacks €14-25, mains €23-35).

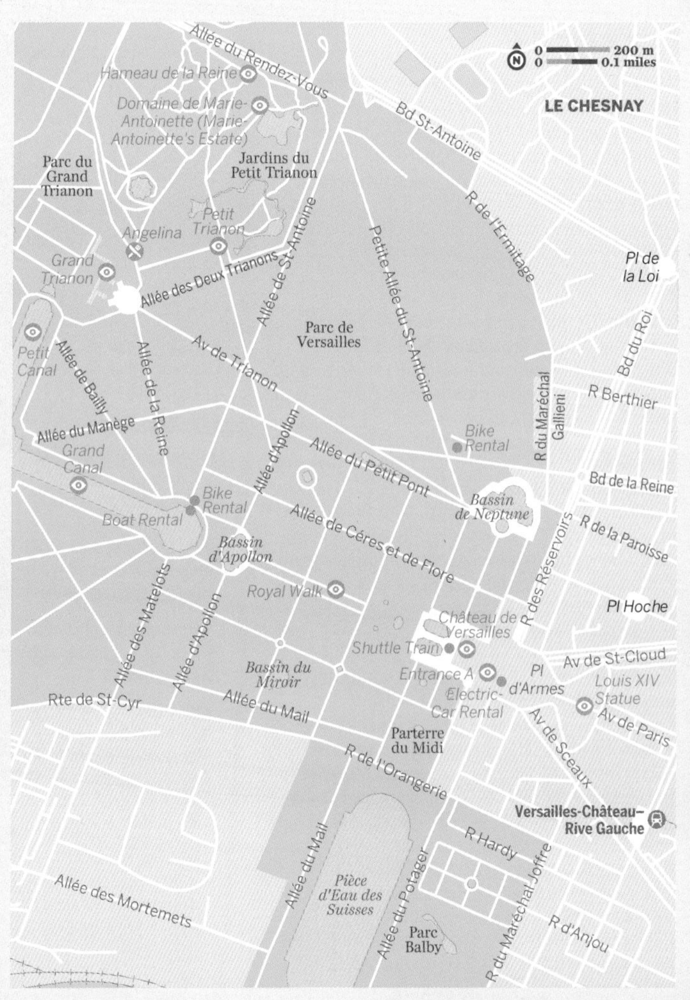

0 200 m
0 0.1 miles
LE CHESNAY
Allée du Rendez-Vous
Hameau de la Reine
Domaine de Marie-Antoinette (Marie-Antoinette's Estate)
Parc du Grand Trianon
Jardins du Petit Trianon
Petit Trianon
Angelina
Grand Trianon
Allée des Deux Trianons
Allée de St-Antoine
Petite Allée du St-Antoine
Bd St-Antoine
R de l'Ermitage
Pl de la Loi
Bd du Roi
Parc de Versailles
Petit Canal
Allée de Bailly
Allée de la Reine
Av de Trianon
R du Maréchal Gallieni
R Berthier
Allée du Manège
Grand Canal
Allée d'Apollon
Bike Rental
Allée du Petit Pont
Bd de la Reine
Bike Rental
Boat Rental
Bassin de Neptune
R de la Paroisse
Allée de Céres et de Flore
R des Réservoirs
Bassin d'Apollon
Royal Walk
Pl Hoche
Château de Versailles
Allée des Matelots
Allée d'Apollon
Shuttle Train
Av de St-Cloud
Bassin du Miroir
Entrance A
Pl d'Armes
Louis XIV Statue
Electric-Car Rental
Rte de St-Cyr
Allée du Mail
Av de Paris
Av de Sceaux
Parterre du Midi
R de l'Orangerie
Versailles-Château–Rive Gauche
R Hardy
Allée du Mail
Allée du Potager
R du Maréchal Joffre
Pièce d'Eau des Suisses
Allée des Mortemets
Parc Balby
R d'Anjou

château's magnificent **gardens** (except during musical events admission free; ⏲gardens 9am-8.30pm Apr-Oct, 8am-6pm Nov-Mar, park 7am-8.30pm Apr-Oct, 8am-6pm Nov-Mar). The best view over the rectangular pools is from the Hall of Mirrors. Pathways include the Royal Walk's verdant 'green carpet', with smaller paths leading to leafy groves.

The Canals

The **Grand Canal**, 1.6km long and 62m wide, is oriented to reflect the setting sun. It's traversed by the 1km-long **Petit Canal**, forming a cross-shaped body of water with a perimeter of over 5.5km.

Marie-Antoinette's Estate

Northwest of the main palace is the **Domaine de Marie-Antoinette** (Marie-Antoinette's Estate; adult/child €10/free, with passport ticket free; ⏲noon-6.30pm Tue-Sun Apr-Oct, to 5.30pm Tue-Sat Nov-Mar). Tickets include the Grand and Petit Trianon palaces, and the **Hameau de la Reine** (Queen's Hamlet), a mock village of thatched cottages where Marie-Antoinette played milkmaid.

Trianon Palaces

The pink-colonnaded **Grand Trianon** was built in 1687 for Louis XIV and his family as a place of escape from the rigid etiquette of the court, and renovated under Napoléon I in the Empire style. The ochre-coloured, 1760s **Petit Trianon** was redecorated in 1867 by the consort of Napoléon III, Empress Eugénie, who added Louis XVI-style furnishings.

Amour sculpture from Petit Trianon

Musical Fountain Shows

Try to time your visit for the magical **Grandes Eaux Musicales** (adult/child €9/7.50; ⏲11am-noon & 3.30-5pm Tue, Sat & Sun mid-May–late Jun, 11am-noon & 3.30-5pm Sat & Sun Apr–mid-May & Jul-Oct) or the after-dark **Grandes Eaux Nocturnes** (adult/child €24/20; ⏲from 8.30pm Sat mid-Jun–mid-Sep), 'dancing water' displays set to music composed by baroque- and classical-era composers.

The Best of Paris

Paris's Best Walks

Paris's Best...

Place de la Concorde (p60)

Best Walks
Left Bank Literary Loop

The Walk

It wasn't only Paris' reputation for liberal thought and relaxed morals that lured writers in the early 20th century – Left Bank Paris was cheap and, unlike Prohibition-era America, you could drink to your heart's content. This walk through the area's long-gentrified streets takes in pivotal places from the era.

Start Rue du Cardinal Lemoine; M Cardinal Lemoine

Finish Rue Notre Dame des Champs; M Vavin

Length 6.5km; three hours

Take a Break

The route is littered with cafes and brasseries with literary associations, including favourites of Jean-Paul Sartre and Simone de Beauvoir **Les Deux Magots** (p162) and **Café de Flore** (p164), Hemingway's favoured **Brasserie Lipp** (p160) and **La Closerie des Lilas** (p162), and other literary-luminary magnets such as **Le Dôme** (p160).

BRUCE YUANYUE BI / LONELY PLANET IMAGES ©

Shakespeare & Company (p142)

❶ Rue du Cardinal Lemoine

Walk southwest along rue du Cardinal Lemoine, peering down the passageway at **No 71**, where James Joyce finished *Ulysses* in apartment E. From 1922 to 1923, Ernest Hemingway lived at **No 74**.

❷ Paul Verlaine's Garret

Hemingway wrote in a top-floor garret of a hotel at **39 rue Descartes** – the same hotel where the poet Paul Verlaine died. Ignore the incorrect plaque.

❸ George Orwell's Boarding House

In 1928 George Orwell stayed in a boarding house above **6 rue du Pot de Fer**, which he called 'rue du Coq d'Or' in *Down and Out in Paris and London* (1933).

❹ Jack Kerouac's Hotel

The **Relais Hôtel du Vieux Paris** at 9 rue Gît le Cœur was a favourite of poet Allen Ginsberg and Beat writer Jack Kerouac in the 1950s.

5 Shakespeare & Company

The original **Shakespeare & Company** (p142) bookshop stood at 12 rue de l'Odéon, where owner Sylvia Beach lent books to Hemingway and published *Ulysses* for Joyce in 1922. It was closed during WWII's Nazi occupation.

6 Henry Miller's Room

Henry Miller stayed on the 5th floor of **36 rue Bonaparte** in 1930; he wrote about the experience in *Letters to Emil* (1989).

7 Oscar Wilde's Hotel

The former Hôtel d'Alsace (now **L'Hôtel**; p205), 13 rue des Beaux-Arts, is where Oscar Wilde died in 1900.

8 Hemingway's First Night in Paris

Hemingway spent his first night in the city at the **Hôtel d'Angleterre**, 44 rue Jacob.

9 Gertrude Stein's Home

Ezra Pound and Hemingway were among those entertained at **27 rue de Fleurus**, where Gertrude Stein lived with Alice B Toklas.

10 Rue Notre Dame des Champs

Pound lived at **70bis rue Notre Dame des Champs**, while Hemingway's first apartment in this area was above a sawmill at **No 113**.

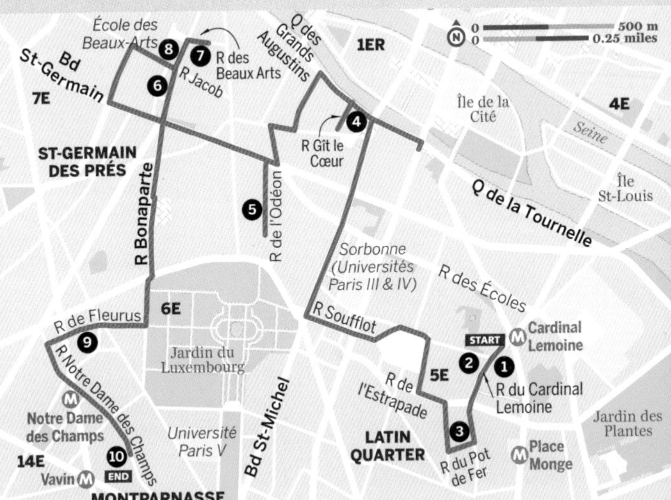

Best Walks Seine-Side Romantic Meander

The Walk

The world's most romantic city has no shortage of beguiling spots, but the Seine and its surrounds are Paris at its most seductive. On this walk you'll pass graceful gardens, palaces, intimate parks, a flower market and an enchanting bookshop. Descend the steps along the quays wherever possible to stroll along the water's edge.

Start Place de la Concorde; Ⓜ Concorde

Finish Jardin des Plantes; Ⓜ Gare d'Austerlitz

Length 7km; three hours

Take a Break

The Seine's islands – Île de la Cité and Île St-Louis – have plenty of enticing places to eat and/or drink, such as **Café Saint Régis** (p125), as well as some picturesque picnic spots. Or simply leave it to serendipity (which is, after all, the essence of every great romance).

Jardin des Tuileries (p60)

1 Jardin des Tuileries

After taking in the panorama from **place de la Concorde** (p60), stroll through the **Jardin des Tuileries** (p60).

2 Jardin du Palais Royal

Browse the arcades flanking the **Jardin du Palais Royal** (p61), adjoining the 17th-century palace where Louis XIV once lived.

3 Cour Carrée

Walk through the **Jardin de l'Oratoire** to the Cour Carrée courtyard of the **Louvre** (p50) and exit at the **Jardin de l'Infante** (Garden of the Princess).

4 Square du Vert Galant

From the **Pont Neuf** (p122), take the steps to the park at Île de la Cité's tip, **Square du Vert Galant**, before ascending to place du Pont Neuf to cross place Dauphine.

5 Marché aux Fleurs Reine Elizabeth II

Parisians have been buying bouquets at the

Marché aux Fleurs Reine Elizabeth II (p127), newly renamed in honour of Britain's Queen Elizabeth II, for centuries. Choose carefully: tradition has it that chrysanthemums are only for cemeteries, carnations bring bad luck, and yellow roses imply adultery.

6 Shakespeare & Company

Amid handpainted quotations, make a wish in the wishing well, leave a message on the 'mirror of love' or curl up with a volume of poetry in the reading library of the magical bookshop **Shakespeare & Company** (p142).

7 Berthillon

Cross **Pont de l'Archevêché** to Île de la Cité, then take **Pont St-Louis** to Île St-Louis and share an ice cream from *glacier* (ice-cream maker) **Berthillon** (p123).

8 Musée de la Sculpture en Plein Air

Along quai St-Bernard, wander among more than 50 late-20th-century unfenced sculptures by artists such as César and Brancusi at the **Musée de la Sculpture en Plein Air** (p138; Open-Air Sculpture Museum).

9 Jardin des Plantes

End your romantic meander at the tranquil **Jardin des Plantes** (p136). For the ultimate denouement, cruise back along the Seine by Batobus.

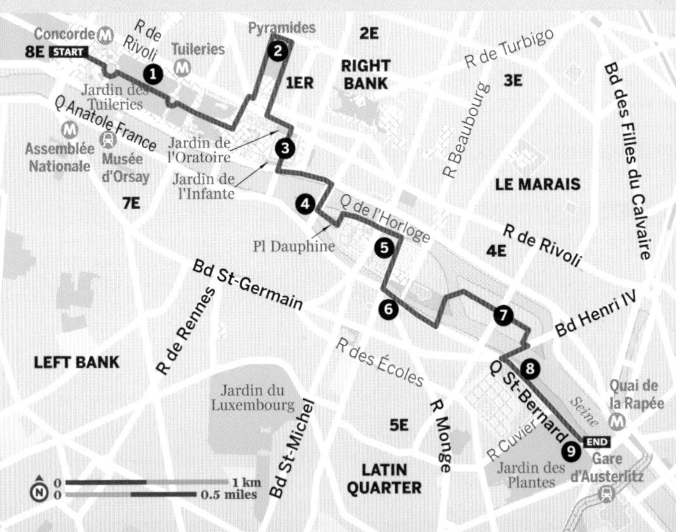

Best Walks
Right Bank Covered Passages

The Walk

Stepping into the *passages couverts* (covered shopping arcades) of the Right Bank is the best way to get a feel for what life was like in early-19th-century Paris. Around half a century later, Paris had around 150 of these decorated arcades. This walking tour is tailor-made for a rainy day, but it's best avoided on a Sunday, when some arcades are shut tight.

Start Galerie Véro Dodat; Ⓜ Palais Royal–Musée du Louvre

Finish Passage Verdeau; Ⓜ Le Peletier

Length 3km; two hours

Take a Break

Like visitors 150 years ago, on this walk you can dine and drink within the arcades as well as shop and even attend the theatre. For a two-Michelin-starred meal, book ahead to dine at **Passage 53** (p65) inside the Passage des Panoramas.

Galerie Vivienne

❶ Galerie Véro Dodat

At 19 rue Jean-Jacques Rousseau, **Galerie Véro Dodat** retains its 19th-century skylights, ceiling murals, Corinthian columns, tiled floor, gas globe fittings (now electric) and shopfronts including furniture restorers.

❷ Galerie Vivienne

Built in 1826, **Galerie Vivienne** is decorated with floor mosaics and bas-reliefs on the walls. Don't miss wine shop **Legrand Filles & Fils**, **Wolff et Descourtis**, selling silk scarves, and **Emilio Robba**, one of the most beautiful flower shops in Paris.

❸ Galerie Colbert

Enter this 1826-built passage, featuring a huge glass dome and rotunda, from rue Vivienne. Exit on rue des Petits Champs (and check out the fresco above).

❹ Passage Choiseul

This 1824-built, 45m-long passage has scores of shops including many specialising in discount and vintage clothing, beads and costume jewellery as well as cheap eateries. Comedies are performed at the **Théâtre des Bouffes Parisiens**, which backs onto the passage's northern end.

5 Passage des Panoramas

From 10 rue St-Marc, enter Paris' oldest covered arcade (1800), the first to be lit by gas (1817). It was expanded in 1834 with four interconnecting passages – Feydeau, Montmartre, St-Marc and Variétés – and is full of eateries and unusual shops, such as autograph dealer **Arnaud Magistry**. Exit at 11 bd Montmartre.

6 Passage Jouffroy

Enter at 10-12 bd Montmartre into passage Jouffroy, Paris' last major passage (1847). There's a wax museum, the **Musée Grévin**, and wonderful boutiques including bookshops, silversmiths and **M&G Segas**, where Toulouse-Lautrec bought his walking sticks. Exit at 9 rue de la Grange Batelière.

7 Passage Verdeau

Cross the road to 6 rue de la Grange Batelière to the last of this stretch of covered arcades. There's lots to explore: vintage comic books, antiques, old postcards and more. The northern exit is at 31bis rue du Faubourg Montmartre.

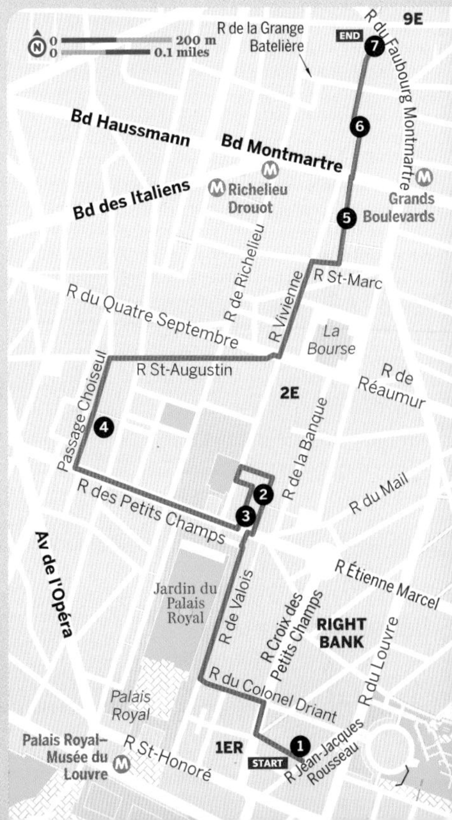

Best **Museums**

The cultured French capital has well over 100 museums, harbouring treasures from throughout the ages. There's everything from major national institutions to super-specialised museums highlighting a single, sometimes offbeat, subject. Temporary exhibitions take place in diverse venues – keep an eye out for what's on while you're in town.

Planning Your Visit

Most museums close one day a week, generally Monday or Tuesday; many open late one or more nights a week – usually the least crowded time to visit. You'll also save time by purchasing tickets online where possible. Remember that the cut-off for entry to museums is typically half an hour to an hour before the official closing times (including times listed in this guide). Audioguides are sometimes included with admission but often incur an extra charge.

National Museums Free Entry

If you can, time your trip to be here on the first Sunday of the month, when you can visit the *musées nationaux* (national museums; www.rmn.fr, in French) as well as a handful of monuments for free (some during certain months only). Temporary exhibitions still incur a charge.

City Museums Free Entry

You can visit the permanent collections of most *musées municipaux* (city-run museums; www.paris.fr) for free any time. Temporary exhibitions incur a charge.

NEIL SETCHFIELD / GETTY IMAGES ©

☑ Top Tips

- Save money by investing in a Paris Museum Pass (p210) or Paris City Passport (p210) or taking advantage of combination tickets.
- Museum admission is often reduced during certain times or on certain days.
- Museums generally charge extra for temporary exhibitions but often offer a discounted combined rate with their permanent collections.

Best Impressionist Collections

Musée d'Orsay France's national museum for impressionist and related

Musée d'Orsay (p148)

artistic movements is a must. (p148)

Musée de l'Orangerie Monet conceived a stunning cycle of his *Water Lilies* series especially for this building. (p60)

Best Modern- & Contemporary-Art Museums

Musée National d'Art Moderne The country's national modern- and contemporary-art museum, located within the striking Centre Pompidou. (p91)

Musée d'Art Moderne de la Ville de Paris Paris' modern-art museum spans the 20th century to the present day. (p44)

Dalí Espace Montmartre Showcases the work of the surrealist master. (p79)

Best Photography Museums

Jeu de Paume France's national photography centre. (p60)

Maison Européenne de la Photographie Excellent photography exhibits. (p96)

Best Sculpture Museums

Musée Rodin Rodin's former mansion-set workshop and its rose gardens contain his masterworks. (p26)

Musée de la Sculpture en Plein Air Over 50 late-20th-century unfenced sculptures by artists including César and Brancusi. (p138)

Worth a Trip

Secluded in the Duke of Valmy's former hunting lodge, the intimate **Musée Marmottan** (☎01 44 96 50 33; www.marmottan.fr; 2 rue Louis Boilly, 16e; adult/child €10/5; ⏰10am-6pm Tue-Sun, to 8pm Thu; Ⓜ La Muette) houses the world's largest collection of Claude Monet's works, including *Impression: Sunrise* (1872), after which impressionism was named, plus paintings by Gauguin, Sisley, Renoir, Degas and Manet.

Best Architecture

Several key eras define Paris' cityscape. From the 11th-century, magnificent cathedrals and palaces were built. Baron Haussmann's demolition of the city's disease-ridden streets made way for boulevards lined by neoclassical buildings. And, after the art nouveau movement, additions centred on French presidents' bold *grands projets* (great projects). For an architectural overview, visit the Cité de l'Architecture et du Patrimoine.

Haussmann's Renovation

Paris' appearance today is largely the work of Baron Georges-Eugène Haussmann (1809–91). Under Napoléon III, Haussmann completely rebuilt swathes of Paris between 1853 and 1870, replacing chaotic narrow streets (easy to barricade in an uprising) with arrow-straight, wide thoroughfares, including the 12 avenues radiating out from the Arc de Triomphe.

Art Nouveau Influence

Art nouveau swept through the Parisian cityscape from the mid-19th century until WWI, leaving its mark on architecture, interior design, furniture and graphics. Sinuous swirls, curls and floral tendrils characterise this 'new art' movement; materials that supported its signature motifs included wrought iron, glass, richly grained timbers and marble.

Rising Skyline

The outrage over the construction of the 1970s eyesore Tour Montparnasse prompted a clampdown on skyscrapers. However due to Paris' chronic lack of housing space, the city council recently approved raising height limits to 180m in some areas. Advocates include Pritzker Prize–winning French architect Jean Nouvel (b 1945).

FUTURE LIGHT / GETTY IMAGES ©

Best Medieval Marvels

Notre Dame This incomparable medieval cathedral is the city's heart in every sense. (p114)

Musée National du Moyen Âge The 15th-century Hôtel de Cluny is a medieval treasure. (p130)

Best Art Nouveau Splendours

Eiffel Tower Paris' 'iron lady' is art nouveau at its best. (p24)

Abbesses metro entrance Hector Guimard's finest remaining metro entrance.

Galeries Lafayette Beautiful department store topped by a stunning stained-glass dome. (p70)

Opéra Bastille (p107), architect Carlos Ott

Best Grands Projets

Centre Pompidou Former president Georges Pompidou's now-beloved cultural centre sparked a furore when it was unveiled in 1977. (p90)

Louvre glass pyramid IM Pei's pyramid, instigated by former president François Mitterrand, likewise created an uproar in 1989. (p50)

Opéra Bastille Mitterrand oversaw a slew of other costly *projets*, including the city's second, state-of-the-art opera house. (p107)

Best Jean Nouvel Buildings

Musée du Quai Branly President Jacques Chirac's pet *projet*, designed by Nouvel. (p31)

Institut du Monde Arabe The building that established Nouvel's reputation blends modern and traditional Arab elements with Western influences. (p136)

Fondation Cartier Pour l'Art Contemporain Stunning contemporary-art space. (p158)

Best Contemporary Structures

Cinémathèque Française Frank Gehry–designed postmodern stunner housing two cinema museums and presenting screenings. (p145)

Forum des Halles Epicentral shopping mall now topped by a giant rainforest-inspired canopy. (p71)

Worth a Trip

The futuristic glass-and-chrome urban jungle of the La Défense business district rises just northwest of the *Périphérique* (ring road), reached by a regular metro ticket. Its dramatic gateway is the 110m-high Carrara-marble-and-granite **Grande Arche** (1 Parvis de la Défense; M La Défense); there's an architecture **museum** (www.ladefense.fr; 15 place de la Défense; admission free; M La Défense) and info centre nearby.

Best History

Paris' history is a saga of battles, bloodshed, grand-scale excesses, revolution, reformation, resistance, renaissance and constant reinvention. But this epic is not just consigned to museums and archives: reminders of the capital's and the country's history are evident all over the city.

Early Beginnings

Paris was born in the 3rd century BC, when the Parisii tribe of Celtic Gauls settled on Île de la Cité. Julius Caesar ended centuries of conflict between the Gauls and Romans in 52 BC. Christianity was introduced in the 2nd century AD; in 508 Frankish king Clovis I united Gaul and made Paris his seat.

Conflicts

In the 12th century Scandinavian Vikings pushed towards Paris, heralding the Hundred Years' War with Norman England, which resulted in England gaining control of France in 1420. In 1429 Joan of Arc rallied French troops to defeat the English.

Revolution

The excesses of Louis XIV and his heirs triggered an uprising of Parisians on 14 July 1789, which kick-started the French Revolution. The government was consolidated in 1799 under Napoléon Bonaparte, who then conquered most of Europe before his defeat at Waterloo.

Reformation & Beyond

At the behest of Napoléon III, Baron Haussmann reshaped the cityscape. However, when Parisians heard of Napoléon III's capture in the war with Prussia in 1870, they demanded a republic. It gave rise to the glittering belle époque ('beautiful era'), which advanced arts and sciences.

Best Roman Legacies

Musée National du Moyen Âge Incorporates the remains of Gallo-Roman baths c AD 200. (p130)

Crypte Archéologique du Parvis Notre Dame Remains of the Gallo-Roman town of Lutetia. (p119)

Arènes de Lutèce Gladiatorial 2nd-century amphitheatre. (p138)

Best Medieval Milestones

Notre Dame Completed in the early 14th century. (p114)

Louvre Immense 12th-century fort-turned-palace-turned-museum. (p50)

Sainte-Chapelle Consecrated in 1248. (p122)

Panthéon (p136)

Sorbonne University founded in 1253. (p138)

Musée National du Moyen Âge Partly housed in the 15th-century Hôtel de Cluny. (p130)

Best Revolutionary Sights

Place de la Bastille Site of the former prison stormed on 14 July 1789, mobilising the Revolution. (p99)

Versailles The October 1789 March on Versailles forced the royal family to leave the château. (p167)

Place de la Concorde Louis XVI and his queen, Marie-Antoinette, were among thousands guillotined where the obelisk now stands. (p60)

Conciergerie Marie-Antoinette was one of the aristocrats tried and imprisoned here. (p122)

Parc du Champ de Mars This former military training ground was the site of revolutionary festivals. (p32)

Best Parisian History Attractions

Musée Carnavalet Chronicles the history of Paris. (p96)

Forum des Images Archive of films set in Paris, plus newsreels, documentaries and advertising. (p69)

Best Burial Places

Père Lachaise The world's most visited cemetery, with famous graves and time-honoured tomb traditions. (p109)

Cimetière du Montparnasse More famous graves, south of St-Germain des Prés. (p158)

Cimetière de Montmartre Yet more famous graves, west of Sacré-Cœur. (p79)

Les Catacombes Prowl the skull- and bone-packed tunnels of Paris' creepy ossuary. (p158)

Panthéon France's greatest thinkers are laid to rest in this immense mausoleum. (p136)

Best Parks & Gardens

If Paris' cafes are the city's communal lounge rooms, its parks, gardens and squares are its backyards. The larger parks are idyllic for strolling or simply soaking up the sunshine, with plenty of seating as well as kiosks and cafes, while small, secret gardens are tucked between historic stone buildings or even perched in the middle of the Seine.

Best Traditional Gardens

Jardin du Luxembourg Paris' most popular park. (p150)

Jardin des Tuileries Part of Paris' historic axis and as classical as it gets. (p60)

Versailles Designed by André Le Nôtre, the château's gardens are fit for a king. (p169)

Best Parks

Promenade Plantée The world's first elevated park, atop a disused railway viaduct. (p99)

Jardin des Plantes Paris' botanic gardens include peony and rose gardens, an alpine garden, greenhouses and more. (p136)

Parc des Buttes Chaumont Hilly, forested haven with grottoes, waterfalls, a lake and an island. (p87)

Place des Vosges Paris' prettiest square, ringed by cloisters, with a park at its centre. (p98)

Best Hidden Gems

Square du Vert Galant Romantically situated on the tip of the Île de la Cité.

Jardin de la Nouvelle France Enchanting little oasis between some of Paris' busiest boulevards. (p45)

Île aux Cygnes A tree-shaded walkway runs the length of the city's little-known third island. (p32)

MING TANG-EVAN / LONELY PLANET ©

Top Tips

- Opening hours vary seasonally – check closing times posted at park gates to avoid being locked in.
- Look out for *murs végétaux* (vertical gardens) popping up around the city, such as outside the Musée du Quai Branly (p31).
- Ecominded city initiatives will see Paris become even greener, with many open areas being created.

Best Of the Seine

La ligne de vie de Paris (the lifeline of Paris), the Seine, sluices through the city, spanned by 37 bridges. Its Unesco World Heritage–listed riverbanks offer picturesque promenades, parks, activities and events, including sandy summertime beaches. After dark, watch the river dance with the watery reflections of city lights and tourist-boat flood lamps. You are in Paris.

Riverbank Rejuvenation

The riverbanks have been reborn with the creation of Les Berges de Seine (p156). On the Right Bank, east of the Hôtel de Ville, 1.5km of former expressway now incorporates walkways and cycleways. Even more revolutionary is the completely car-free 2.3km stretch of the Left Bank from the Pont de l'Alma to the Musée d'Orsay, with sporting equipment, games, events and floating gardens on artificial islands.

Paris Plages

Palm trees, bars, cafes, sun lounges, parasols, water sprays and sand line the river from mid-July to mid-August during the 'Paris Beaches'.

Best River Cruises

Bateaux-Mouches (www.bateauxmouches.com; Port de la Conférence, 8e; ⌚Apr-Dec; adult/child €13.50/5.50; Ⓜ Alma Marceau) The largest river-cruise company in Paris and a favourite with tour groups. Cruises (70 minutes) run regularly from 10.15am to 11pm April to September and 13 times a day between 11am and 9pm the rest of the year. Commentary is in French and English. It's located on the Right Bank, just east of the Pont de l'Alma.

Vedettes de Paris (www.vedettesdeparis.fr; Port de Suffren, 7e; adult single/return €8/14) It might be a small company, but its one-hour sightseeing cruises on smaller boats are second to none. It runs themed cruises too, including imaginative 'Paris mystery' tours for kids and boats along the river to Notre Dame.

PAWEL LIBERA / GETTY IMAGES ©

Best Churches

Some of the city's most magnificent buildings are its churches and other places of worship. Not only exceptional architecturally and historically, they also contain exquisite art, artefacts and other priceless treasures. And best of all, entry to general areas within them is, in most cases, free.

Classical Concerts

Paris' beautiful, centuries-old stone churches have magnificent acoustics and provide a meditative backdrop for classical-music concerts. Posters outside churches advertise upcoming events with ticket information, or visit www.ampconcerts.com, where you can make online reservations. Tickets cost around €23 to €30.

Etiquette

Bear in mind that, although many of Paris' places of worship are also major tourist attractions, Parisians come here to pray and celebrate significant events on religious calendars as part of their daily lives. Be respectful: keep noise to a minimum, obey photography rules (check signs), dress appropriately and try to avoid key times (eg Mass) if you're sightseeing only.

Best Landmark Churches

Notre Dame The city's mighty Gothic cathedral is without equal. (p114)

Sacré-Cœur Paris' domed basilica lords over the city. (p74)

Église St-Sulpice Featured in *The Da Vinci Code,* with frescoes by Eugène Delacroix. (p156)

Église St-Germain des Prés Built in the 11th century, this is Paris' oldest church. (p156)

Best Churches for Classical Concerts

Sainte-Chapelle Concerts provide the perfect opportunity to appreciate Sainte-Chapelle's beauty. (p122)

Église de la Madeleine Renowned for its monumental organ. (p60)

Église St-Eustache Concerts have long been a tradition at this beautiful central church. (p61)

Best Non-Christian Places of Worship

Mosquée de Paris Paris' 1920s art deco, Moorish tiled mosque has a wonderful tearoom and *hammam* (steambath). (p137)

Guimard Synagogue Art nouveau synagogue. (p99)

Best Panoramas

Paris is a photographer's dream. In addition to close-up shots of local street life, there are spectacular vantage points where you can snap vistas of the city – from the top of monuments, on hilltops, in vast squares and on bridges. Even without a camera, the views are unforgettable. Stroll around and you'll find your own favourite panoramas of Paris.

Best Buildings with a View

Eiffel Tower Not only the city's most iconic building but also its highest. (p24)

Tour Montparnasse The saving grace of this otherwise-hideous high-rise is its panoramic observation deck. (p158)

Arc de Triomphe Climb to the top for the best views along Paris' historic axis. (p38)

Centre Pompidou Captivating views of Paris, including the Eiffel Tower. (p90)

Galeries Lafayette Incredible views of Paris unfold from this department store's rooftop – and they're free! (p70)

Le Printemps This magnificent department store also has mesmerising rooftop views for free. (p70)

Cité de l'Architecture et du Patrimoine Amazing Eiffel Tower views unfurl from the windows and terrace out front. (p42)

Best Open Spaces with a View

Île aux Cygnes Walk west to east along this artificial island for breathtaking Eiffel Tower views. (p32)

Promenade Plantée Get a bird's-eye view of local Parisian life three storeys up along this elevated park. (p99)

DAN HERRICK /GETTY IMAGES ©

Top Tips

▶ For transport with a view, hop on a Batobus (p208) or regular bus. Scenic bus routes include lines 21 and 27 (Opéra–Panthéon), line 29 (Opéra–Gare de Lyon), line 47 (Centre Pompidou–Gobelins), line 63 (Musée d'Orsay–Trocadéro), line 73 (Concorde–Arc de Triomphe) and line 82 (Montparnasse–Eiffel Tower).

Best **Eating**

France pioneered what is still the most influential style of cooking in the Western world and Paris is its showcase *par excellence*. Colours, textures and garnishes are impeccably arranged everywhere from simple restaurants to *haute cuisine* establishments helmed by legendary chefs. The city doesn't have its own 'local' cuisine but is the crossroads for France's regional produce and flavours.

Evolving Trends

In addition to classical French fare, look out for cuisines from around the globe. Neobistros offer some of Paris' most exciting dining options. Generally small and relatively informal, they're run by young, talented chefs who aren't afraid to experiment. Exclusively vegetarian establishments are emerging but still rare.

Dining Times

Breakfast (usually a baguette with butter and jam, and strong coffee) is seen as a mere precursor to lunch, the traditional main meal, starting around 12.30pm. Most restaurants open for dinner around 7pm or 7.30pm. Some high-end restaurants close at weekends, and many places close in August.

Menus

Eateries usually serve a *plat du jour* (dish of the day) at lunch (and occasionally at dinner), as well as *menus* (fixed-price meals) of an *entrée* (starter), *plat* (main course) and *fromage* (cheese) or dessert or both. These offer infinitely better value than ordering à la carte. Meals are often considerably cheaper at lunch than dinner.

CARLOS SANCHEZ PEREYRA / GETTY IMAGES ©

☑ Top Tips

- Tap water is safe and free of charge; ask for *une carafe de l'eau* (jug of water).
- Doggie bags/boxes of leftovers aren't 'done', as the dining experience and the food are considered inseparable.
- Booking ahead (up to a couple of months) for popular and/or high-end places – is recommended.

Best Bistros

Le 6 Paul Bert Dazzling dishes that change daily. (p101)

Le Pantruche Superb, great-value modern French cuisine. (p80)

Fresh baguettes

Bones Signature small plates or stunning multicourse menus in stripped-back surrounds. (p102)

Frenchie Hidden alleyway bistro serving sensational *menus*. (p63)

Le Miroir Stylish, creative bistro fare. (p85)

Best Gastronomic Extravaganzas

Restaurant David Toutain Mind-blowing mystery degustation menus. (p32)

Yam'Tcha Exquisitely fused French and Asian flavours, paired with teas. (p65)

La Tour d'Argent Centuries-old establishment overlooking Notre Dame serving signature pressed duck. (p139)

Best Picnic Fare

JSFP Traiteur Salads, terrines, pâté and amazing quiches. (p159)

CheZaline Baguettes filled with seasonal ingredients. (p104)

Choux d'Enfer Sweet and savoury *choux* (pastry puffs) by Alain Ducasse and Christophe Michalak. (p33)

Worth a Trip

Hugo Desnoyer (☎01 46 47 83 00; www.hugodesnoyer.fr; 28 rue du Docteur Blanche, 16e; menu €50, mains €16-32; ⏰7am-8pm Tue-Fri, 7am-7.30pm Sat; Ⓜ Jasmin) is Paris' most famous butcher. Settle down to a *table d'hôte* feast of homemade terrines, quiches, foie gras and cold cuts followed by premium meat at his shop in the 16e.

Best Markets

Nowhere encapsulates Paris' village atmosphere more than its markets. Not simply places to shop, the city's street markets are also social gatherings for the entire neighbourhood. Residents toting quintessentially Parisian canvas shopping bags on wheels chat with neighbours, fellow shoppers and stallholders and pick up culinary tips. Flea markets are full of antique, vintage and new treasures.

Street Markets

Nearly every little quarter has its own street market, held at least once a week, where tarpaulin-topped trestle tables bow beneath spit-roasted poultry, seafood on beds of crushed ice, meat, cheeses, sun-ripened fruit and vegetables, and pâtés, preserves and other delicacies. Many markets also sell clothes, accessories, homewares and more. *Marchés biologiques* (organic markets) are also sprouting up across Paris.

Flea Markets

Exquisite antiques, vintage and retro clothing, jewellery, bric-a-brac, cheap brand-name clothing, footwear, African carvings, DVDs and electronic items are laid out at the city's colourful flea markets. Watch out for pickpockets! Just north of Montmartre, Marché aux Puces de St-Ouen (www.marcheauxpuces-saintouen.com) has more than 2500 stalls.

MING TANG-EVANS / LONELY PLANET ©

☑ Top Tips

- No street markets take place on Monday.
- The website www.paris.fr lists every market by *arrondissement*, including speciality markets.

Best Markets

Marché Bastille One of the city's largest, liveliest street markets laden with quality produce. (p103)

Marché aux Enfants Rouges Paris' oldest covered market, with communal tables for lunch. (p93)

Marché aux Puces d'Aligre Central flea market adjoining the wonderfully chaotic Marché d'Aligre. (p102)

Best For Kids

Parisians adore *les enfants* (children) and welcome them with open arms just about everywhere. You'll notice French kids are generally quiet and polite, and you'll be expected to make sure yours are, too. But kids can still burn off plenty of energy: central Paris' residential design means you'll find playground equipment in parks and squares throughout the city.

Dining with Kids

Many restaurants accept little diners (confirm ahead). Children's menus aren't widespread, however, and most restaurants don't have highchairs. In fine weather, pick up sandwiches and crêpes from a street stall or pack a market-fresh picnic and head to the city's parks and gardens.

Accommodating Kids

Parisian buildings' limited space often means premium-priced family-size accommodation – apartments may be more economical. Check availability and costs for a *lit bébé* (cot).

Amusement Parks

Just outside central Paris are several amusement parks. The most high-profile is Disneyland Resort Paris (www.disneylandparis.com); French alternatives include Parc Astérix (www.parcasterix.fr) and, for tots, the adorable Jardin d'Acclimatation (www.jardindacclimatation.fr).

Best Attractions for Kids

Le Grand Rex Kids can become movie stars on entertaining behind-the-scenes tours. (p69)

Aquarium de Paris Cinéaqua Shark tank! (p44)

ESCUDERO PATRICK / GETTY IMAGES ©

☑ Top Tips

▶ Children under four travel free on public transport and generally receive free admission to sights. Discounts vary for older kids (aged up to 18) – anything from a euro off to free.

▶ Be extra vigilant crossing roads as Parisian drivers frequently ignore green pedestrian lights.

Jardin du Luxembourg Pony rides, puppet shows and more. (p150)

Vedettes de Paris Special 'Paris Mystery' Seine cruises for kids. (p185)

Best Drinking

For Parisians, drinking and eating go together like wine and cheese, and the line between a cafe, *salon de thé* (tearoom), bistro, brasserie, bar and even a *bar à vins* (wine bar) is blurred, while the line between drinking and clubbing is often nonexistent – a cafe that's quiet mid-afternoon might have DJ sets in the evening and dancing later on.

Cafe Culture

Paris' cafes have long been the city's communal lounge rooms: places to meet friends, read, write, philosophise, flirt and fall in - and out of - love.

Coffee

If you order *un café* (a coffee), you'll be served a single shot of espresso. A *café allonge* is lengthened with hot water, a *café au lait* comes with milk and a *café crème*, lengthened with steamed milk, is the closest to a latte. The city is in the throes of a coffee revolution, with local roasteries like Belleville Brûlerie and Coutume priming cafes citywide for outstanding brews made by professional baristas, often using cutting-edge extraction techniques.

Wine

Wine is easily the most popular beverage in Paris and house wine invariably costs less than bottled water. *Les vins naturels* (natural wines) contain little or no sulphites.

Cocktails

Cocktail bars are undergoing a resurgence.

MING TANG-EVANS / LONELY PLANET ©

Top Tips

- Many establishments have a tiered pricing structure, with coveted terrace seats more expensive than perching at the counter.
- Most places serve at least small plates; it's normally fine to order coffee/alcohol if you're not dining.
- The French rarely go drunk-wild and tend to frown upon it.

Best Neighbourhood Cafes

Le Pure Café Still as quintessentially Parisian as Ethan Hawke's character found it in *Before Sunset*. (p104)

Le Baron Rouge (p102)

La Fée Verte Absinthe specialist. (p105)

Le Progrès Montmartre local. (p83)

Best Coffee

Coutume Artisan roasters of premium beans, with a fab flagship cafe. (p34)

La Caféothèque Maze of a coffee house with serious tasting notes and seating made for lounging all day. (p106)

Lockwood Belleville-roasted beans. (p68)

Telescope It may be small, but it packs a punch. (p68)

Best Wine Bars

Le Baron Rouge Wonderfully convivial barrel-filled spot. (p102)

Taverne Henri IV Island-set stalwart serving cheese and charcuterie. (p126)

Au Sauvignon With an original zinc bar. (p162)

Le Garde Robe Excellent, affordable natural wines. (p67)

Best Cocktail Bars

Harry's New York Bar Knockout cocktails from the inventor of the Bloody Mary. (p67)

Le Mary Céleste Ultrafashionable Marais cocktail bar. (p93)

Experimental Cocktail Club Fabulous cocktails in a setting that exudes spirit and soul. (p68)

Best
Nights Out

From sipping cocktails in swanky bars to carving up cutting-edge clubs, rocking to live bands, being awed by operas, ballets and classical concerts, entertained by films, dazzled by cabarets; intrigued by avant-garde theatre productions or listening to smooth jazz or stirring *chansons*, a night out in Paris promises to be a night to remember.

Nightclubs

Paris' residential make-up means clubs aren't ubiquitous. Still, electronica, laced with funk and groove, remains its strong suit. DJs tend to have short stints in venues – check www.tribudenuit.com. Salsa and Latino also maintain a huge following. Admission to clubs is free to around €20.

Jazz, Chansons & Cabarets

Paris has some fantastic venues for jazz and *chansons* (heartfelt, lyric-driven music typified by Édith Piaf). Tickets to major cabaret spectacles start from around €90 (€130 with lunch, €150 with dinner) and usually include a half-bottle of Champagne.

Opera, Ballet, Theatre & Classical Music

France's Opéra National de Paris and Ballet de l'Opéra National de Paris perform at the Palais Garnier and Opéra Bastille opera houses. Virtually all theatre productions are in French but sometimes have English-language subtitles.

Cinema

Pariscope and *L'Officiel des Spectacles* (at newsstands on Wednesday) list screening times. Tickets cost around €11 for adults (€13 for 3D). Foreign films screened in their original language with French subtitles are labelled 'VO' *(version originale)*; films labelled 'VF' *(version française)* are dubbed in French.

RUSM / GETTY IMAGES ©

☑ Top Tips

- Paris Nightlife (www.paris-nightlife.fr) is an all-encompassing listings site.
- On the day of a performance, tickets are often available at half price (plus commission of about €3) at Kiosque Théâtre Madeleine (p69).
- Fnac (www.fnac.fr) sells a wide range of entertainment and sport tickets.

Best Nightclubs

Point Éphémère Edgy club and performance venue booking exceptional emerging and established DJs, artists and bands. Ubercool. (p87)

Moulin Rouge (p85)

Rex Club Paris' first dedicated techno club is still cutting edge and has a phenomenal sound system. (p68)

Social Club Subterranean nightclub with superb DJs and live bands. (p67)

Le Nouveau Casino Intimate concerts and top DJs play electro, pop, deep house and rock. (p87)

Best Jazz Clubs

Café Universel Brilliant array of live jazz and blues concerts. (p142)

Le Caveau de la Huchette Always entertaining medieval-cellar venue. (p142)

Best Cabarets

Moulin Rouge The home of the can-can is touristy but spectacular all the same. (p85)

Au Lapin Agile Historic and authentic, in the heart of Montmartre. (p77)

Worth a Trip

An abandoned railway station east of Bastille has been transformed into the alternative club **La Flèche d'Or** (www.flechedor.fr; 102bis rue de Bagnolet, 20e; vary; M Alexandre Dumas or Gambetta), hosting some of the hottest DJs and live musicians (especially reggae and rock) in town.

Best Gay & Lesbian Paris

There's less of a defined gay and lesbian 'scene' here than in other cities where it's more underground. While Le Marais – particularly around the intersection of rues Ste-Croix de la Bretonnerie and des Archives – is the mainstay of gay and lesbian nightlife, venues throughout the city attract a mixed crowd.

Background

Paris was the first-ever European capital to vote in an openly gay mayor when Bertrand Delanoë was elected in 2001, and the city itself is very open – same-sex couples commonly display affection in public and checking into a hotel room is unlikely to raise eyebrows. In 2013, France became the 13th country in the world to allow same-sex marriage (and adoption by same-sex couples). Typically, at least one partner needs to be a resident to get married here.

Festivities

Gay pride peaks during late June's Gay Pride March (www.gaypride.fr, in French), with over-the-top floats and festivities.

STEVE ALLEN / GETTY IMAGES ©

Top Tips

Useful resources:

- Centre Gai et Lesbien de Paris Île de France (www.cglparis.org)
- Paris-Gay.com (www.paris-gay.com)

Best Gay & Lesbian Bars

Le Tango Mingle with a cosmopolitan gay and lesbian set in a historic 1930s dancehall. (p105)

Open Café The wide terrace is prime for talent-watching. (p106)

3w Kafé Flagship cocktail bar-pub on a street with several lesbian bars. (p106)

Quetzal Perennial favourite; cruisy at all hours. (p106)

Best For Free

Paris' national museums offer free entry on the first Sunday of the month (some during certain months only), and permanent exhibits at city museums are free (temporary exhibitions incur a charge). A handful of Paris' national monuments also have free entry on the first Sunday of the month (also some in certain months only), including those listed below.

Walking in Paris for Free

Paris is an eminently walkable city, with beautiful parks and gardens, awe-inspiring architecture, markets, buskers' performances and fashion boutiques (well, window shopping never goes out of style) to check out along the way. For a free walking tour, contact Paris Greeters (p201) for a personalised excursion led by a resident volunteer.

Cycling in Paris (Almost) for Free

If you'd rather free-wheel around Paris, the Vélib' (p208) system costs next to nothing for a day's subscription, and the first 30 minutes of each bike rental is free.

MATT MUNRO / LONELY PLANET ©

Best Free Sights

Louvre Free entry on the first Sunday of the month October to March. (p50)

Arc de Triomphe Free entry to the top on the first Sunday of the month November to March. (p38)

Notre Dame Free entry to the towers on the first Sunday of the month November to March. (p114)

Versailles Free château entry on the first Sunday of the month November to March. (p167)

Père Lachaise This vast celebrity-filled cemetery is free to wander around (p109)

Maison Européenne de la Photographie Free from 5pm every Wednesday year round. (p96)

Best Fashion

Home to iconic labels like Chanel and Dior, Paris' can claim fashion as its forte. Yet, although its well-groomed residents mean the city can look and feel like a giant catwalk, fashion here is about style and quality rather than status or brand names. Most shops close at least one or two days a week, usually Sunday and Monday.

Fashion Districts

Shopping opportunities exist throughout the city, but certain neighbourhoods have especially concentrated options. Look for luxury flagship stores in the Triangle d'Or (Golden Triangle; bordered by avenues Georges V, Champs-Élysées and Montaigne) and St-Germain des Prés. The increasingly hip haut Marais and Canal St-Martin are fertile grounds for experimental designers.

Arcades & Department Stores

Paris' **covered passages** are treasure chests of exquisite boutiques, while the city's *grands magasins* (department stores) sell high-quality wares.

Speciality Shops

What sets Paris apart is its incredible array of speciality shops dedicated to individual items such as hats, gloves, handbags, umbrellas, stockings and tights, and chic children's wear.

Fashion Shows

Haute couture (high fashion) and *prêt-à-porter* (ready-to-wear) fashion-show tickets are like hen's teeth, even among fashion media. For some catwalk action, reserve ahead to attend free weekly fashion shows at Galeries Lafayette.

☑ Top Tips

- Paris' *soldes* (sales) generally take place over five weeks, starting in mid-January and again in mid-June.

Best Department Stores

Galeries Lafayette Quality men's, women's and kids' clothing. (p70)

Le Printemps Grand department store. (p70)

Le Bon Marché Incorporates a stellar array of designers. (p153)

Best Fashion Boutiques

La Citadelle Multidesigner Montmartre shop with some real finds. (p85)

Galeries Lafayette (p70)

La Boutique Extraordinaire Exquisite, hand-knitted garments. (p93)

Shine Stocks a discerning selection of up-and-coming designers' clothing. (p93)

Surface to Air Edgy, up-to-the-minute clothing. (p93)

Best Accessories

A La Recherche De Jane Handmade men's and women's hats. (p165)

Pauline Pin Super-soft, super-stylish handbags made in Le Marais. (p93)

Alexandra Sojfer Handcrafted umbrellas. (p153)

Best Secondhand, Vintage & Discount Boutiques

Didier Ludot Couture creations of yesteryear. (p70)

L'Habilleur Discount designer wear. (p93)

Frivoli Brand-name cast-offs by the Canal St-Martin. (p87)

Kiliwatch New and used streetwear; vintage hats and boots. (p71)

Best Concept Stores

Gab & Jo The country's first-ever concept store stocking only made-in-France items including homewares and more. (p71)

Merci Multilevel store with profits donated to charity. (p92)

Worth a Trip

For previous seasons' collections, surpluses and seconds by name-brand designers such as Sonia Rykiel, save money at discounted outlet stores along **rue d'Alésia**, 14e, particularly west of the Alésia metro station between av de Maine and rue Raymond-Losserand. Shops here pop up regularly and close just as often, so you can never be sure what you'll find.

Best **Multicultural Paris**

Paris might be the bastion of French culture, but these days that definition incorporates myriad nationalities who call this cosmopolitan city home. Throughout the capital you'll find vibrant hubs of cultural life that make up *mondial* (multicultural) Paris. Visiting grocery stores, delis, markets, shops and places of worship as you explore the city offers a mini world tour.

Multicultural Background

Waves of immigration over the centuries, including a large number of immigrants from France's former colonies since the middle of last century, have given rise to an exhilarating mix of ethnicities, cuisines and the arts – and to debates like the 2004 ban at state-run schools on Muslim headscarves (and all other religious symbols, such as crucifixes) in favour of secularism, and the controversial 2011 ban on women wearing burqas in public (France was the first European country to impose one). Under French law, censuses can't ask questions about ethnicity or religion, but they do collect country-of-birth statistics, which confirm Paris as one of the most multicultural cities in Europe.

IMAGES ETC LTD / GETTY IMAGES ©

Best Mondial Museums

Musée du Quai Branly Indigenous art, artefacts, music and more from every continent bar Europe. (p31)

Institut du Monde Arabe Arabian arts are displayed in stunning surrounds; also hosts concerts and film screenings. (p136)

Musée Guimet des Arts Asiatiques Exceptional collection of Asian art and artefacts. (p42)

Louvre Antiquities from Greece and Egypt and other extraordinary global treasures. (p50)

La Pinacothèque Look out for *mondial* exhibitions at Paris' top private museum. (p62)

Best Tours

Paris Greeters (www.parisgreeters.fr; by donation) See Paris through local eyes with these two- to three-hour city tours. Volunteers lead groups (up to a maximum of six people) to their favourite spots in the city. Minimum two weeks' notice needed.

THATLou (☎06 86 13 32 12; www.thatlou.com; per person excluding admission fees Louvre/d'Orsay €25/35) Treasure hunts in English or French for groups of two people or more in the Louvre, Musée d'Orsay (THATd'Or) and streets of the Latin Quarter (THATrue). Participants form teams and play alone or against another team, and have to photograph themselves in front of 20 to 30 works of art ('treasure'). Hunts usually last up to two hours.

Paris Walks (☎01 48 09 21 40; www.paris-walks.com; adult/child €12/8) Engaging and informative walking tours in English focusing on various quarters or themes (art, fashion, chocolate, the French Revolution etc).

Fat Tire Bike Tours (☎01 56 58 10 54; www.fattirebiketours.com; 24 rue Edgar Faure; M La Motte Picquet Grenelle) Popular day- and night-time city tours. Bike tours start from €30. Ask about entertaining 'segway' tours on gyroscopic two-wheeled contraptions.

Canauxrama (www.canauxrama.com; adult/student & senior/4-12yr €16/12/8.50) Barges travel between Port de Plaisance de Paris–Arsenal, 12e, and Bassin de la Villette, 19e, (and vice versa) along Canals St-Martin and l'Ourcq, including an illuminated underground section, taking 2½ hours one way. Discounted online bookings.

NICOLAS MCCOMBER / GETTY IMAGES ©

Meeting the French (www.meetingthefrench.fr) Make-up workshops, backstage cabaret tours, fashion-designer showroom visits, French table decoration or embroidery classes, market tours, and baking with a Parisian baker are among these unique tours and behind-the-scenes experiences.

L'Open Tour (www.parisopentour.com; one-day pass adult/child €31/16) Whirlwind hop-on, hop-off city tours aboard open-deck buses, with four different circuits and 50 stops.

Best
Cooking & Wine-Tasting Courses

If dining in the city's restaurants whets your appetite, Paris has stacks of cookery schools offering courses for all budgets and levels of ability. Where there's food in Paris, wine is never more than an arm's length away; plenty of places offer wine tastings and instruction for beginners through to connoisseurs.

Best Culinary Classes

Cook'n With Class (www.cooknwithclass.com) Nine international chefs, small classes and a Montmartre location.

École Le Cordon Bleu (www.cordonbleu.edu) One of the world's foremost culinary-arts schools.

La Cuisine Paris (http://lacuisineparis.com) A variety of courses from bread, croissants and *macarons* to market classes and 'foodie walks'.

Le Foodist (www.lefoodist.com) Cooking classes, wine pairings and hosted dinners in the Latin Quarter.

Best Wine-Appreciation Sessions

Ô Château (www.o-chateau.com; 68 rue Jean-Jacques Rousseau, 1er) Wine aficionados can thank this young, fun, cosmopolitan *bar à vins* for bringing affordable tasting to Paris. Sign up in advance for an intro to French wine (€30) or a guided cellar tasting in English over lunch (€75) or dinner (€100).

Musée du Vin (www.museeduvinparis.com; 5 sq Charles Dickens, 16e; 10am-6pm Tue-Sun) In addition to its displays, Paris' wine museum offers instructive tastings (€63 for two hours).

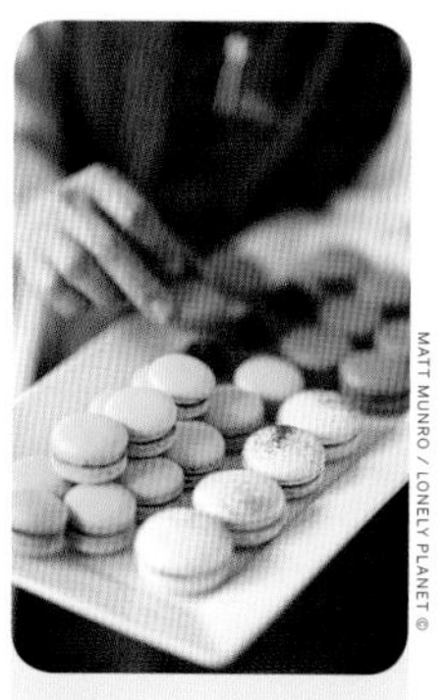

MATT MUNRO / LONELY PLANET ©

☑ Top Tips

▶ Even if you're only here on a lightning-quick trip, there are plenty of short-course options, but book well ahead.

▶ Cooking schools and wine-tasting establishments often run classes in English or offer at least some level of translation – check when you book.

Survival Guide

Survival Guide

Before You Go

When to Go

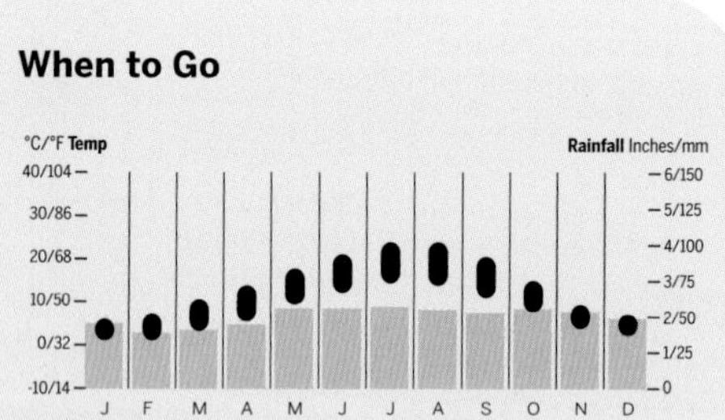

➡ Winter (Nov–Feb) Cold and dark, occasional snow. Museums are quieter and accommodation prices are lower.

➡ Spring (Mar–May) Mild, sometimes wet. Major sights start getting busier; parks and gardens begin to come into their own.

➡ Summer (Jun–Aug) Warm to hot, generally sunny. Main tourist season. Some businesses close for August.

➡ Autumn (Sep–Nov) Mild, generally sunny. Cultural life moving into top gear after the summer lull.

Book Your Stay

☑ **Top Tip** Accommodation outside central Paris is marginally cheaper than within the city itself, but it's almost always a false economy, as travelling into the city consumes time and money. Choose somewhere within Paris' 20 *arrondissements* (city districts), where you can experience Parisian life from the moment you step out the door.

➡ Paris' accommodation is often *complet* (full) well in advance. Reservations are recommended any time of year and are essential during the warmer months (April to October) and all public and school holidays.

➡ Even the best Paris hotel rooms tend to be small. Cheaper hotels may not have lifts (elevators); air conditioning is rare.

➡ Paris levies a *taxe de séjour* (tourist tax) of €0.20 up to €1.50 per person per night (normally added to your bill).

➡ Breakfast is rarely included; cafes often offer better value.

➡ To live like a Parisian, consider renting a short-stay apartment, for example through Airbnb (www.airbnb.com).

Useful Websites

Lonely Planet (www.lonelyplanet.com/france/paris/hotels) Reviews of Lonely Planet's top choices.

Paris Hotel Service (www.parishotelservice.com) Boutique hotel gems.

Paris Hotel (www.hotels-paris.fr) Well-organised hotel booking site with lots of user reviews.

Guest Apartment Services (www.guestapartment.com) Romantic apartment rentals on and around Paris' islands.

Room Sélection (www.room-selection.com) Select apartment rentals centred on Le Marais.

Paris Attitude (www.parisattitude.com) Thousands of apartment rentals, professional service, reasonable fees.

Best Budget

Cosmos Hôtel (www.cosmos-hotel-paris.com) Brilliant value, footsteps from Le Marais' nightlife.

Hôtel du Nord – Le Pari Vélo (www.hoteldunord-leparivelo.com) Bric-a-brac charm and bike hire.

Mama Shelter (www.mamashelter.com) Philippe Starck–designed hipster haven with a cool in-house pizzeria.

Hôtel St-André des Arts (01 43 26 96 16) Great St-Germain location without the price tag.

St Christopher's (www.st-christophers.co.uk/paris-hostels) Modern hostel amenities in two convenient locations.

BVJ Monceau (www.bvjhotel.com) Brand new hostel in a former *hôtel particulier* (private mansion) steps from the Champs Élysées.

Best Midrange

Edgar (www.edgarparis.com) Twelve individually themed rooms, each by a different artist or designer.

Hôtel Emile (www.hotel-emile.com) Breathtaking rooftop views steal hearts at this Marais trendsetter.

Le Citizen Hotel (www.lecitizenhotel.com) Modern and tech-savvy, with a minimalist design.

Hôtel Jeanne d'Arc (www.hoteljeannedarc.com) Like a family home in a quiet Marais backstreet.

Hôtel Amour (www.hotelamourparis.fr) Stylish romantic getaway.

Best Top End

L'Hôtel (www.l-hotel.com) The stuff of romance, Parisian myths and urban legends.

Hôtel Fabric (www.hotelfabric.com) Stylish ode to the 19th-century textile industry in the Oberkampf area.

Hôtel Molitor (www.mltr.fr) Stunningly restored art deco swimming pool with gallery-style poolside rooms.

Hotel Crayon (www.hotelcrayon.com) Line drawings, retro furnishings and coloured-glass shower doors.

➡ **Le Pradey** (www.lepradey.com) The last word in luxury hotel design.

Arriving in Paris

☑ **Top Tip** For the best way to get to your accommodation, see p17.

Charles de Gaulle

Paris' largest international airport, **Aéroport de Charles de Gaulle** (CDG; www.aeroportsdeparis.fr), commonly called 'Roissy' in French after the suburb in which it's located, is 28km northeast of central Paris. Its terminals are linked by free CDGVAL shuttle trains – check www.easycdg.com for info.

Train

Terminals T2 and T3 are served by the RER B line (€9.50, approx 50 minutes, every 10 to 15 minutes), which connects with the Gare du Nord, Châtelet–Les Halles and St-Michel–Notre Dame stations in the city centre. Trains run from 5am to 11pm; there are fewer trains on weekends. Follow the signs 'Paris by Train'.

Bus

There are six bus lines.

Les Cars Air France line 2 (€17, 1¼ hours, every 20 minutes, 6am to 11pm) Links the airport with the Arc de Triomphe. Children aged two to 11 years pay half price.

Les Cars Air France line 4 (€17.50, every 30 minutes, 6am to 10pm from CDG, 6am to 9.30pm from Paris) Links the airport with Gare de Lyon (50 minutes) in eastern Paris and Gare Montparnasse (55 minutes) in southern Paris. Children aged two to 11 years pay half price.

Roissybus (€10.50, 45 to 60 minutes, every 15 minutes, 5.30am to 11pm) Links the airport with Opéra.

RATP bus 350 (€5.70, 50 minutes, every 30 minutes, 5.30am to 11pm) Links the airport with Gare de l'Est in northern Paris.

RATP bus 351 (€5.70, 60 minutes, every 30 minutes, 5.30am to 11pm) Links the airport with place de la Nation in eastern Paris.

Noctilien bus 140 & 143 (€7.60 or four metro tickets, hourly, 12.30am to 5.30pm) Part of the RATP night service, Noctilien has two buses that go to CDG: bus 140 from Gare de l'Est, and 143 from Gare de l'Est and Gare du Nord.

Taxi

A taxi to the city centre takes 40 minutes. During the day pay around €50; the fare increases 15% between 5pm and 10am and on Sundays. Only take taxis at a clearly marked rank. Never follow anyone who approaches you at the airport and claims to be a driver.

Orly

Located 19km south of central Paris, **Aéroport d'Orly** (ORY; ☎01 70 36 39 50; www.aeroportsdeparis.fr) is closer than CDG. However, it's not as frequently used by international airlines, and public transportation options aren't quite as straightforward.

➡ **Train** There is no direct train to/from Orly; you'll need to change halfway.

RER B (€10.90; 35 minutes, every four to 12 minutes) This line connects Orly with the St-Michel–Notre Dame, Châtelet–Les Halles and Gare du Nord stations in the city centre. In order to get from Orly to the

RER station (Antony), you must first take the Orlyval automatic train. The service runs from 6am to 11pm (fewer on weekends). You only need one ticket to take the two trains.

Bus

Air France bus 1 (€12.50, one hour, every 20 minutes 5am to 10.20pm from Orly, 6am to 11.20pm from Invalides) This bus runs to/from the Gare Montparnasse (35 minutes) in southern Paris, Invalides in the 7e, and the Arc de Triomphe. Children aged two to 11 years pay half price.

Orlybus (€7.50, 30 minutes, every 15 minutes, 6am to 11.20pm from Orly, 5.35am to 11.05pm from Paris) This bus runs to/from the metro station Denfert Rochereau in southern Paris, making several stops en route.

Tram

Tramway T7 (€1.70, every six minutes, 40 minutes, 5.30am to 12.30am Monday to Saturday, 6.30am to 12.30am Sunday) Links Orly with Villejuif-Louis Aragon metro station in southern Paris; buy tickets from the machine at the tram stop as no tickets are sold on board.

Taxi

➡ A taxi to the city centre takes roughly 30 minutes. During the day, pay between €40 and €55; the fare increases by 15% between 5pm and 10am and on Sundays.

Beauvais

➡ Located 75km north of Paris, the **Aéroport de Beauvais** (BVA; ☎08 92 68 20 66; www.aeroportbeauvais.com) is served by a few low-cost flights. Before you snap up that bargain, consider if the post-arrival journey is worth it.

➡ The Beauvais shuttle (€17, 1¼ hours) links the airport with metro station Porte de Maillot. See the airport website for details and tickets.

Gare du Nord

➡ The highly civilised **Eurostar** (www.eurostar.com) whisks you between Paris' Gare du Nord and London's St Pancras Station in around 2¼ hours. Through-ticketing is available to/from many regional UK stations.

➡ For connections from Paris' Gare du Nord to Brussels–Midi, Amsterdam CS and Cologne's Hauptbahnhof, see **Thalys** (www.thalys.com).

Other Mainline Train Stations

➡ Paris has five other stations for long-distance trains, each with its own metro station: Gare d'Austerlitz, Gare de l'Est, Gare de Lyon, Gare Montparnasse and Gare St-Lazare; the station used depends on the direction from Paris.

➡ Contact **Voyages SNCF** (www.voyages-sncf.com) for connections throughout France and continental Europe.

Gare Routière Internationale de Paris–Galliéni

➡ The city's international bus terminal, **The Gare Routière Internationale de Paris–Galliéni** (☎08 92 89 90 91; 28 av du Général de Gaulle; **M** Galliéni), is in the inner suburb of Bagnolet.

➡ Services throughout Europe are provided by **Eurolines** (☎08 92 89 90 91; www.eurolines.eu).

Getting Around

Bicycle

☑ **Best for...** sightseeing and exercise.

The **Vélib'** (http://en.velib.paris.fr) bike share scheme puts 20,000-odd bikes at the disposal of Parisians and visitors to get around the city. There are some 1800 stations throughout the city, each with anywhere from 20 to 70 bike stands. The bikes are accessible around the clock.

➡ To get a bike, you first need to purchase a one-/seven-day subscription (€1.70/8), either at the terminals found at docking stations or online.

➡ The terminals require a credit card with an embedded smartchip (even then, some foreign-chip-enabled credit cards don't work). Alternatively, purchase a subscription online.

➡ After you authorise a deposit (€150) to pay for the bike (should it go missing), you'll receive an ID number and PIN code and you're ready to go.

➡ Bikes are rented in 30-minute intervals: the first half-hour is free, the second is €2, the third and each additional half-hour are €4. If you return a bike before a half-hour is up and then take a new one, you will not be charged.

➡ If the station you want to return your bike to is full, log in to the terminal to get 15 minutes for free to find another station.

➡ Bikes are geared to cyclists aged 14 and over, and are fitted with gears, an antitheft lock with key, reflective strips and front and rear lights. Bring your own helmet (they are not required by law).

Boat

☑ **Best for...** scenery.

To combine Seine sightseeing with transportation, the **Batobus** (www.batobus.com; Port de Solférino, 7e; 10am-9.30pm Apr-Aug, to 7pm rest of year; 1-/2-day pass €16/18) is a handy hop-on, hop-off service stopping at eight key destinations: the Eiffel Tower, Musée d'Orsay, St-Germain des Prés, Notre Dame, Jardin des Plantes, Hôtel de Ville, the Louvre and the Champs-Élysées. Boats dock every 20 to 25 minutes.

Bus

☑ **Best for...** sightseeing, parents with prams/buggies and people with limited mobility.

➡ Frequent bus services run from around 5.30am to 8.30pm (some lines to 12.30am). The number of routes is reduced at night and on Sundays. Timetables and route information is available from Paris' transit authority, **RATP** (www.ratp.fr), which also runs the metro and RER.

➡ After the metro closes **Noctilien** (www.noctilien.fr) night buses operate; the website has information and maps. Routes cover most of the city; look for blue 'N' or 'Noctilien' signs at bus stops. Tickets cost the same as one metro/bus ticket for short journeys; longer journeys require two or more tickets.

Metro & RER

☑ **Best for...** general travel throughout Paris.

➡ Paris' underground network, run by the RATP, consists of two separate but linked systems: the metro and the RER suburban train line. The metro has 14 numbered lines; the RER has five main lines, designated A to E and then numbered, which pass through the city centre.

➡ Each metro line has a different colour, number and final destination. Signs in stations indicate the way to the platform for your line. The direction signs on each platform indicate the terminus. On lines that split into several branches, the terminus served by each train is indicated on the cars, and signs on each platform give the number of minutes until the next train.

➡ Signs marked *correspondance* (transfer) show how to reach connecting trains. At stations with many intersecting lines, such as Châtelet and Montparnasse Bienvenüe, the connection can take a long time.

➡ Each metro line has its own schedule, but trains usually start at around 5.30am, with the last train beginning its run between 12.35am and 1.15am (2.15am on Friday and Saturday).

Tickets & Passes

➡ The same **RATP** tickets are valid on the metro, RER (within the city limits, ie zone 1), buses, trams and the Montmartre funicular. A ticket – called **Le Ticket t+** – costs €1.70 (half-price for children aged four to nine years) if bought individually and €13.70 for adults for a *carnet* (book) of 10. Ticket windows accept most credit cards but machines don't accept all credit cards (even some chip-enabled cards).

➡ One ticket lets you travel between any two metro stations – no return journeys – for a period of 1½ hours, with unlimited transfers. A single ticket can be used to transfer between daytime buses and trams, but not from the metro to bus or vice versa.

➡ Keep your ticket until you exit the station or risk a fine.

➡ If you're staying in Paris for a week or more, ask at metro station offices about rechargeable **Navigo** (www.navigo.fr) passes.

Taxi

☑ **Best for...** travelling with luggage and for reaching destinations not located near public transport stops.

➡ You'll find taxi ranks near major intersections.

➡ The *prise en charge* (flagfall) is €2.50. Within the city limits, it costs €1 per kilometre for travel between 10am and 5pm Monday to Saturday (*Tarif A*; white light on meter). At night (5pm to 10am), on Sunday from 7am to midnight and in the inner suburbs the rate is €1.24 per kilometre (*Tarif B*; orange light on meter). Travel in the outer suburbs is at *Tarif C*, €1.50 per kilometre.

➡ There's a €3 surcharge for taking a fourth passenger, but drivers may refuse for insurance reasons. The first piece of baggage is free; additional pieces over 5kg cost €1 extra.

➡ Avoid 'freelance' – ie illegal – cabs.

➡ To order a taxi, call or reserve online with **Taxis G7** (☎3607; www.taxisg7.fr), **Taxis Bleus** (☎01 49 36 10 10; www.taxis-bleus.com) or **Alpha Taxis** (☎01 45 85 85 85; www.alphataxis.com).

Essential Information

Business Hours

☑ **Top Tip** Final entry to attractions such as monuments and museums is generally half an hour to an hour before official closing times.

Opening hours Fluctuate constantly; check ahead to be sure.

Closed The month of August (for many places).

Shops & businesses In general, closed on Sunday and often Monday; some also close for lunch (around 12.30pm to 2.30pm).

Large shops Often open until around 10pm once a week.

Banks Open from 9am to 1pm and 2pm to 5pm Monday to Friday, some Saturday mornings.

Restaurants Typically noon to 2pm and 7.30pm to 10.30pm.

Museums The majority close one day a week; some open late one night a week.

Discount Cards

☑ **Top Tip** Almost all museums and monuments in Paris have discounted tickets *(tarif réduit)* for students and seniors (generally over 60 years), provided you have a valid ID.

➡ If you plan on visiting a lot of museums, pick up a **Paris Museum Pass** (http://en.parismuseumpass.com) or a **Paris City Passport** (www.parisinfo.com); the latter also includes public transport and various extras. The passes get you into 60-odd venues in and around Paris, bypassing (or reducing) long ticket queues. Both passes are available from the Paris Convention & Visitors Bureau (p212).

➡ Mobilis and Paris Visite passes are valid on the metro, RER, SNCF's suburban lines, buses, night buses, trams and Montmartre funicular railway. No photo is needed, but write your card number on the ticket. Passes are sold at larger metro and RER stations, SNCF offices in Paris, and the airports.

➡ The Mobilis card allows unlimited travel for one day and costs €6.80 (two zones) to €16.10 (five zones). Buy it at any metro, RER or SNCF station in the Paris region. Depending on how many times you plan to hop on/off the metro in a day, a *carnet* might work out cheaper.

➡ Paris Visite allows unlimited travel as well as discounted entry to certain museums and other discounts and bonuses. The 'Paris+Suburbs+Airports' pass includes transport to/from the airports and costs €22.85/34.70/48.65/59.50 for one/two/three/five days. The cheaper 'Paris Centre' pass, valid for zones 1 to 3, costs €10.85/17.65/24.10/34.70 for one/two/three/five days. Children aged four to 11 years pay half price.

Electricity

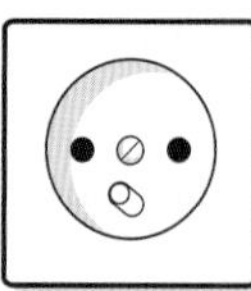

230V/50Hz

Emergency

Ambulance (SAMU; ☎15)

Fire (☎18)

Police (☎17)

EU-wide emergency (☎112)

Money

➡ France uses the euro (€). For updated exchange rates, check www.xe.com.

➡ Visa is the most widely accepted credit card, followed by MasterCard. American Express and Diners Club cards are accepted only at more exclusive establishments. Some restaurants don't accept credit cards.

➡ Many automated services, such as ticket machines, require a chip-and-PIN credit card. Ask your bank for advice before you leave.

Public Holidays

New Year's Day (Jour de l'An) 1 January

Easter Sunday (Pâques) Late March/April

Easter Monday (Lundi de Pâques) Late March/April

May Day (Fête du Travail) 1 May

Victory in Europe Day (Victoire 1945) 8 May

Ascension Thursday (L'Ascension) May (the 40th day after Easter)

Whit Monday (Lundi de Pentecôte) Mid-May to mid-June (seventh Monday after Easter)

Bastille Day (Fête Nationale) 14 July

Assumption Day (L'Assomption) 15 August

All Saints' Day (La Toussaint) 1 November

Armistice Day (Le Onze Novembre) 11 November

Christmas Day (Noël) 25 December

Money-Saving Tips

➡ Many museums are free on at least the first Sunday of the month.

➡ Consider investing in a transport and/or museum pass.

➡ Stock up on fresh food at the markets and food shops, then head to a park for a picnic.

➡ Short-stay apartments can work out to be considerably cheaper than a hotel room.

➡ The city has hundreds of wi-fi points offering two-hour sessions from 7am and 11pm at public spaces including parks, libraries and municipal buildings. Locations are mapped at www.paris.fr/wifi.

Safe Travel

➡ Pickpockets prey on busy places; *always* stay alert to the possibility of someone surreptitiously reaching for your pockets or bags.

➡ In an increasingly common ruse, scammers pretend to 'find' a gold ring (after subtly dropping it on the ground) then offer it to you as a diversionary tactic to pickpocket or demand money. Don't fall for it!

➡ Paris has a high incidence of beggars; if someone approaches you and you're not willing or able to give money, simply say '*désolé*' ('sorry').

Dos & Don'ts

➡ Greet or farewell anyone you interact with, such as shopkeepers, with '*Bonjour (bonsoir* at night)/*Au revoir*'.

➡ Particularly in smaller shops, staff may not appreciate you touching the merchandise until invited to do so.

➡ *Tu* and *vous* both mean 'you' but *tu* is used only with people you know very well, children or animals. Use *vous* until you're invited to use *tu*.

➡ You'll have an more rewarding experience if you address locals in French, even if all you say is '*Parlez-vous anglais*?' (Do you speak English?)

➡ The metro is safe to use until it closes, including for women travelling alone, but stations best avoided late at night include the long passageways of Châtelet–Les Halles and Montparnasse–Bienvenüe, as well as Château Rouge, Gare du Nord, Strasbourg St-Denis, Réaumur–Sébastopol and Stalingrad. *Bornes d'alarme* (alarm boxes) are located in the centre of each metro and RER platform and in some station corridors.

Telephone

➡ Check with your provider before you leave about roaming costs and/or ensure your phone's unlocked to use a French SIM card (available in Paris).

➡ France doesn't use separate area codes – you always dial the full 10-digit number. Drop the initial ☎0 if calling France from abroad.

➡ Country code ☎33

➡ International access code (from France) ☎00

Toilets

☑ **Top Tip** Take advantage of the toilets before you leave any monument or museum – they're well maintained and incur no extra charge.

➡ Public toilets in Paris are signed *toilettes* or WC.

➡ Self-cleaning cylindrical toilets on Parisian pavements are open 24 hours and are free of charge. Look for the words *libre* (available; green-coloured) or *occupé* (occupied; red-coloured).

➡ Cafe staff don't appreciate you using their facilities if you're not a paying customer (a coffee can be a good investment). Fast-food chains usually require door codes, which are printed on receipts. In older cafes and bars, you may find a *toilette à la turque* (Turkish-style toilet), the French term for a squat toilet.

➡ There are free public toilets in front of Notre Dame cathedral, near the Arc de Triomphe, east down the steps at Sacré-Cœur, at the northwestern entrance to the Jardin des Tuileries and in some metro stations.

➡ Other good bets are major department stores or big hotels.

Tourist Information

The main branch of the **Paris Convention & Visitors Bureau** (Office du Tourisme et des Congrès de Paris; Map p58; www.parisinfo.com; 27 rue des Pyramides, 1er; ⌚9am-7pm May-Oct, 10am-7pm Nov-Apr; Ⓜ Pyramides) is 500m northwest of the Louvre.

Elsewhere in Paris, the phone number and website is the same as for the main office.

Gare de l'Est Welcome Desk (place du 11 Novembre 1918, 10e; ⌚8am-7pm Mon-Sat; Ⓜ Gare de l'Est) Inside Gare de l'Est train station, facing platforms 1–2.

Gare de Lyon Welcome Desk (20 blvd Diderot, 12e; ⌚8am-6pm Mon-Sat; Ⓜ Gare de Lyon) Inside Gare de Lyon train station, facing platforms L–M.

Gare du Nord Welcome Desk (18 rue de Dunkerque, 10e; ⌚8am-6pm; Ⓜ Gare du Nord) Inside Gare du Nord station, under the glass roof of the Île de France departure and arrival area (eastern end of station).

Montmartre Welcome Desk (Map p78; opposite72 bd Rochechouart, 18e; ⌚10am-6pm; Ⓜ Anvers) At the foot of Montmartre.

Syndicate d'Initiative de Montmartre (Map p78; ☎01 42 62 21 21; www.montmartre-guide.com; 21 place du Tertre, 18e; ⌚10am-6pm; Ⓜ Abbesses) Locally run tourist office and shop on Montmartre's most picturesque square. It sells maps of Montmartre and organises tours daily at 2.30pm.

Travellers with Disabilities

➡ Paris' antiquated architecture, including much of the metro, means unfortunately that *fauteuil roulent* (wheelchair) access is severely limited, and ramps are rare. Newer hotels, museums and public facilities must (by law) provide access. Many restaurants have only partial access, and restaurant bathrooms may not accommodate wheelchairs or provide rails – ask when you book.

➡ The **Paris Convention & Visitors Bureau** (www.parisinfo.com; 27 rue des Pyramides, 1er; 9am-7pm May-Oct, 10am-7pm Nov-Apr) has excellent information for travellers with disabilities and impairments. For information about accessible cultural venues, surf **Accès Culture** (www.accesculture.org).

➡ Available from the **Syndicate des Transports d'Île de France** (☎08 10 64 64 64; www.stif-idf.fr), the *Guide Practique à l'Usage des Personnes à Mobilité Réduite* has details of wheelchair accessibility for all forms of public transport. Its info service, **Info Mobi** (www.infomobi.com), is especially useful.

Visas

➡ There are generally no entry requirements for nationals of EU countries. Citizens of Australia, the USA, Canada and New Zealand don't need visas to visit France for up to 90 days.

➡ Except for citizens of a handful of other European countries (including Switzerland), everyone, including South African citizens, needs a Schengen Visa, named for the Schengen Agreement that has abolished passport controls among 22 EU countries (with four more to follow) and has also been ratified by the non-EU governments of Iceland, Liechtenstein, Norway and Switzerland.

➡ Check www.france.diplomatie.fr for the latest visa regulations and your closest French embassy.

Language

The sounds used in spoken French can almost all be found in English. There are a couple of exceptions: nasal vowels (represented in our pronunciation guides by 'o' or 'u' followed by an almost inaudible nasal consonant sound 'm', 'n' or 'ng'), the 'funny' *u* sound ('ew' in our guides) and the deep-in-the-throat *r*. Bearing these few points in mind and reading our pronunciation guides below as if they were English, you'll be understood just fine. The markers (m) and (f) indicate the forms for male and female speakers respectively.

To enhance your trip with a phrasebook, visit **lonelyplanet.com**. Lonely Planet iPhone phrasebooks are available through the Apple App store.

Basics

Hello.
Bonjour. bon·zhoor

Goodbye.
Au revoir. o·rer·vwa

How are you?
Comment allez-vous? ko·mon ta·lay·voo

I'm fine, thanks.
Bien, merci. byun mair·see

Please.
S'il vous plaît. seel voo play

Thank you.
Merci. mair·see

Excuse me.
Excusez-moi. ek·skew·zay·mwa

Sorry.
Pardon. par·don

Yes./No.
Oui./Non. wee/non

I don't understand.
Je ne comprends pas. zher ner kom·pron pa

Do you speak English?
Parlez-vous anglais? par·lay·voo ong·glay

Eating & Drinking

..., please.
..., s'il vous plaît. ... seel voo play

A coffee	*un café*	un ka·fay
A table for two	*une table pour deux*	ewn ta·bler poor der
Two beers	*deux bières*	der bee·yair

I'm a vegetarian.
Je suis végétarien/végétarienne. (m/f) zher swee vay·zhay·ta·ryun/vay·zhay·ta·ryen

Cheers!
Santé! son·tay

That was delicious!
C'était délicieux! say·tay day·lee·syer

The bill, please.
L'addition, s'il vous plaît. la·dee·syon seel voo play

Shopping

I'd like to buy ...
Je voudrais acheter ... zher voo·dray ash·tay ...

I'm just looking.
Je regarde. zher rer·gard

How much is it?
C'est combien? say kom·byun

It's too expensive.
C'est trop cher. say tro shair

Can you lower the price?
Vous pouvez baisser le prix? voo poo·vay bay·say ler pree

Emergencies

Help!
Au secours! o skoor

Call the police!
Appelez la police! a·play la po·lees

Call a doctor!
Appelez un médecin! a·play un mayd·sun

I'm sick.
Je suis malade. zher swee ma·lad

I'm lost.
Je suis perdu/perdue. (m/f) zhe swee pair·dew

Where are the toilets?
Où sont les toilettes? oo son lay twa·let

Time & Numbers

What time is it?
Quelle heure est-il? kel er ay til

It's (eight) o'clock.
Il est (huit) heures. il ay (weet) er

It's half past (10).
Il est (dix) heures et demie. il ay (deez) er ay day·mee

morning	*matin*	ma·tun
afternoon	*après-midi*	a·pray·mee·dee
evening	*soir*	swar

yesterday	*hier*	yair
today	*aujourd'hui*	o·zhoor·dwee
tomorrow	*demain*	der·mun

Monday	*lundi*	lun·dee
Tuesday	*mardi*	mar·dee
Wednesday	*mercredi*	mair·krer·dee
Thursday	*jeudi*	zher·dee
Friday	*vendredi*	von·drer·dee
Saturday	*samedi*	sam·dee
Sunday	*dimanche*	dee·monsh

1	*un*	un
2	*deux*	der
3	*trois*	trwa
4	*quatre*	ka·trer
5	*cinq*	sungk
6	*six*	sees
7	*sept*	set
8	*huit*	weet
9	*neuf*	nerf
10	*dix*	dees
100	*cent*	son
1000	*mille*	meel

Transport & Directions

Where's ...?
Où est ...? oo ay ...

What's the address?
Quelle est l'adresse? kel ay la·dres

Can you show me (on the map)?
Pouvez-vous m'indiquer (sur la carte)? poo·vay·voo mun·dee·kay (sewr la kart)

I want to go to ...
Je voudrais aller à ... zher voo·dray a·lay a ...

Does it stop at (Amboise)?
Est-ce qu'il s'arrête à (Amboise)? es·kil sa·ret a (om·bwaz)

I want to get off here.
Je veux descendre ici. zher ver day·son·drer ee·see

Behind the Scenes

Send Us Your Feedback

We love to hear from travellers – your comments help make our books better. We read every word, and we guarantee that your feedback goes straight to the authors. Visit **lonelyplanet.com/contact** to submit your updates and suggestions.

Note: We may edit, reproduce and incorporate your comments in Lonely Planet products such as guidebooks, websites and digital products, so let us know if you don't want your comments reproduced or your name acknowledged. For a copy of our privacy policy visit lonelyplanet.com/privacy.

Our Readers

Many thanks to the travellers who wrote to us with useful advice and anecdotes:

Alex Thomas, Bob Schermer, Geoffrey Dunbar, Lisa Wilkie, Michael Rodin, Mitch Greenhill, Priya Mishra

Catherine's Thanks

Merci to my fellow award-winning Paris authors Chris Pitts and Nicola Williams, to Julian, and the innumerable Parisians who offered insights and inspiration. At LP, thanks especially to Kate Morgan and James Smart. As ever, *merci encore* to my parents, brother, *belle-sœur* and *neveu* for my lifelong love of Paris.

Acknowledgments

Cover photograph: Eiffel Tower, Philip Lee Harvey/Getty.

This Book

This 4th edition of *Pocket Paris* was coordinated by Catherine Le Nevez and researched and written by Catherine Le Nevez, Christopher Pitts and Nicola Williams. This guidebook was commissioned in Lonely Planet's London office and produced by the following:

Destination Editors James Smart, Kate Morgan **Product Editors** Anne Mason, Alison Ridgway **Regional Senior Cartographer** Valentina Kremenchutskaya **Book Designer** Mazzy Prinsep **Assisting Editors** Sarah Bailey, Stephanie Ong **Cover Researcher** Naomi Parker **Thanks to** Dan Corbett, Penny Cordner, Helvi Cranfield, Anna Harris, Elizabeth Jones, Claire Murphy, Claire Naylor, Karyn Noble, Ellie Simpson, Lyahna Spencer, Lauren Wellicome, Tony Wheeler

Index

See also separate subindexes for:

Eating p220
Drinking p221
Entertainment p221
Shopping p221

Sights p000
Map Pages **p000**

Sights p000
Map Pages **p000**

Eating

Sights p000
Map Pages **p000**

Drinking

Entertainment

Shopping

Sights p000
Map Pages **p000**